PRO/CON VOLUME 8

U.S. FOREIGN POLICY

Published 2003 by Grolier,
a division of Scholastic Library Publishing
90 Sherman Turnpike
Danbury, Connecticut 06816

© 2003 The Brown Reference Group plc

Library of Congress Cataloging-in-Publication Data
Pro/con
  p. cm
Includes bibliographical references and index.
  Contents: v. 7. The Constitution – v. 8. U.S. Foreign Policy – v. 9. Criminal Law and
the Penal System – v.10. Health – v. 11. Family and Society – v. 12. Arts and Culture.
  ISBN 0-7172-5753-3 (set : alk. paper) – ISBN 0-7172-5754-1 (vol. 7 : alk. paper) –
ISBN 0-7172-5755-X (vol. 8 : alk. paper) – ISBN 0-7172-5756-8 (vol. 9 : alk. paper) –
ISBN 0-7172-5757-6 (vol. 10 : alk. paper) – ISBN 0-7172-5758-4 (vol. 11 : alk. paper)
ISBN 0-7172-5759-2 (vol. 12 : alk. paper)
  1. Social problems. I. Scholastic Publishing Ltd Grolier (Firm)

HN17.5 P756 2002
361.1–dc21
                                                                      2001053234

Printed and bound in Singapore

SET ISBN 0-7172-5753-3
VOLUME ISBN 0-7172-5755-X

For The Brown Reference Group plc
Project Editor: Aruna Vasudevan
Editors: Sally McFall, Chris Marshall, Phil Robins, Lesley Henderson, Jane
Lanigan, Leon Gray, Fiona Plowman
Consultant Editor: Charles Doran, Andrew W. Mellon Professor of
International Studies, The School of Advanced International Relations,
John Hopkins University
Designer: Sarah Williams
Picture Researchers: Clare Newman, Susy Forbes
Set Index: Kay Ollerenshaw

Managing Editor: Tim Cooke
Design Manager: Lynne Ross
Production Manager: Alastair Gourlay

GENERAL PREFACE

"All that is necessary for evil to triumph is for good men to do nothing."
—Edmund Burke, 18th-century English political philosopher

Decisions

Life is full of choices and decisions. Some are more important than others. Some affect only your daily life—the route you take to school, for example, or what you prefer to eat for supper—while others are more abstract and concern questions of right and wrong rather than practicality. That does not mean that your choice of presidential candidate or your views on abortion are necessarily more important than your answers to purely personal questions. But it is likely that those wider questions are more complex and subtle and that you therefore will need to know more information about the subject before you can try to answer them. They are also likely to be questions where you might have to justify your views to other people. In order to do that you need to be able to make informed decisions, be able to analyze every fact at your disposal, and evaluate them in an unbiased manner.

What is *Pro/Con*?

Pro/Con is a collection of debates that presents conflicting views on some of the more complex and general issues facing Americans today. By bringing together extracts from a wide range of sources—mainstream newspapers and magazines, books, famous speeches, legal judgments, religious tracts, government surveys—the set reflects current informed attitudes toward dilemmas that range from the best way to feed the world's growing population to gay rights, from the connection between political freedom and capitalism to the fate of Napster.

The people whose arguments make up the set are for the most part acknowledged experts in their fields, making the vast difference in their points of view even more remarkable. The arguments are presented in the form of debates for and against various propositions, such as "Is Pornography Art?" or "Is U.S. Foreign Policy Too Interventionist?" This question format reflects the way in which ideas often occur in daily life: in the classroom, on TV shows, in business meetings, or even in state or federal politics.

The contents

The subjects of the six volumes of *Pro/Con 2—The Constitution, U.S. Foreign Policy, Criminal Law and the Penal System, Health, Family and Society*, and *Arts and Culture—* are issues on which it is preferable that people's opinions are based on information rather than personal bias.

Special boxes throughout *Pro/Con* comment on the debates as you are reading them, pointing out facts, explaining terms, or analyzing arguments to help you think about what is being said.

Introductions and summaries also provide background information that might help you reach your own conclusions. There are also comments and tips about how to structure an argument that you can apply on an everyday basis to any debate or conversation, learning how to present your point of view as effectively and persuasively as possible.

VOLUME PREFACE
U.S. Foreign Policy

Every nation has a foreign policy to address the needs of its citizens in the world community. In the first decades of the American republic U.S. foreign policy centered around Britain and France—the former colonial powers—and its close neighbors Mexico and Canada. As the economy expanded, the United States turned its attention farther afield. Successful military campaigns against Mexico (1846-1848) and Spain (1898) gave the United States influence in the Americas and the Caribbean.

Following its vital, although initially reluctant, role in the defeat of Germany and its allies in both World War I (1914-1918) and World War II (1939-1945), the United States emerged as a major world power. In the 20 years or so after the latter war much of U.S. military policy was focused on defeating the spread of communism. The collapse of the Soviet Union and the end of the Cold War left the United States as the world's only superpower. Many people feel that the United States therefore has a duty to protect democracy and freedom on the international stage, but others disagree. The question of how the United States relates to the world—whether on globalization, defense, human rights, or sanctions—remains crucial in defining its foreign policy.

Learning from history
Many people suggest that U.S. foreign policy centers around national interests, with little regard for the international community. They suggest that the main objective of it is to ensure that the United States remains the world's main power and authority. Former Secretary of State Madeleine Albright once warned that "the greatest danger to America is the possibility that we will fail to hear the example of our World War II and Cold War generations; that we may forget the history of this century; that problems abroad, if left unattended, will all too often come home to America."

Critics of U.S. foreign policy argue that many of its current problems stem from the fact that its interventionist policies have ignored the wishes of other countries. Some even claim that the terrorist action of September 11, 2001—the day of the worst acts of terrorism the United States has ever seen—may in some way have been the result of its foreign policy.

As attention turned away from the shocking images and appalling eyewitness stories, serious questions were asked: Who was responsible for this horrendous attack? What had the United States done to inspire such hatred? Could its overly interventionist stance have provoked such action? What could the United States do to change matters?

Living in a modern world
In order to make any decision about politics, it is essential to have accurate, informed information.

The subjects in *U.S. Foreign Policy* focus on 16 important topics, with 32 articles by experts on a range of subjects extending across the U.S. relationship to the modern world, trade, developing countries, and the serious question of terrorism.

HOW TO USE THIS BOOK

Each volume of *Pro/Con* is divided into sections, each of which has an introduction that examines its theme. Within each section are a series of debates that present arguments for and against a proposition, such as whether or not the death penalty should be abolished. An introduction to each debate puts it into its wider context, and a summary and key map (see below) highlight the main points of the debate clearly and concisely. Each debate has marginal boxes that focus on particular points, give tips on how to present an

argument, or help question the writer's case. The summary page to the debates contains supplementary material to help you do further research.

Boxes and other materials provide additional background information. There are also special spreads on how to improve your debating and writing skills. At the end of each book is a glossary and an index. The glossary provides explanations of key words in the volume. The index covers all twelve books, so it will help you trace topics throughout this set and the previous one.

background information
Frequent text boxes provide background information on important concepts and key individuals or events

summary boxes
Summary boxes are useful reminders of both sides of the argument..

further information
Further Reading lists for each debate direct you to related books, articles, and websites so you can do your own research.

other articles in the *Pro/Con* series
This box lists related debates throughout the *Pro/Con* series.

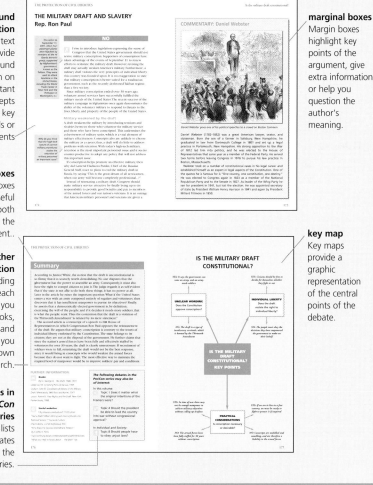

marginal boxes
Margin boxes highlight key points of the argument, give extra information, or help you question the author's meaning.

key map
Key maps provide a graphic representation of the central points of the debate.

CONTENTS

THE UNITED STATES' POSITION IN THE WORLD

INTRODUCTION

The United States is the third most populous and fourth largest country in the world. Since the disintegration of the Soviet Union in 1991 it has been the world's only superpower. Its influence on global politics, economics, and culture can be seen everywhere—a fact for which it has been both praised and criticized.

U.S. foreign policy was central to international politics throughout the 20th century. It remained so at the start of the 21st century, in the aftermath of terrorist attacks on New York and Washington, D.C., on September 11, 2001. President George W. Bush subsequently declared a war against terrorism in which the United States would take the lead in orchestrating international action or act unilaterally if necessary. The ensuing diplomatic and military action led many people to reflect on the United States' position as a world leader. The topics in this section look at four important aspects of this subject.

The beginnings

The history of U.S. involvement in foreign affairs is relatively short. For the first decades of the young republic—and throughout much of the 19th century—the United States largely confined its international activity to relations with its neighbors, Canada and Mexico. It also asserted, in the Monroe Doctrine of 1833, its dominion throughout the Americas.

Following the end of the Civil War in 1865, however, the United States experienced rapid industrial and economic expansion that was accompanied by more international involvement. Alaska and Hawaii became acquired territories, while victory in the Spanish–American War (1898) gave the United States control of the Philippines, Puerto Rico, and Guam.

The building of the Panama Canal to link the Pacific and Atlantic oceans and control of the Panama Canal Zone in 1903 further increased the United States' international importance. The United States entered the 20th century as an economically important power. Its dominance was strengthened by World War I (1914-1918), in which U.S. troops played a vital part in the final defeat of Germany and its allies. Despite a general desire to remain aloof from European conflicts, the United States found itself reluctantly dragged into international affairs, culminating in its campaigns in World War II (1939-1945) in Europe and the Pacific.

An interventionist policy?

After the end of World War II in 1945 the United States became increasingly involved in international affairs and played a key role in setting up the United Nations (UN) that same year. It also quickly emerged as a leader in the struggle against communism known as the Cold War, when relations were strained with both the Soviet Union and China. The fight against communism resulted in U.S. military intervention in foreign conflicts such as Korea (1950-1953) and Vietnam (1961-1975).

U.S. foreign policy in the latter half of the 20th century continued to be interventionist both covertly, as in its funding of rebel groups in Nicaragua and Panama in the 1980s, and overtly, as

Peace and order

While some people believe that direct intervention in foreign affairs—through military action or economic pressure—is the best way for the United States to influence other countries, others argue that the United States should break off relations with nations whose politics or religions it disagrees with. In some cases people believe that such a break in relations would influence a foreign government to instigate change far more successfully than direct U.S. interference. Supporters of breaking off relations with unfavorable regimes,

> "In the beginning,
> all the world was America."
>
> —JOHN LOCKE (1632–1704), ENGLISH POLITICAL THEORIST

in military action in Grenada (1983), Libya (1989), and Afghanistan (2001-2002). This interventionism has been the subject of much debate. Many people argue that no nation has the right to interfere in another country's affairs unless it represents a direct threat to that nation. Other people counter that the United States is part of the international community and should take the lead in trying to prevent unacceptable behavior, such as oppression or civil rights abuses.

The first two topics in this section examine aspects of this question. In the first topic Irving Kristol and Barbara Conry debate whether the United States has an obligation to defend democracy and freedom overseas. In the second topic Congressman Ron Paul and Steven R. David specifically look at whether U.S. foreign policy is too interventionist.

however, believe that the United States does not have a duty to police other countries' affairs and should not worry about the results of its actions.

This matter became urgent after the September 11 attacks and led to attention being focused particularly on fundamentalist Islamic nations. Critics argue that the United States should break off relations with these regimes, which often have poor human rights records and a history of sponsoring terrorist activity. Stephen Zunes and Reuel Marc Gerecht examine this subject in Topic 3.

Although the United States turned to the UN for support during the 1991 Gulf War and after it launched the War on Terror more than a decade later, U.S.-UN relations have on occasions been strained. William H. Luers and Max Boot debate this relationship in Topic 4.

Topic 1

DOES THE UNITED STATES HAVE A DUTY TO PROTECT DEMOCRACY AND FREEDOM OVERSEAS?

YES
"A POST-WILSONIAN FOREIGN POLICY"
AMERICAN ENTERPRISE INSTITUTE, AUGUST 1996
IRVING KRISTOL

NO
FROM "U.S. 'GLOBAL LEADERSHIP': A EUPHEMISM FOR WORLD POLICEMAN"
POLICY ANALYSIS NO. 267, FEBRUARY 5, 1997
BARBARA CONRY

INTRODUCTION

For over a century the United States has been the world's leading superpower thanks to its economic supremacy, advanced technology, and vast resources. It played a leading role in winning both world wars. It is the senior partner in the North Atlantic Treaty Organization (NATO), and its support is vital to the survival of the United Nations (UN). But is the United States obliged to use its power? Every nation has the right to take action overseas in order to protect its interests. Does the special status of the United States, however, require it to protect values, such as democracy and freedom, in other parts of the world?

Foreign policy has long reflected a combination of idealism and self-interested realism. The idealist streak began early in history. It was the intention of the Framers of the Constitution to create not just a new nation, but a republic that would inspire other peoples seeking self-government. But while the United States has often cast itself as the champion of freedom and democracy, its leaders have had to balance this idealism against the political practicalities of its widespread strategic and economic interests.

The complexity of the issue is illustrated by U.S. actions throughout the 20th century.

When President Woodrow Wilson proposed his famous Fourteen Points as the principles on which to end World War I (1914–1918), for example, Europe's leaders condemned his unrealistic idealism. Wilson also helped create the League of Nations, an international forum that would make war a thing of the past. Americans, however, disillusioned with Europe's conflicts, rejected Wilson's idealism in the 1920 presidential election. The victorious candidate, Warren G. Harding, promised instead a policy of isolationism, or noninvolvement in foreign affairs.

> *"America ... knows that by once enlisting under other banners than her own ... she would no longer be the ruler of her own spirit."*
> —JOHN QUINCY ADAMS
> (1767–1848), SIXTH PRESIDENT

During the 1920s and 1930s, as Europe and the Soviet Union fell under the grip of extremism, the United States remained neutral. Faced with an expansionist Japan in the Pacific, however, President Franklin D. Roosevelt changed this policy in the late 1930s, arguing that the United States should become the "arsenal of democracy." This approach—and U.S. entry into World War II (1939-1945)— was widely supported by Americans.

After 1945 political and military rivalry between the United States and the Soviet Union and its communist allies developed into the Cold War. The United States found itself both hailed as the champion of democracy and condemned for intervening in the affairs of other nations. In the late 1950s, for example, it was drawn into a civil war between communists and others in Vietnam.

To those who prosecuted the war, it seemed essential to protect U.S. interests from the spread of communism; to many critics it was an unjust conflict with no purpose.

Since the Cold War ended in the early 1990s, the United States has remained at the forefront of intervention overseas, such as in the 1991 Persian Gulf War against Iraq, the UN peacekeeping missions in the Balkans in the early 1990s, and the battles in Afghanistan following the September 11, 2001, terrorist attacks on New York and Washington, D.C.

Critics, however, point out that such missions do not always produce results compatible with U.S. values. The victory of the U.S.-led coalition in the Gulf, for example, left Saddam Hussein as the Iraqi dictator and restored to government in Kuwait the autocratic royal family. And although the United States introduced its own choice of leader in Afghanistan, with a view to returning the country to democracy, its military actions also strengthened the position of Afghan warlords, who threatened to disrupt the peaceful transfer of power.

Another criticism of U.S. involvement overseas is that it is selective, tending to tie in with special interests, such as access to the oil fields of the Persian Gulf. Supporters respond that not even a superpower can solve all the injustices of the world: Intervention must be selective. Critics, however, point out contradictions in U.S. policy. They claim, for example, that the United States has not put pressure on some of its trading partners, such as China and some Latin American states, to improve their poor record on human rights.

The following articles offer two views of America's role in the world. The first argues that America should support U.S. ideals worldwide, the second that the role of global policeman is too costly.

A POST-WILSONIAN FOREIGN POLICY
Irving Kristol

Everyone from American scholars to foreign statesmen finds American foreign policy very puzzling. And so the basic tenor of all commentaries on this policy, at any time and from any source, tends to be critical. When was the last time you read an enthusiastic endorsement of American foreign policy? I have no such recollection.

The truth is that American foreign policy is *necessarily* always perplexing. This has nothing to do with the inadequacies of our presidents or State Departments. Such inadequacies surely exist but they are, as it were, built into their mission and the way they are compelled to execute it. In short, confusion is inescapable. The reason is that American foreign policy is truly exceptional, formed in a way that is quite different from that of other nations.

The author refers to the constitutional limitations built into the exercise of government in the United States. For example, the president is commander in chief of the armed forces, but Congress has the power to declare war.

Uniquely democratic

One does not ordinarily find French or British or German foreign policy to be the subject of such permanent, agitated criticism among those countries' people. That is because the European tradition … has tended to regard foreign policy as the preserve of the state. The British, French, and German foreign offices do not hold our kind of daily televised press briefings, in which newsmen compete to come up with embarrassing questions. They would like to see the United States follow their example. But the United States cannot, because our foreign policy is in thrall to popular opinion. Our foreign policy is uniquely democratic, for better or worse. And our popular opinion is profoundly ambivalent when it comes to foreign affairs. It has been so since the founding of the Republic.

Do you agree that U.S. foreign policy is in "thrall to popular opinion"? Some people argue that daily White House press briefings owe more to an active media than to democratic scrutiny. How would you respond to this?

The ambivalence can be summed up this way: The American people see their nation as being an exceptional one, with a very special mission in the world. This mission has an ineradicable moral component—our foreign policy is supposed to make the world a better place for humanity to inhabit. There is consensus on this. But there is no consensus on how this is to be accomplished. The division is basically three-fold, though with some discordant tendencies within each fold.

Briefly, there are those who believe that being an exemplary "city on a hill" should suffice, except when a very narrowly defined "national interest" is clearly at issue; this is what we loosely refer to as isolationism. There are others, however, who think that only an activist participation in world affairs and the creation of a "new world order" dominated by international organizations that promise "collective security" can satisfy our moral ambitions. And there are still others—mainly academics and professionals—who are skeptical about "American exceptionalism" to begin with, and who therefore would like to see American foreign policy to be consistently "pragmatic" and "realistic," with our national interest defined in traditional "balance of power" terms.

All three currents are now visible in American discourse. The "isolationist" impulse seems irrepressible even among those Americans who believe that our national destiny is to be the world's mightiest power. Those quotation marks are justified because there are almost no "isolationists" who will not make an occasional exception for the Western hemisphere, where they can foresee reasons for righteous intervention. And it is worth recalling that it was precisely among the isolationist-minded that anti-Communist enthusiasm during the Cold War was most manifest. Being the world's greatest power inexorably implies resistance to those who challenge this status. A true isolationist would have only a literal conception of national security—a purely defensive definition. Very few such people actually exist. Pat Buchanan sometimes seems like one, but his innate belligerency—another popular American trait—belies the appearance. In power begins inescapable responsibilities and challenges.

The Wilsonian impulse

What can fairly be called the Wilsonian impulse dominates our State Department and such influential post-World War I organizations as the Council on Foreign Relations. Indeed, practically all privately financed membership organizations devoted exclusively to foreign policy are Wilsonian. There are not many of them and their memberships may not be large, but they do attract former foreign-affairs officers, often high and distinguished officials, who are presumed to speak with some authority and who get a disproportionate amount of respectful media coverage.

I say disproportionate because in the past decades the Wilsonian impulse has grown weaker. Very few politicians these days go around saying nice things about the United

John Winthrop (1588–1649), one of the Puritan founders of New England, believed his colony should set an example of Christian morality, like a "CIty on a Hill." The author interprets this phrase nowadays to mean leading by example, not by intervention in other's affairs.

Pat Buchanan (1938–) is a right-wing politician who ran as the Reform Party candidate in the 2000 presidential election. The author argues that while he is generally noninterventionist, Buchanan sometimes supports U.S. involvement. For example, he supports the right to prevent European interference in U.S. politics as first stated in the 1823 Monroe Doctrine.

The "Wilsonian impulse," named for President Woodrow Wilson (1856–1924), is the desire to promote democracy around the world. Go to pages 10–11 for more information on Wilson's foreign policy.

Go to Topic 4 Should the United States show a stronger commitment to the United Nations? on pages 48–59 for an examination of the United Nations.

Nations, while the quotient of nasty references has grown astronomically. All those quaint phrases—"a world without war" or "open covenants openly arrived at," even a universal right to "self-determination"—may still occasionally turn up in commencement addresses, but they are feeble and echoless. A casual reference to the Wilsonian vision as "utopian" rarely provokes vigorous dissent. But the past weighs heavily on American diplomacy, and the State Department does not find it easy to disengage itself publicly from those old commitments to this vision.

A realistic approach

Privately and unofficially, it's another matter. All American administrations, without exception, find themselves discreetly wandering down a third track. The media and policymakers usually describe this as "pragmatism"; academics speak more bluntly of "realism" or "neo-realism." Pragmatism is very much in the American vein, suggesting as it does the adaptation of ideals to reality, not the abandonment of those ideals. Still, this does lead to recurrent denunciations by righteous moralists of American foreign policy as hypocritical, which it inevitably and necessarily is.

Why do you think the author agrees that U.S. foreign policy is hypocritical?

To escape this trap, some policy analysts have forged yet another path, one that affirms commitment to American political and social ideals, which are not always universalist ideals, as the essential guides for our policy. Unlike Wilsonianism, this point of view is nationalist and unilateralist, looking back to Theodore Roosevelt rather than to Woodrow Wilson. It is an ingenious effort to wed realism to idealism, in a uniquely American way. But whether the real world is any more hospitable to American ideals than to the universalist ideals of the United Nations is not at all clear. One suspects that this mixture of idealism and "neorealism" will in its own turn have to plead the exigencies of pragmatism at crucial moments.

President Theodore Roosevelt (1858–1919) believed that the United States should intervene in international politics when its interests were at stake. Some people claim that the spread of democracy around the world is ultimately in the United States' interests. What do you think?

Exasperating enigma

In the end the fundamental problem for American democracy is that its foreign policy is democratic. This is something the world has not witnessed since ancient Athens, where a democratic foreign policy led to one disaster after another. On the other hand, Athens was never the great power the United States is today, and its version of democracy had far fewer ways of shaping, refining, and even sometimes thwarting popular opinion. Still, American foreign policy will surely remain, as it always has been, an exasperating enigma to the rest of the world as well as to our academic analysts, who will never cease to believe that a foreign policy should be analytically coherent.

So we muddle along, intervening spasmodically in various parts of the world, with mixed results. The Gulf War witnessed a most fortuitous confluence of moralistic rhetoric ("resist aggression") and realistic motives (involving oil and Middle East stability), though even in this case the opposition to intervention was stronger than one would have anticipated. In Bosnia, it was media outrage at Serbian atrocities that propelled our reluctant intervention, and no serious person can believe that we are there to establish a peaceful multiethnic Bosnia. We would have much preferred to let our NATO allies cope with Bosnia, but they seem incapable of coping with anything—a fact that our official rhetoric covers up as best it can.

It is because of this internal conflict within the American soul that every administration is attracted to economic sanctions as against military intervention. In most cases these sanctions are ineffectual, but they do give the appearance of attentive action and only a few interest groups pay much attention to them.

With the end of the Cold War, what we really need is an obvious ideological and threatening enemy, one worthy of our mettle, one that can unite us in opposition. Isn't that what the most successful movie of the year, *Independence Day*, is telling us? Where are our aliens when we most need them?

In the 1991 Gulf War the author argues that moral and practical issues justified U.S. involvement. In the conflict in Bosnia (1992–1995) he proposes that the weakness of other nations forced the United States to engage. Find out more about the war in Bosnia by going to http://www. washingtonpost. com/wp-srv/inatl/ longterm/balkans/ overview/ bosnia.htm.

See Topic 7 Should economic sanctions be used to promote human rights? *on pages 86–97.*

Do you think the author would choose a different conclusion were he writing after September 11, 2001?

U.S. "GLOBAL LEADERSHIP": A EUPHEMISM FOR WORLD POLICEMAN
Barbara Conry

"Containment" was formulated in the 1940s to check the expansion of the Soviet Union. The other strategies referred to here were attempts to increase reliance on international laws, partnerships, and institutions following the collapse of the Soviet Union in 1991.

Supporters of U.S. leadership in the 20th century might point to its role in World War II. Critics might mention the U.S. failure in the Vietnam War (1955–1975) to prevent communists from uniting North and South Vietnam.

NO

The U.S. foreign policy community has been grasping for a national security strategy since the end of the Cold War nullified the doctrine of containment. From former president George Bush's proclamation of the "new world order" to the Clinton administration's strategies of "enlargement" and "assertive multilateralism," Washington has found containment a tough act to follow. Gradually, though, a bumper-sticker approach to foreign policy has emerged upon which almost everyone can agree: U.S. "leadership" in world affairs.

Pundits of varying ideological persuasions and high-level policymakers from both parties have embraced the notion of global leadership as a guiding principle of U.S. foreign policy. Former secretary of state Warren Christopher has written, "America must lead.… American leadership is our first principle and a central lesson of this century. The simple fact is that if we do not lead, no one else will." Republican presidential nominee Bob Dole echoed Christopher's sentiments, declaring, "Only the United States can lead on the full range of political, diplomatic, economic, and military issues confronting the world."

… Christopher [and] Dole … have at times had serious disagreements about … foreign policy. Their agreement on the need for U.S. global leadership does not indicate consensus but instead reflects the ambiguity of global leadership as a basis for U.S. strategy. Anyone can invoke the mantra of U.S. global leadership because its meaning is in the mind of the speaker. As Jessica Mathews of the Council on Foreign Relations has pointed out, "Rhetorically, at least, nearly everyone agrees on the undiminished need for American leadership. But the word is used to mask profoundly different views of America's role in the world."

Conflicting definitions of U.S. leadership
There is nothing wrong with "leadership" per se. The United States can and should play a leading role in a number of arenas. Washington's leadership since World War II of the

global trade liberalization process, for example, has
been highly constructive. Such economic leadership
should continue. U.S. moral and cultural leadership—the
American tradition of commitment to such ideals as
democracy, individual liberty, and the other philosophical
foundations of the Constitution—should also continue.
Such American economic and moral leadership is both
beneficial and sustainable.

Today's proponents of "global leadership," however, are
advocating something better described as hegemony than
as leadership. Unlike moral or economic leadership, global
leadership does not envision the United States' leading
by example or through diplomacy. Global leadership is
essentially coercive, relying on "diplomacy" backed by
threats or military action.

Global leadership also entails greater responsibility than
does leadership in the economic or moral and cultural
arenas. U.S. leadership in trade liberalization does not make
the United States responsible for countries that practice
protectionism. Nor does economic leadership demand that
the United States use any means necessary to maintain its
leadership role. Advocates of U.S. political and military
leadership, however, have a much more ambitious view of
the responsibilities global leadership entails and the actions
the United States is obligated to take to preserve its role
as global leader....

Translating leadership into policy

The ambiguity of "leadership" is also one of the reasons it
is so difficult to translate into policy. At its most extreme,
leadership-driven foreign policy suggests that the United
States is responsible to some degree for everyone,
everywhere. It is unlikely that Washington could or would
seek to take the idea to that extreme in terms of policy.
The inescapable dilemma, then, is how to determine which
situations demand Washington's attention and which can be
left to run their course.

The proponents of leadership cannot agree on the
proper criteria for making such decisions.... Advocating
U.S. intervention in the Bosnian war while ignoring other,
similar regional wars is random at best. Such selectivity could,
however, be perceived as having more sinister motives.
Citing more deadly recent conflicts in such places as Sudan,
Cambodia, Rwanda, and Angola, syndicated columnist Doug
Bandow has observed, "For all of the passion exhibited by
those who advocate military intervention to protect Bosnian

> "Hegemony" means domination over other people. The author feels that diplomacy "backed by military threats or action" is not true diplomacy. Do you think that the threat of force is ever justifiable when negotiating?

> Research the conflicts in these nations by going to http://www.cia.gov/cia/publications/factbook/.

Do you think there is a danger that the government—and media—is more concerned with conflicts involving "white Europeans" than, say, Africans?

Muslims, it seems strangely limited. Put bluntly, those who shout the loudest about genocide and war seem to care only when the victims are white Europeans."...

Promise now, pay later

Another policy problem involves the grandiose rhetoric that is a hallmark of global leadership and frequently results in policy dilemmas or embarrassing backpedaling. U.S. officials too often succumb to the temptation to make extravagant promises of future U.S. action—usually at times when the likelihood of having to act on those promises seems remote (or at least beyond the next election)....

During the 1992 presidential election Bill Clinton promised, if elected, to sign laws granting low tariffs on Chinese exports only if China improved its human rights record. After his election Clinton decided not to sign the law, although he continued to press China on human rights. In 1993 the Clinton administration declared that North Korea would not be allowed to develop nuclear weapons, but had to change its position after experts could not rule out that the country already possessed such weapons.

In the cases of both China and North Korea ... [the Clinton administration] overestimated both what it needed to do and what the United States was capable of doing. Human rights and nuclear nonproliferation are worthwhile goals, but they are competing with an array of other foreign policy objectives–many of which are more important. Because of China's immense market potential, trade was a higher priority than human rights. And the risks associated with forcibly denying Pyongyang a nuclear weapons capability— conducting a preemptive strike, for example—were more dangerous than North Korea's possession of a few nuclear devices. The lesson is that U.S. officials should not be seduced by the myth of Washington's omnipotence into making commitments that the United States cannot meet or does not value enough relative to other priorities to meet....

The imperatives of leadership

U.S. global leadership can be a policy straitjacket even in the absence of extravagant rhetoric, creating "imperatives" where there are none.... Given the number of ethnic conflicts that are currently raging and are likely to flare up in the near future—the Stockholm International Peace Research Institute counted 30 major armed conflicts in 1995 alone—that imperative puts too great a claim on American blood and treasure to provide the underpinning for a viable foreign policy. [Warren] Christopher has commented, "Our strength is a blessing, not a burden." The argument that the United States must take action simply because it has the ability to do so, however, carries the implicit assumption that U.S. strength is indeed a burden rather than a blessing.

The author raises a central question: Does the strength of the United States create a duty for it to protect people across the world, or should a government's first responsibility be toward the welfare of its own people?

Global leadership is a tremendously costly proposition.... The U.S. defense budget today totals approximately $265 billion—more than $1,000 each year for every American and more than the combined defense budgets of the other industrial powers. A significant proportion of that spending is linked to American security commitments around the world. NATO costs U.S. taxpayers approximately $60 billion to $90 billion per year; U.S. commitments to Japan, South Korea, and other East Asian allies cost approximately $35 billion to $40 billion per year; and the American commitment to the Persian Gulf region costs at least $40 billion per year. Those commitments, which total between $135 billion and $170 billion annually, are in place largely to preserve American leadership....

Human costs must also be considered. Leadership cannot be achieved through dollar diplomacy and impressive military spending alone. U.S. troops sometimes will have to go into battle to prove American prowess. The American public has demonstrated a meager tolerance of American casualties, especially since the remarkably low body count in the gulf war seemed to suggest that a war could be fought with little bloodshed....

Public skepticism

But the evidence suggests that the American public is not averse to military casualties for the sake of defending vital American interests. The public is intolerant of battlefield losses in military operations that appear to have little or no direct link to U.S. national security. As David Evans of Business Executives for National Security has observed, "The issue really takes on additional sensitivity when there is not a clear and compelling national interest for the government to impose the blood tax on its youth." And, as [the journalist Thomas] Friedman conceded, today's crises do not offer the "compelling moral or strategic appeal" that would raise American tolerance for spilled blood. Public skepticism about sending U.S. troops to Bosnia is consistent with this analysis; polls have indicated that Americans do not believe U.S. vital interests are at stake, and consequently support for the operation is weak....

Given the enormous economic and human costs and the troublesome policy implications associated with leading the world, the supposed benefits of leadership deserve close scrutiny....

See the sidebar on page 52 for more information on NATO.

Some people would respond that the "commitments" the author lists also protect U.S. interests abroad, such as trading partnerships. After the events of September 11, 2001, do you think that maintaining international security has become more important for the United States?

In contrast to the Bosnia operation, public opinion generally backed the sending of troops to Afghanistan in October 2001 to destroy the Al Qaeda network, believed to be behind the terrorist attacks of September 11.

Summary

Irving Kristol argues that the United States is unique in that its foreign policy is broadly shaped by public opinion. While people in other nations are generally content to leave foreign policy to the politicians, the American public believes that the United States has a historical duty to provide a beacon of democratic values to the rest of the world. Kristol argues that the U.S. tradition of idealism, summed up by the internationalist views of President Woodrow Wilson during World War I, has been tempered by the realities of the United States' position as the world's only superpower. That position produces a strange and somewhat inconsistent foreign policy that combines moralistic impulses with realistic motives.

In the "no" article Barbara Conry warns that the U.S. impulse toward assuming "global leadership" can be potentially dangerous: The phrase, she suggests, means different things to different people. She also argues that the form of leadership most likely to emerge is neither democratic nor diplomatic but coercive, since it requires the United States to force other nations to follow its lead. However, because the United States cannot be responsible for all people in all parts of the world, its involvement in foreign conflicts will always appear random or face accusations of bias toward one group of countries rather than another. In the end, she concludes, global leadership is simply too costly to be workable. As well as the financial burden, the public has become increasingly skeptical about sending troops into conflicts in which vital U.S. interests are not directly threatened.

FURTHER INFORMATION:

Books:

Baritz, Loren, *City on a Hill: A History of Ideas and Myths in America*. Westport, CT: Greenwood Press, 1980. Hyland, William G., *Clinton's World: Remaking American Foreign Policy*. Westport, CT: Praeger, 1999.

Articles:

Berger, Samuel R. "A Foreign Policy for a Foreign Age." *Foreign Policy*, November/December 2000, Vol. 79.

Useful websites:

http://www.aei.org/ra/raschn020609.htm
"Bush's Role for America: The World's Top Cop" by William Schneider.
http://www.cato.org/dailys/05-25-00.html
"International Silent Treatment" by Doug Bandow.
http://www.ceip.org/files/publications/
pub_by_date.ASP?p=11

List of articles on U.S. world leadership published by the Carnegie Endowment for International Peace.

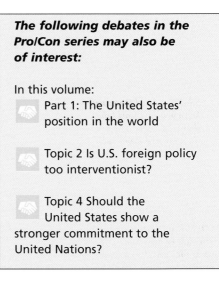

The following debates in the Pro/Con series may also be of interest:

In this volume:
Part 1: The United States' position in the world

Topic 2 Is U.S. foreign policy too interventionist?

Topic 4 Should the United States show a stronger commitment to the United Nations?

DOES THE UNITED STATES HAVE A DUTY TO PROTECT DEMOCRACY AND FREEDOM OVERSEAS?

YES: Now that the Cold War is over, the United States can direct its vast resources to fight against global tyranny and inequality

YES: The Founders intended the United States to be an inspiration to other peoples who aspired to democracy. That tradition should continue.

SUPERPOWER
Should the world's only superpower act as a global policeman?

MORALITY
Does the United States have a moral duty to propagate democratic values?

NO: There are too many conflicts and injustices in the world even for a superpower to oppose. The United States should concentrate on looking after its own interests.

DOES THE UNITED STATES HAVE A DUTY TO PROTECT DEMOCRACY AND FREEDOM OVERSEAS?

KEY POINTS

NO: The United States can set an example to other nations simply by demonstrating the advantages of democracy and liberty. It does not need to actively spread such values.

YES: The United States will thrive best in a world that shares its commitment to freedom and democracy

YES: Many successful U.S. interventions overseas have led to democratic and free-market reforms

INTERESTS
Do U.S. interests and values always go together?

NO: U.S. interests mainly reflect strategic or trade concerns. We can trade as well with repressive regimes or dictatorships as with any other nation.

NO: Despite the rhetoric of its leaders, U.S. policy is purely self-interested even when it is dressed up in moral guise

Topic 2
IS U.S. FOREIGN POLICY TOO INTERVENTIONIST?

YES
FROM "A SAD STATE OF AFFAIRS," SPEECH TO THE U.S. HOUSE OF REPRESENTATIVES,
OCTOBER 25, 2001
REP. RON PAUL

NO
"SAVING AMERICA FROM THE COMING CIVIL WARS"
FOREIGN AFFAIRS, JANUARY/FEBRUARY 1999
STEVEN R. DAVID

INTRODUCTION

The terrorist attacks on the Pentagon and the World Trade Center on September 11, 2001, put U.S. foreign policy firmly in the spotlight. How much was U.S. involvement overseas to blame for provoking the assault? As the most powerful nation in the world, the United States is thought by many people to have not only a duty but an obligation to intervene in the affairs of other countries.

There are a whole host of reasons for such intervention. Some people cite moral and ideological reasons, such as the protection of democracy and the promotion of peace; they argue that the United States is in a position to improve conditions for less fortunate people around the world. Other reasons for intervention overseas are far more practical, however. They include the protection of U.S. trade and strategic interests, the defense of national security, and the desire to fight terrorist activity at its source.

Critics argue that the United States has been far too willing to become overinvolved in the affairs of other countries. In their view terrorist activity, such as the attacks on U.S. embassies overseas in the 1990s and the attacks of September 11, are a direct response to the way in which the United States has conducted its foreign affairs. Is there a need for the United States to become so involved in the affairs of other countries that the lives of American citizens are put at risk?

The United States is a fairly isolated country, locked between the Atlantic and Pacific oceans and bordered only by Canada to the north and Mexico to the south. Historically, the United States adopted an isolationist foreign policy because of its relative geographical safety. In the early years of the republic foreign policy was largely directed toward stabilizing relations with Britain and France, the former colonial powers that still had interests in North America.

Only later did the United States begin to turn its attention from Europe toward its nearer neighbors in the Americas and the Caribbean. During the 19th century, for example, the United States both fought Mexico—it gained California and the Southwest from Mexico by the Treaty of Guadalupe Hidalgo at the end of the Mexican-American War (1846-1848)—and invested heavily in its neighbor, particularly in Mexican railroads and mines. Similar investment in other nations led in the early 20th century to U.S. military incursions in Central America to protect economic interests.

> *"These commitments—hope and order, law and life—unite people across cultures and continents. Upon these commitments depend all peace and progress. For these commitments we are determined to fight."*
>
> —GEORGE W. BUSH,
>
> 43RD PRESIDENT, 2001

When World War I (1914-1918) began, the United States tried to stay neutral. It eventually entered into war in 1917, but only in response to increasing antagonism from Germany. At the outbreak of World War II (1939-1945) the United States again remained neutral until it was brought into the war by the Japanese attack on Pearl Harbor in 1941. In the years following World War II the United States emerged as a superpower. The Cold War (1946-1991) with the Soviet Union cast the United States as the protector of capitalism and democracy versus communism. The desire to combat communism, along with the domino theory—that each state that became communist in turn would influence others until communism reached America's own backyard—meant that the legitimate concerns of U.S. foreign policy now ranged around the world. Thus, for example, the United States became involved in civil wars in Southeast Asia in the late 1950s, a part of the world that few Americans had visited or knew anything about at that time.

In the modern world civil wars, dangerous dictatorships, and terrorist organizations can all have effects that reach far beyond national borders. Supporters of U.S. intervention abroad argue that such threats to national security as Osama Bin Laden's Al Qaeda network justify military engagement overseas. They cite the need to protect U.S. citizens in foreign conflicts and to protect economic interests, such as oil supplies in the Middle East, as further reasons for action. Critics, however, remain skeptical both of the effectiveness of such interventions and of the potential harm they can do to the reputation of the United States.

In the first of the following articles Congressman Ron Paul argues that U.S. foreign policy is often far too interventionist, unbalanced, and ill conceived. In the second article Steven R. David, on the other hand, counters that more intervention is needed now to prevent problems in the future.

A SAD STATE OF AFFAIRS
Rep. Ron Paul

YES

It breaks my heart to see what is happening to our country today. All Americans have grieved over the losses suffered on 9/11. The grief for those who lost loved ones is beyond description....

There are some who, in addition to feeling this huge sense of personal loss that all Americans share, grieve for other serious and profound reasons. For instance, many thoughtful Americans are convinced that the tragedy of 9/11 was preventable. Since that might be true, this provokes a tragic sadness, especially for those who understand how the events of 9/11 needlessly came about.

The reason why this is so sad and should be thoroughly understood is that so often the ones who suggest how our policies may have played a role in evoking the attacks are demonized as unpatriotic and are harshly dismissed as belonging to the "blame America crowd."

Those who are so anxious to condemn do not realize that the policies of the American Government, designed by politicians and bureaucrats, are not always synonymous with American ideals. The country is not the same as the Government. The spirit of America is hardly something for which the Government holds a monopoly on defining. America's heart and soul is more embedded in our love of liberty, self-reliance, and tolerance than by our foreign policy, driven by powerful special interests with little regard for the Constitution.

Throughout our early history, a policy of minding our own business and avoiding entangling alliances, as George Washington admonished, was more representative of American ideals than those we have pursued for the past 50 years. Some sincere Americans have suggested that our modern interventionist policy set the stage for the attacks of 9/11, and for this, they are condemned as being unpatriotic.

This compounds the sadness and heartbreak that some Americans are feeling. Threats, loss of jobs, censorship and public mockery have been heaped upon those who have made this suggestion. Freedom of expression and thought, the bedrock of the American Republic, is now too often condemned as something viciously evil. This should cause freedom-loving Americans to weep from broken hearts....

Do you think that after the 9/11 attacks Americans paid enough attention to trying to understand why the United States was a terrorist target?

Do you agree that foreign policy reflects more the concerns of interest groups rather than the spirit and letter of the Constitution? What interest groups might they be?

Freedom of expression is enshrined in the First Amendment to the Constitution.

Trouble in the Middle East

We already hear of plans to install and guarantee the next government of Afghanistan. Getting Bin Laden and his gang is one thing, nation-building is quite another. Some of our trouble in the Middle East started years ago when our CIA put the Shah in charge of Iran. It was 25 years before he was overthrown, and the hatred toward America continues to this day. Those who suffer from our intervention have long memories.

Our support for … Saudi Arabia, with our troops occupying what most Muslims consider sacred land, is hardly the way to bring peace to the Middle East. A policy driven by our fear of losing control over the oil fields in the Middle East has not contributed to American Security. Too many powerful special interests drive our policy in this region, and this does little to help us preserve security for Americans here at home.

Critics suggest that U.S. support for Saudi Arabia reflects a double standard in its foreign policy. The Saudi regime has a long record of human rights abuses and is known to have funded terrorist organizations.

As we bomb Afghanistan, we continue to send foreign aid to feed the people suffering from the war. I strongly doubt if our food will get them to love us or even be our friends. There is no evidence that the starving receive the food. And too often it is revealed that it ends up in the hands of the military forces we are fighting. While we bomb Afghanistan and feed the victims, we lay plans to install the next government and pay for rebuilding the country. Quite possibly, the new faction we support will be no more trustworthy than the Taliban, to which we sent plenty of aid and weapons in the 1980s. That intervention in Afghanistan did not do much to win reliable friends in the region.

The United States spent billions of dollars backing the Mujahideen ("soldiers of God")—Islamic freedom fighters opposed to the Soviet invasion of Afghanistan from 1979 to 1989. In 1996 Mujahideen leaders established the fundamentalist Taliban as the ruling body of Afghanistan.

It just may be that Afghanistan would be best managed by several tribal factions, without any strong centralized government and without any outside influence, certainly not by the UN. But then again, some claim that the proposed Western financed pipeline through northern Afghanistan can only happen after a strong centralized pro-Western government is put in place.…

I happen to believe that winning this battle against the current crop of terrorists is quite achievable in a relatively short period of time. But winning the war over the long term is a much different situation. This cannot be achieved without a better understanding of the enemy and the geopolitics that drive this war. Even if relative peace is achieved with a battle victory over Osama Bin Laden and his followers, other terrorists will appear from all corners of the world for an indefinite period of time if we do not understand the issues.

You can find out more about Osama Bin Laden and his terrorist network Al Qaeda on Marshall Brain's website How Stuff Works at www. howstuffworks.com/ bin-laden.htm.

Changing our current foreign policy with wise diplomacy is crucial if we are to really win the war and restore the sense of tranquility to our land that now seems to be so far in our distant past. Our widespread efforts at peacekeeping and nation-building will only contribute to the resentment that drives the fanatics. Devotion to internationalism and a one-world government only exacerbates regional rivalries. Denying that our economic interests drive so much of what the West does against the East impedes any efforts to diffuse the world crisis that already has a number of Americans demanding nuclear bombs to be used to achieve victory. A victory based on this type of aggressive policy would be a hollow victory indeed.

An excuse to attack our liberties and privacy

I would like to draw analogy between the drug war and the war against terrorism. In the last 30 years, we have spent hundreds of billions of dollars on a failed war on drugs. This war has been used as an excuse to attack our liberties and privacy. It has been an excuse to undermine our financial privacy while promoting illegal searches and seizures with many innocent people losing their lives and property. Seizure and forfeiture have harmed a great number of innocent American citizens.

Another result of this unwise war has been the corruption of many law enforcement officials. It is well known that with the profit incentives so high, we are not even able to keep drugs out of our armed prisons. Making our whole society a prison would not bring success to this floundering war on drugs. Sinister motives of the profiteers and gangsters, along with prevailing public ignorance, keeps this futile war going.

Illegal and artificially high priced drugs drive the underworld to produce, sell and profit from this social depravity. Failure to recognize that drug addiction, like alcoholism, is a disease rather than a crime, encourages the drug warriors in efforts that have not and will not ever work. We learned the hard way about alcohol prohibition and crime, but we have not yet seriously considered it in the ongoing drug war.

Corruption associated with the drug dealers is endless. It has involved our police, the military, border guards and the judicial system. It has affected government policy and our own CIA. The artificially high profits from illegal drugs provide easy access to funds for rogue groups involved in fighting civil wars throughout the world.

For the first 140 years of our history, we had essentially no Federal war on drugs, and far fewer problems with drug addiction and related crimes was a consequence. In the past 30 years, even with the hundreds of millions of dollars spent on the drug war, little good has come of it. We have vacillated from efforts to stop the drugs at the source to severely punishing the users, yet nothing has improved.

This analogy is highly appropriate. In many cases the United States is fighting a common enemy—terrorist groups such as the Revolutionary Armed Forces of Colombia (FARC) and Al Qaeda have been linked to drug trafficking.

The author implies that making drugs legal would be the best way to win the drug war. But wouldn't it be an admission of defeat?

Each year, the U.S. federal government spends $19.2 billion on the war on drugs, a rate of about $609 per second.

This war has been behind most big government police powers of the last 30 years, with continual undermining of our civil liberties and personal privacy. Those who support the IRS's efforts to collect maximum revenues and root out the underground economy have welcomed this intrusion, even if the drug underworld grows in size and influence.

The drug war encourages violence. Government violence against nonviolent users is notorious and has led to the unnecessary prison overpopulation. Innocent taxpayers are forced to pay for all this so-called justice. Our drug eradication project (using spraying) around the world, from Colombia to Afghanistan, breeds resentment because normal crops and good land can be severely damaged. Local populations perceive that the efforts and the profiteering remain somehow beneficial to our own agenda in these various countries.

Drug dealers and drug gangs are a consequence of our unwise approach to drug usage. Many innocent people are killed in the crossfire by the mob justice that this war generates. But just because the laws are unwise and have had unintended consequences, no excuses can ever be made for the monster who would kill and maim innocent people for illegal profits. But as the violent killers are removed from society, reconsideration of our drug laws ought to occur.

Understanding the policies that incite hatred

A similar approach should be applied to our war on those who would terrorize and kill our people for political reasons. If the drug laws, and the policies that incite hatred against the United States, are not clearly understood and, therefore, never changed, the number of drug criminals and terrorists will only multiply.

Without some understanding of what has brought us to the brink of a worldwide conflict, and reconsideration of our policies around the globe, we will be no more successful in making our land secure and free than the drug war has been in removing drug violence from our cities and towns....

Without an understanding of why terrorism is directed towards the United States, we may well build a prison for ourselves with something called homeland security while doing nothing to combat the root causes of terrorism. Let us hope we figure this out soon.

We have promoted a foolish and very expensive domestic war on drugs for more than 30 years. It has done no good whatsoever. I doubt our Republic can survive a 30-year period of trying to figure out how to win this guerilla war against terrorism. Hopefully, we will all seek the answers in these trying times with an open mind and understanding.

How does the war on drugs undermine civil liberties? See Volume 7 Topic 14 Are random drug tests of athletes constitutional? on pages 178–189.

Between 1996 and 1998 cultivation of the coca plant in Colombia rose by 50 percent despite the aggressive spray campaigns. Coca farmers moved the coca plantations to increasingly remote areas in response to the spraying.

SAVING AMERICA FROM THE COMING CIVIL WARS
Steven R. David

In the early 1990s, when David was writing, the breakup of the federation of Yugoslavia sparked widespread ethnic conflicts in the Balkans, prompting intervention by the international community.

The author refers to the U.S.-sponsored 1995 Dayton Peace Accord, which brought to an end the conflict in Bosnia.

The Korean War (1950–1953) was sparked when communist North Korea invaded South Korea in 1950. A similar conflict occurred between communist North Vietnam and South Vietnam (1950–1975). The United States intervened in both in an attempt to prevent the spread of communism.

NO

Recent events have given the lie to the conventional wisdom on civil wars: that they are private matters which great powers may simply ignore. Over the past ten years, America has again and again found itself in the middle of foreign, internal conflicts, from Haiti to Somalia. And nowhere has the focus been so acute or the consequences as immediate as in the Balkans. The United States and its Western allies have worked hard—though with limited success—to end the wars that erupted when Yugoslavia collapsed. Western interests were directly implicated; concern over humanitarian abuses, the risk of war spreading to neighboring states, and the future of NATO itself justified American and European intervention. Dayton seemed to win a fragile peace for Bosnia. But the threat of war in Europe now looms as likely as ever, as elections return Bosnian hard-liners to office and the uprising simmers in Kosovo. The prospects of achieving a lasting peace in the region are slim, and these problems are likely to vex American policymakers for years to come.

The attention paid by the West to the wars in the former Yugoslavia should come as no surprise. Only recently have superpowers refrained from involvement in internal conflicts. Traditionally the case has been just the opposite. And with good reason: revolutions in France, Russia, and China sparked profound changes in the international system that remain with us today. During the Cold War, internal conflicts in Korea and Vietnam drew the United States into costly interventions, while domestic strife in El Salvador and Nicaragua dominated American foreign policy through the 1980s. For the Soviet Union, internal wars provided the source for both one of Moscow's greatest victories (Cuba) and one of its most costly defeats (Afghanistan).

Since the collapse of the USSR (brought on in part by the Afghan disaster) and the end of the Cold War, new questions must be asked about civil wars and American interests. Proxy fights between Russia and America are no longer likely. The domino effect is no longer a concern. Though wars within states continue to outnumber those fought between them, many now argue that the United States should turn its back on these internal squabbles. These civil wars, they argue, are the domestic affairs of poor, weak countries, not important enough to merit American involvement. Getting enmeshed in complicated disputes and age-old hatreds will sap American resources—and for no good reason.

There is something to this view. Most civil wars do not directly threaten the United States or its allies. While recent internal conflicts have raised humanitarian concerns, none has seriously affected American security or economic interests. This, however, was largely a matter of luck. The United States should recognize a vital and sobering truth: that Russia, Mexico, and Saudi Arabia all now stand on the brink of civil war, conflicts that would have devastating consequences for the United States. These consequences are not the traditional dangers of state-to-state aggression, such as outside attack or invasion. Though largely ignored by scholars and policymakers, who remain fixated on the idea of international conflict, internal war has emerged as a principal threat to security in the post-Cold War world.

If the United States ignores disputes that do not directly threaten national security, it runs the risk of appearing not to care. However, intervention often brings charges of imperialist exploitation. How can the United States win?

The end of the world (as we know it)

Conflicts fought within borders of a single state send shock waves far beyond their frontiers. To begin with, internal wars risk destroying assets the United States needs. Were the Persian Gulf oil fields destroyed in a Saudi civil war, the American economy (and those of the rest of the developed world) would suffer severely. Internal wars can also unleash threats that stable governments formerly held in check. As central governments weaken and fall, weapons of mass destruction may fall into the hands of rogue leaders or anti-American factions. More directly, internal wars endanger American citizens living and traveling abroad. Liberia will not be the last place America sends helicopters to rescue its stranded citizens. Finally, internal wars, when they erupt on U.S. borders, threaten to destabilize America itself. U.S. intervention in Haiti was spurred, in large part, by fear of the flood of refugees poised to enter the United States.

Visit Princeton University's Woodrow Wilson School of Public and International Affairs website to read a report on the U.S. intervention in Haiti: www.wws. princeton.edu/ ~cases/papers/ haiti.html.

All of these dangers are grave enough to warrant consideration; what makes them even more serious is the fact that their impact on America is largely unintended. Being unintended, the spill-off effects of civil wars are not easily deterred, which creates unique challenges to American interests. U.S. policymakers have traditionally tried to sway foreign leaders through a simple formula: ensure that the

In September 2002 George W. Bush justified the use of preemptive strikes against any regime thought to possess weapons of mass destruction. Many legal experts argue that preemptive strikes violate international law.

benefits of defying America are outweighed by the punishment that the United States will inflict if defied. That calculus, however, no longer applies when there is no single, rational government in place to deter. This raises the cost to America; if the United States (or any country) cannot deter a threat, it must turn to actual self-defense or preemption instead. Unlike deterrence, these strategies are enormously difficult to carry out and in some cases (such as preventing the destruction of the Saudi oil fields) would be impossible. Without deterrence as a policy option, Washington loses its most effective means of safeguarding its interests.

Where are these new threats likely to crop up? And which should the United States be concerned with? Two criteria must guide policymakers in answering these questions. First is the actual likelihood of civil war in any particular state. American interests would be endangered by a war in Canada, but the prospect is so improbable it can safely be ignored. Second is the impact of a civil war on the United States; would it threaten vital American security and economic concerns? Future conflict in Sierra Leone may be plausible, but it would have such a negligible impact on the United States that it does not justify much attention.

Only three countries, in fact, meet both criteria: Mexico, Saudi Arabia, and Russia. Civil conflict in Mexico would produce waves of disorder that would spill into the United States, endangering the lives of hundreds of thousands of Americans, destroying a valuable export market, and sending a torrent of refugees northward. A rebellion in Saudi Arabia could destroy its ability to export oil, the oil on which the industrialized world depends. And internal war in Russia could devastate Europe and trigger the use of nuclear weapons.

These countries include Indonesia, Venezuela, the Philippines, Egypt, Turkey, Israel, and China, among others.

Of course, civil war in a cluster of other states could seriously harm American interests.... In none, however, are the stakes as high or the threat of war as imminent....

Arming America

Lack of attention to the threat of civil wars by U.S. policymakers and academics has meant a lack of response and policy options. This does not mean, however, that Washington can or should do nothing at all. As a first measure, American policymakers should work with governments of threatened states to prevent domestic conflict from erupting. Though the inadvertent side effects of internal conflicts cannot be deterred, the outbreak of civil war itself may be discouraged. Doing so may require unambiguous and generous American support for a regime

Is it the responsibility of the United States to work with the governments of troubled states, or is it the job of the United Nations?

that finds itself under assault. Or it may require Washington to ease out unsustainable leaders (the Philippines' Marcos or Indonesia's Suharto) once their time has clearly passed. Either way, the difficulties of preventing internal war pale in comparison to the problems of coping with its effects....

Fundamentally, Washington must recognize that future threats will be qualitatively different from traditional challenges. During the Cold War, an enormous amount of military, economic, and scholarly effort went into deterring a Soviet invasion of Western Europe. America did not then hesitate to protect itself. The prospect of internal war erupting in key states is now just as likely as was that of Soviet troops pouring through the Fulda Gap, and the consequences would be just as catastrophic. And yet the U.S. government gives internal war only a tiny fraction of the attention it once paid to the Soviet threat. With the Cold War over and internal wars virtually the only form of battle being fought, scholars and policymakers need to shift gears and recognize that not all threats to security are deliberate, purposeful acts of a coherent enemy that can be deterred with the right policy. Civil wars could inadvertently unleash catastrophic harms. Because these risks are so hard to prevent, they must now get the attention they so urgently deserve.

What do you think the United States can do to prepare itself for civil war in states that could harm American interests?

Summary

To what extent should the United States intervene in foreign affairs? In the first article Ron Paul argues that U.S. foreign policy is often too interventionist. While the United States is far too willing to use military intervention in foreign disputes, it fails to achieve long-term objectives of peace and stability. Paul believes that U.S. foreign policy is unbalanced and often guided by economic interests, and that resentment against this may be the driving force behind terrorist attacks such as those of September 11, 2001. He warns politicians and policymakers not to repeat the mistakes of the war on drugs, where hard-line policies have actually increased drug usage and violent behavior. In conclusion Paul calls for a better understanding of the reasons why foreign policies breed resentment toward the United States. Only then can the United States begin to combat the root causes of terrorism.

In the second article Steven R. David argues that U.S. foreign policy is not interventionist enough. Civil wars and regional rivalries have far-reaching consequences that can directly affect U.S. interests, for example, by destroying valuable economic assets or threatening national security. David suggests that the United States has been slow to recognize the dangerous consequences of new conflicts abroad. Particularly where there is no recognized government in a country and where diplomacy fails, David argues, the United States must turn to actual self-defense or preemptive strikes, since it is much better to tackle a problem earlier than to deal with its consequences later on. In conclusion David suggests that U.S. foreign policy requires a shift toward deterrence to prevent future threats to American interests and security.

FURTHER INFORMATION:

Books:

Carter, Ralph G., *Contemporary Cases in U.S. Foreign Policy: From Terrorism to Trade.* Washington, D.C.: Congressional Quarterly, 2001.

Gelb, Leslie H., et al., *Intervention and American Foreign Policy.* New York: Council on Foreign Relations Press, 2001.

Joes, Anthony James (ed.), *Saving Democracies: U.S. Intervention in Threatened Democratic States.* Westport, CT: Praeger, 2000.

Litwak, Robert S., *Rogue States and U.S. Foreign Policy: Containment after the Cold War.* Baltimore, MD: Johns Hopkins University Press, 2000.

Peters, Ralph, *Beyond Terror: Strategy in a Changing World.* Mechanicsburg, PA: Stackpole Books, 2002.

Pillar, Paul R., and Michael H. Armacost, *Terrorism and U.S. Foreign Policy.* Washington, D.C.: The Brookings Institution, 2001.

Useful websites:

www.afpc.org
Bulletins, articles, and analysis on contemporary issues in foreign policy from the American Foreign Policy Council.

www.policyalmanac.org/world
Comprehensive links and background information on U.S. foreign policy and national security issues.

The following debates in the Pro/Con series may also be of interest:

In this volume:
 Topic 14 Does terrorism arise from the problem of "failed states"?

IS U.S. FOREIGN POLICY TOO INTERVENTIONIST?

YES: U.S. foreign policy actively protects economic assets abroad

YES: The United States preempts major threats to national security wherever they may come from

ECONOMY
Does U.S. foreign policy help strengthen the economy?

NATIONAL SECURITY
Does U.S. foreign policy strengthen national security?

NO: U.S. foreign policy only looks for short-term solutions. It does not create long-term economic stability.

NO: U.S. intervention breeds the resentment that drives fanatics

IS U.S. FOREIGN POLICY TOO INTERVENTIONIST?
KEY POINTS

YES: U.S. foreign policy champions the democratic cause as a model for world stability

YES: U.S. foreign policy aims to prevent weapons of mass destruction from falling into dangerous hands

GLOBAL STABILITY
Does U.S. foreign policy create a safer world?

NO: U.S. foreign policy often fails to remove dangerous dictators or repressive regimes. These same threats may crop up again.

NO: U.S. foreign policy breeds strong anti-Western sentiment, laying the foundations for future conflict

HOW TO MAKE A SPEECH

"Speech is power: Speech is to persuade,
to convert, to compel."

—RALPH WALDO EMERSON (1803–1882), POET AND ESSAYIST

A good speech is informative, interesting, and concise. Learning how to convey your message to an audience is an invaluable life skill. These two pages will help you prepare, structure, and deliver a speech that captures an audience's attention. With practice your speeches will improve, and you will be able to apply your speaking skills to other areas of your life.

The following points will help you prepare and deliver a speech in any situation:

1. Know your audience
It is important to find out what kind of audience you will be talking to.
• Are they old or young?
• Are they predominantly male or female?
• Are they culturally mixed?
Take these factors into account when preparing your speech—it is vital that the audience understands your references, language, and humor.

2. Know your subject
Thorough research on your subject will enable you to speak confidently.
• Use a variety of research tools such as the library, Internet, and encyclopedias to ensure accuracy.
• Try to obtain up-to-date statistics.
• Make a list of possible questions that may arise.

3. Practice
Once you have written your speech (see opposite), it is important to practice.
• Use a mirror: Think about how your body language can help convey your message. For example, use gestures to emphasize important points.
• Tape yourself: Think about the clarity of your delivery and ways to reduce any poor grammar or unnecessary sounds, such as "er" or "um."
• Family or friends: Rehearse in front of them, and ask for constructive criticism.

4. Delivery
Before finally giving your speech, think about how you will deliver it.
• Consider using relevant visual aids to support your speech.
• Use your voice effectively. Vary the pitch and tone. Do not mumble. Project clearly so that people at the back of the room can hear everything you say.
• Stand straight with your shoulders back to help you appear more confident.

STRUCTURING YOUR SPEECH

When writing your speech, split it into three main sections: introduction, body, and conclusion. Rather than writing the speech out word for word, write short sentences on cue cards to prompt you (remember to number the cards in order!). Doing this will make your speech sound more spontaneous and accessible and will give you an opportunity to make more eye contact with the audience.

Introduction

Your opening remarks will set the tone of your speech. Try to grab the attention of your audience from the outset, for example, with an outrageous (but not offensive) statement, a rhetorical question, or a joke. Engaging with the audience at the beginning will encourage them to listen to the rest of your speech. Keep the introduction short, but make sure you briefly explain what you intend to discuss in the main body of your speech.

Body

This is the main part of the speech. Explain your points, ideas, and information in a helpful, logical way. Choose from the following approaches:
* Discuss your ideas as a series of points. It is important to keep the audience's attention, so try to make each point as clear and concise as possible.
* Use a handout to outline your main points. List a few key headings that you can refer to in your speech. If handwritten, make sure the handout is legible!
* Use a whiteboard or overhead projector to make a "mind-map." Write the main topic in the middle, and draw branches to key points with further branches from them to more minor points. Practice drawing your mind-map beforehand.
* Support your ideas with case studies, examples, anecdotes, and visual aids.

Conclusion

Your final comments are important and should contain the key ideas you want your audience to take away with them. Reiterate your main points clearly. Try to end your speech on an upbeat note, with a question or an interesting point.

POINTS TO REMEMBER WHEN SPEAKING

* Avoid repetition of words and phrases. Be concise and clear.
* Rhetorical questions may encourage your audience to think independently.
* Use "I" and "you," and make eye contact to build a more intimate relationship with the audience.
* Anecdotes, quotations, and statistics lend authority to your speech.
* Ask yourself, "Is this speech interesting, concise, and effective"?
* Monitor time: How long can you speak without it being boring?

Topic 3
SHOULD THE UNITED STATES HAVE RELATIONS WITH FUNDAMENTALIST REGIMES?

YES
"IRAN: TIME FOR DÉTENTE"
FOREIGN POLICY IN FOCUS, POLICY BRIEFS, NOVEMBER 1999, VOL. 4, NO. 28
STEPHEN ZUNES

NO
FROM "ON TO IRAN!"
AMERICAN ENTERPRISE INSTITUTE, FEBRUARY 18, 2002
REUEL MARC GERECHT

INTRODUCTION

Fundamentalism can be defined as a movement that rigidly adheres to a set of basic principles or beliefs. In line with this definition there have been many fundamentalist regimes in history, from the medieval Holy Roman Empire to the communist Soviet Union. Since the late 1970s, however, a number of Islamic countries—most notably Iran— have practiced a form of religious government that can be described as fundamentalist.

Islamic fundamentalism is a fairly modern movement that stresses a literal interpretation of the Koran, the Muslim equivalent of the Christian Bible. While it is a fairly modern school of Islamic thought, fundamentalism has its roots in the 18th century, when Muhammad 'Abd al-Wahab (1703–1792) called for a return to fundamental Islamic values—the so-called "pillars of Islam." These values grew more popular

in the 19th century in response to European involvement in the Muslim world. Many Muslims embraced the cultural and economic influences of the West in an attempt to build powerful secular societies. Others argued that Western influence had a negative effect on traditional Islamic values and opposed control by nations they viewed with suspicion.

Support for the European Islamic model gained momentum when the Ottoman Empire—the Muslim empire of the Turks—crumbled after World War I (1914–1918). New Muslim states, such as Iraq, Jordan, and Saudi Arabia, emerged. In the years following World War II (1939–1945), France and Britain withdrew from North Africa, liberating Muslim states such as Algeria and Sudan. While the West still played a vital role in supporting these independent nations, new influences, such as Arab nationalism and socialism, started to develop. By the late 1960s the Muslim world was increasingly frustrated with Western involvement in its internal affairs. Interest in fundamentalism grew.

"Criticism of the government's policies is not bad, but when someone attempts to undermine the foundations of the government, it is treason and not freedom of expression."
—AYATOLLAH ALI KHAMENEI, IRANIAN RELIGIOUS LEADER, 1998

In 1979 Islamic fundamentalism was established as a political force in Iran when Shah Muhammad Reza Pahlavi was overthrown by the Muslim cleric Ayatollah Ruhollah Khomeini (1900–1989). Unlike Iran's secular government under the shah, the new religious authorities enforced Islamic codes of behavior and dress and suppressed Western influences. Khomeini inspired Islamic fundamentalists everywhere, from the Muslim Brotherhood in Egypt to the Islamic Salvation Front in Algeria. Fundamentalist states were also established in Sudan in 1989 and in Afghanistan in 1996 in the aftermath of the war with the Soviet Union.

Iran–U.S. relations worsened in the months after Khomeini's accession. Demanding the extradition of the shah from his exile in the United States, Iranian students held 52 Americans hostage in the U.S. embassy in the nation's capital, Tehran. It was not until Khomeini's death in 1989 that Iran tempered its policies toward the West. The country's former president, al-Udhma Khameini, was declared the new spiritual leader, while Ali Akbar Hashemi Rafsanjani became the Iranian president. But despite Rafsanjani's moves toward economic liberalization and appeasing Western governments, the U.S. position toward Iran has continued to be hostile. U.S. officials link Iran to terrorist groups such as Hezbollah. Millions of dollars have been spent on intelligence operations, and tough economic sanctions—on oil and trade—have been imposed in an effort to undermine the Iranian government.

Critics of U.S. policy toward Iran, such as Stephen Zunes in his article "Iran: Time for Détente," believe that the anti-American sentiments of Iran's Islamic regime are a direct result of U.S. interference in the Middle East. They argue that economic sanctions are unlikely to change the Iranian position and have a devastating effect on the country. Through diplomacy the United States could press Iran to end policies the West deems unacceptable, such as the suspected funding of terrorists.

Advocates of current U.S. foreign policy toward Iran, such as Reuel Marc Gerecht in his article "On to Iran!" believe that hostile policies are the only way to deal with tyrannical regimes. While many people think that anti-American sentiment has cooled since the democratic election of President Khatami in 1997, others believe that Khatami is a front for hard-line Iranian clerics with terrorist links. Supporters of current U.S. policy suggest that diplomatic relations can only be resumed when the extreme element of the Iranian regime is removed.

IRAN: TIME FOR DÉTENTE
Stephen Zunes

YES

An effective way to begin is to state the main point of your argument at the start. The keystone of Zunes's argument is the dual standard of U.S.–Iran policy: The United States supports other Middle Eastern regimes that are also guilty of the crimes of which it accuses Iran.

✓ …Although the misdeeds of the Iranian regime are indeed numerous, the first major problem with U.S. policy is that most U.S. accusations against the Iranians seem to be grossly exaggerated. Iran's activities are not substantially worse than those of other nations in the region, including governments considered close allies of the United States. Thus Washington's policy is based on a series of false assumptions, and it compromises U.S. credibility, even when its concerns have a legitimate basis.

Although Iran has certainly trained, financially supported, and funneled arms to extremist Islamic groups and to the repressive government in Sudan, U.S. charges of direct Iranian responsibility for specific terrorist acts against Israeli and American targets are highly dubious. Indeed, Iranian support for such groups has declined significantly in recent years. Iran's terrorism beyond its borders has always been primarily directed at exiled dissidents, not against the U.S. or Israel. Similarly, Iran's potential as a nuclear power has been greatly exaggerated, with the Clinton administration even overruling the more modest conclusions of its own agencies. The foreign diplomatic community in Teheran and the president of the International Atomic Energy Agency appear to agree that Iran's motivations in building a nuclear reactor are peaceful.

The "dangers" Iran poses

Sunni Muslims make up the majority in most Islamic countries except Iran, which is dominated by Shi'ite Muslims. A split between the two groups occurred early in Islamic history over leadership of the community. Other differences over community organization and legal practices followed, but the two groups share the same doctrine.

Iran's immediate post-revolutionary zeal to export its ideology was short-lived, as internal problems and outside threats deflected the attention of its leadership. In addition, Iranians are culturally and religiously very different from the Sunni Arabs that dominate the Middle East. Indeed, the hierarchical structure of Shi'ism limits the revolution's appeal as a model for other Middle Eastern states.

There is little evidence to suggest aggressive Iranian designs in the Persian Gulf, either. Iran has not threatened—nor does it have any reason for provoking—a confrontation over sea lanes, because it is at least as dependent as its neighbors on unrestricted navigation. In fact, Iran has been dramatically reducing its military spending due to financial problems. Additionally, despite increased Iranian procurement of sophisticated missiles, Arab gulf states have similar missile capabilities, supplementing the U.S. Navy as an effective deterrent force.

The second major problem with U.S. policy is that efforts to isolate and overthrow the Iranian government are not based on legal grounds. The U.S. has avoided urging the UN to support its sanctions, because Washington knows there is no legal basis for such actions, and it would thus fail to get any support. Unlike international sanctions against the former apartheid government of South Africa or the current military junta in Burma, sanctions against Iran are not predicated on significant legal or moral imperatives. As with similar extraterritorial efforts regarding Cuba, U.S. attempts to pressure other nations to get tough with Iran have alienated even America's strongest allies, who consider such efforts to be in violation of World Trade Organization principles.

Do you think it is right that the United States can take action against states that it does not favor, even if such action is illegal?

Similarly, U.S. efforts to subvert the Iranian government are contrary to international legal conventions that recognize sovereign rights and principles of nonintervention. They run directly counter to the Algiers Declaration of 1981, under which the U.S. unequivocally pledged not to intervene politically or militarily in the internal affairs of Iran. The U.S. is [also] obligated under the Nuclear Nonproliferation Treaty to allow signatory states in good standing (like Iran) to have access to peaceful nuclear technology.

Having accused the United States of acting illegally against Iran, Zunes backs up his argument with specific examples of why U.S. action is illegal.

The third major problem is that current U.S. policy fails to make the Iranian regime act more in accord with international standards of human rights. The idea that U.S. sanctions can create sufficient economic pressure on Iran to topple the regime has never been realistic, because European and Japanese allies hold most of Iran's foreign debt and would never cooperate in such a self-defeating policy. Clinton's 1995 executive order banning trade with Iran took place without consultation with other countries, who simply absorbed the trade to the detriment of American businesses.

It seems that U.S. hostility toward Iran is based less on a rational calculation of the threat Teheran poses to U.S. interests than on a reactive stance toward any regime that challenges American hegemony. Iran serves, along with other so-called "rogue" states, as an opportunity for U.S. political leaders to appear tough and as a rationalization for continued high levels of military spending.

Do you agree with the author that the real reason the United States is hostile to Iran is because it is such a high-profile opponent of American values and politics?

Though Iranians as a whole, reflected in key segments of their government, appear willing to support increasing cooperation with the West, U.S. policy has so offended nationalist sentiments that it has had the ironic impact of enhancing the credibility of the hard-line elements. Each escalation in U.S. sanctions, rhetoric, or military presence in the Persian Gulf becomes a self-fulfilling prophecy as Iranians consider themselves increasingly under siege.

See Topic 10 Has the United States exploited Latin America? on pages 124–135 of this volume.

The double standards in U.S. policy are also a major factor behind the policy's failure. The history of U.S. support for terrorist groups in Latin America and elsewhere lends little credibility to Washington's antiterrorist crusade against Iran. Likewise, U.S. support for Saudi Arabia and Washington's ambivalence toward the Taliban government of Afghanistan lend little credence to [U.S.] concerns over Iran's notorious human rights record and rigid interpretation of Islamic law....

Toward a new foreign policy

During pro-reformist demonstrations in Iran that were savagely suppressed by rightist elements in July 1999, both the Clinton administration and its congressional critics remained largely silent, with the State Department only making a terse statement in calling for Iranian recognition of international human rights standards. One reason for this quiescence was the fear that more open U.S. support of the students might lead to a hard-line backlash. Supporting efforts at liberalizing the regime rather than overthrowing it entirely would be a more realistic, legal, and moral option, as well as one more likely to restore American credibility....

Zunes strengthens his argument by suggesting clear alternative measures that the United States could take toward Iran.

There are three major areas where U.S. policy toward Iran could improve. First, a broader coordination in the formulation of policy is essential. On the domestic level, policy toward Iran should no longer be directed primarily by the Pentagon and national security managers but should include the perspectives of State Department area specialists, Iranian-American intellectuals, and others knowledgeable about the country. On the international level, the U.S. must reverse its unilateralism and should coordinate policy with the Europeans and others who share U.S. concerns. Enforcing already-existing safeguards against nuclear proliferation would be one particularly important area for such efforts.

Unilateral action affects only one side or party, as opposed to multilateral action in which many sides participate.

Similarly, the U.S. should work through the UN and should support other multilateral efforts to create a new security regime for the region rather than simply fueling the arms race and exacerbating the suspicions and bellicose rhetoric between Iran and the Arab gulf states. The U.S. must also seriously consider the perspectives of the democratic opposition in Iran. Although the Iranian opposition—which supports the arms embargo and opposes direct support for the government until moderate forces consolidate their hold

"Bellicose" means eager to fight or warlike.

and liberalize further—is somewhat divided, most strenuously oppose the U.S.-led economic embargo against Iran.

Second, the U.S. must scrap its double standards. Rather than targeting only Iran, the Clinton administration must pressure Saudi Arabia and other regimes in the Middle East to end their human rights abuses. Once the need for evenhandedness is recognized, there are a number of potential agreements that could be solidified between the U.S. and Iran. For example, Washington could propose ending its support for Israeli occupation forces in southern Lebanon in return for an end to Iranian support of the Lebanese Hezbollah resisting that occupation. Similarly, the best way to stop any procurement of nuclear weapons by Iran is to support a nuclear weapons-free zone in the Middle East. Such a move would require both the withdrawal of U.S. nuclear forces from the region and a pledge by Washington to pressure Israel to dismantle its nuclear arsenal. Iran has long supported such a nuclear-free zone agreement.

Third, U.S. policy must include a carrot as well as a stick. There has been a great reluctance to reward Iran for good behavior, in part as a reaction to the misguided policies of the Reagan administration, which sent arms to hard-line elements in the Iranian military. To maximize its policy impact, Washington should let Teheran know just which Iranian policies will result in rewards or punishments.

Making reasonable demands

Similarly, the U.S. must ascertain which of its demands for policy changes in Iran are reasonable and realistic. For example, given both the widespread support among Iranians for the Palestinians and the growing realization that the current framework of the negotiations are to the Palestinians' disadvantage, insisting upon Iranian governmental support of the U.S.-brokered Middle East peace process is unrealistic.

Iran will continue to play an important and unique role in the politics of the region based on its own perceived self interests. Despite persistent efforts to isolate Iran, the U.S. cannot change that reality. It is important that Washington find a way to encourage Iran to become a more responsible member of the community of nations and to end its repression against legitimate dissent. This will require, however, that America reevaluate its policies toward both Iran and the Middle East as a whole. Détente between the U.S. and Iran is necessary if there is to be peace and security in the region. The current antagonistic relationship between the two countries serves neither's long-term interests.

The Israeli Army occupied South Lebanon in 1978 after Palestinian guerillas based there attacked northern Israel. Israel's invasion prompted UN Security Council Resolution 425, which called for Israel's complete and unconditional withdrawal. For more see www.mideastfacts.com/israel_lebanon.overview.html.

Do you think that there is a realistic possibility of a nuclear-free zone agreement in the Middle East? If not, why not?

"Détente" is a French word that means the easing of strained relations.

ON TO IRAN!
Reuel Marc Gerecht

To read Bush's 2002 State of the Union address, go to www. whitehouse.gov/ stateoftheunion/.

"Evanesce" means disappear. Does the author's choice of words aid or hinder his argument?

Khatami was elected president in 1997 with the promise of wide political and social reforms. To read Khatami's CNN interview, go to www.salamiran. org/events/ Interview/text.html.

"Foggy Bottom" is a historic district of Washington, D.C., but the author is referring to the city's political community.

NO

President George W. Bush's stunningly forceful State of the Union address has probably forever altered U.S.-Iranian relations. It may provoke a redrawing of the intellectual map of the Middle East, giving liberal democracy its best chance in the region since the end of World War II. In following through on his promise to counter and preempt hostile Iranian actions, the president will likely accelerate the collapse of the clerical regime. This is a good thing, for unless the regime falls, the Islamic Republic's penchant for tyranny, terrorism, and unconventional weaponry will not evanesce. As the sad experience of the "moderate" president Mohammad Khatami gives ample evidence, the clerical regime isn't evolving into a humane, "Islamic democracy." Indeed, we may well be watching the clerics immerse themselves again in a wave of anti-American terrorism....

The false promise of Khatami

Khatami's election and his "dialogue-of-civilizations" interview on CNN in January 1998 whetted hopes at State that the cold war between Washington and Tehran, and the tension between us and our allies, might be over. A good-guy-Khatami-versus-bad-guy-Khamenei view took hold at Foggy Bottom, as it did in the American business community and academe. They all embraced Khatami more eagerly than they had Ali Akbar Hashemi Rafsanjani, the cleric who first dampened the revolutionary fires inside his country.

This philo-Khatami attitude continued past September 11, which is astonishing since the Iranian president had long since become politically irrelevant in Tehran and the clerical town of Qom. He had repeatedly failed to throw down the gauntlet at those in the regime who were harassing journalists, students, government employees, and women—all important voices in the "civil society" coalition that twice elected Khatami. He was, as an Iranian who'd known him from childhood once remarked, "a chicken," which was one of the most important reasons why Rafsanjani, the first "moderate" president of the republic and the second most powerful mullah in Iran, decided to back him in 1997. With Khatami in the presidency, there would be no radical change.

Nevertheless, the State Department saw the Afghan war as an excellent opportunity to build a bridge to the clerical regime, since the enemy (the Iranians) of my enemy (the Taliban) ought to be my friend. With the department's Policy Planning boss Richard Haass in the lead, State began sending signals to Tehran, and to Congress, that Iran was being helpful to America's antiterrorist coalition. U.S. officials were favorably impressed with Iran's promise to undertake search-and-rescue missions for any American pilot downed over Iranian territory…. In Washington, some U.S. officials spoke with hushed awe of the intelligence Tehran provided about the whereabouts of Taliban leaders and Osama Bin Laden. And the clerics didn't sabotage the Bonn conference on Afghanistan's political future. All in all, according to Ambassador Haass, the Iranians were playing a "constructive" role in Afghanistan.

Is this "an enemy of my enemy is my friend" viewpoint an appropriate basis for a country's foreign policy? What problems might it create?

Iranian support an illusion

This was nonsense. The "pro-American drift" (*Washington Post*) of the Iranian government during the Afghan war was an illusion—Persian realpolitik, as fear of American airpower dovetailed with Western hopefulness and gullibility. The clerics in Tehran, attentive students of history who keenly understand the anti-American ideological underpinnings of their regime, knew that the American enemy of a Muslim foe must remain *the* enemy. In the war against the Taliban, the clerics actually gave us little to nothing. Allowing U.S. warplanes and helicopter crews overflight and search-and-rescue rights in Iranian airspace would have been something; offering to aid a hypothetically downed pilot was not. (The Iranians probably would have returned any stranded U.S. pilot—B-52s and smart bombs concentrate the mind—but it might not have been the quickest homeward voyage.) And Tehran's providing information about the whereabouts of senior Taliban and Al Qaeda officials isn't particularly compelling evidence of friendly intentions. Whatever they gave us obviously wasn't top-drawer stuff since most of the leadership of the Taliban and Al Qaeda appear to have escaped. Also, if the clerics could get Americans to bomb Taliban leaders they hate, this again seems most sensible and sound—a bit like getting Washington to give you anti-tank missiles in exchange for liberating American hostages whom your foreign proxies kidnapped….

Gerecht employs a classic debating technique. He presents the opposing argument and then completely demolishes it.

"Realpolitik" means practical politics.

Gerecht's sarcastic reference is to the 1986 arms-for-hostages scandal between the United States and Iran. For more information go to www. washington-report. org/backissues/0994/ 9409008.htm.

Many U.S. officials and Iran experts have believed for nearly a decade that the Iranian regime has retired from anti-American terrorism. The Iranian intelligence service might regularly murder expatriates in Europe and the Middle East, and Tehran might send lethal aid to Hezbollah, Hamas, and the Palestinian Islamic Jihad for their attacks against Israelis and Jews, these experts think, but the clerics no longer really want to attack the United States. By the 1990s, Iranian intelligence and the Revolutionary Guard Corps, and their faithful followers in the Lebanese Hezbollah, particularly its voraciously lethal security chief Imad Mughniyah, had stopped blowing up embassies and Marine barracks and kidnapping and killing American citizens and U.S. officials. The clerics were, so the reasoning went, tired of the battle against the "Great Satan." Thermidor had arrived. The mullahs now preferred trade to terrorism. After America's war against Iraq, they were scared of U.S. military power. The Europeans, who were all over Iran trying to find a way to make a profit, kept telling Americans how the country had changed. One just had to ignore the occasional expatriate killing spree, the clerical regime's penchant for supporting radical Palestinians, and its weapons-of-mass-destruction programs, which were justified in any case since Saddam Hussein was still right next door. The mullahs would outgrow their bad habits, we were told, as the regime aged and democratized.

The Khobar Towers bombing

The 1996 bombing at Khobar Towers in Dhahran, Saudi Arabia, that killed 19 American soldiers threw a kink into this analysis, but the election of Mohammad Khatami arrived just in time to quiet serious reflection on that bloody episode the summer before. As one think-tanker remarked offhandedly, it was not wise to underscore probable Iranian complicity in the Khobar bombing for fear of derailing Khatami's reform movement and the "thaw" in U.S.-Iranian relations. Though this was an absurd and dangerous analysis of Iranian culture and the clerical system—the "be-nice-and-the-moderates-might-win" approach to Middle Eastern power politics—the view was quite widespread in the Clinton administration.

Given the op-eds and think-tank papers written just before and during the Afghan war … this détentist view of commerce and politics still has currency in establishment circles. This perspective, again, is astonishing since Mohammad Khatami … was a political irrelevancy in Iran even before his reelection in June 2001. The clerical ruling class had coalesced decisively around Khamenei. And the truth be told: Khatami and Khamenei do not in all probability significantly differ on whether the United States, by its very nature, is harmful to the Islamic Republic.

During the French Revolution Thermidor was the eleventh month in the French revolutionary calendar. It marked the downfall of Robespierre and the end of the Reign of Terror on 9 Thermidor (July 27, 1794).

Khobar Towers was a facility housing U.S. and allied forces supporting the coalition air operation over Iraq.

"Op-eds" are the opinion/editorial columns in newspapers and magazines.

In Iran the president ranks second in the hierarchy of power to the supreme religious leader, who has the final say in matters of state.

It is also stupefying that anyone, 24 years after the revolution, still believes that trade could have a moderating effect on the clerical regime's behavior. The Middle Eastern mercantile tradition, like the Italian, sees war and commerce as compatible. Rafsanjani and Khamenei, who have probably authorized every Iranian terrorist operation since the early 1980s, have advocated increasing U.S.-Iranian commerce. Both favored the Conoco oil-and-gas deal canceled by the Clinton administration in 1995…. They'd love to buy oil-drilling equipment, big electric turbines, and high technology from the United States, not to mention American military equipment, if they could get their hands on it.

In spring 1995 the U.S. oil firm Conoco won a $600 million contract to develop Iran's Sirri Island oil field in the Persian Gulf. After pressure from the Israel lobby President Clinton signed an executive order cutting off all U.S. business with Iran.

The mullahs have been trading with the Western Europeans for 20 years while killing dozens of Iranian expatriates on European soil. If the Americans start to act like Europeans—engage in trade and a "critical dialogue" regardless of clerical behavior—why should the mullahs moderate their comportment? Laissez-faire trade blended with political rationalism inevitably drops you to the lowest common denominator, which is where the clerics, first-rate realpoliticians with a sharp ideological edge, operate against Westerners most effectively.

"Laissez-faire" is a policy of noninterference of government in politics or the economy.

Nonetheless, it is likely that the State Department, the Europeans, influential voices in the American business and foreign-policy communities, and the American academic crowd specialized in the Middle East will resist the logic of President Bush's "axis of evil" address. A return to non-belligerent dialogue, even if indirect and haphazard, will appear to many as a more reasonable approach.

After all, Iran really hasn't changed its spots since September 11. The clerical regime has been seriously seeking nuclear weapons since the end of the Gulf War in 1991. Its ballistic missile program is even older. Tehran has been giving money and weaponry to Palestinian radicals and the Lebanese Hezbollah for years….

The Bush administration ought to want to unnerve the ruling clerics, and embolden Iran's people, by letting all know that America, as President Bush declared in his State of the Union address, favors real popular government in Iran. The administration must not, under any circumstances, reach out to "moderate" and "pragmatic" mullahs to the detriment of the Iranian people. This strategy is fool's gold. All we would be doing is reaching out to the head of the powerful Expediency Council, Ali Akbar Hashemi Rafsanjani, who is indeed a moderate, pragmatic, and *powerful* cleric. And if Rafsanjani reaches back, he will most certainly beat us black and blue….

Summary

Many Americans equate Islamic fundamentalism with terrorism, and in the wake of the attacks in New York and Washington, D.C., on September 11, 2001, this view is perhaps not surprising. But the driving force behind this terrorism is the extremist groups that hide behind fundamentalist regimes. In itself fundamentalism is not the threat. Nevertheless, extremist activities have put U.S. relations with the Muslim world under enormous pressure.

In the first article Stephen Zunes suggests that U.S. foreign policy toward a now democratic Iran is characterized by hostility. He suggests that the United States has based its policy on exaggerated accusations about Iran's nuclear capabilities and links to terrorism. Zunes points to U.S. support for Saudi Arabia—another fundamentalist regime with a bad human rights record—as a double standard in its policy. He concludes by urging the United States to develop a foreign policy toward Iran to encourage peace in the Middle East.

In the second article Reuel Marc Gerecht suggests that President George W. Bush was right when he included Iran in the "axis of evil" during his State of the Union address in 2002. While many people think that Iran's moderate president Khatami has tempered the oppressive regime, Gerecht believes otherwise. He claims that Khatami is a puppet for hard-line clerics who maintain links with terrorist organizations such as Hezbollah and continue in their quest for nuclear weapons. Gerecht concludes that the U.S. government should maintain tough economic sanctions and foreign policy to undermine Iran's ruling clerics. Only when a real and popular government rules in Iran should U.S. foreign policy change.

FURTHER INFORMATION:

Books:

Bill, James, *The Eagle and the Lion: The Tragedy of American-Iranian Relations*. New Haven, CT: Yale University Press, 1988.

Davidson, Lawrence, *Islamic Fundamentalism*. Westport, CT: Greenwood Press, 1998.

Mackey, Sandra, *The Iranians: Persia, Islam and the Soul of a New Nation*. New York: Plume Press, 1998.

Articles:

Amirahmadi, Hooshang, "US–Iran Relations: From Confrontation to Modus Vivendi"? *CIRA Bulletin*, vol. 14, no. 2, September 1998.

Razi, Gholam Hossein, "The Nature of U.S. Opposition to Iran: A Framework for Foreign Policy Analysis." *Iranian Journal of International Affairs*, vol. 10, no. 3, Fall 1998.

Useful websites:

www.cmcu.net
The Center for Muslim–Christian Understanding site.
www.mpac.org
The Muslim Public Affairs Council represents the interests of Muslims in the United States.

> **The following debates in the Pro/Con series may also be of interest:**
>
> In this volume:
> Topic 16 Should the United States take more responsibility for promoting peace in the Middle East?

SHOULD THE UNITED STATES HAVE RELATIONS WITH FUNDAMENTALIST REGIMES?

YES: Only through diplomacy can the United States communicate disagreements with the policies of fundamentalist regimes and encourage more acceptable ones

YES: Alienating fundamentalist regimes makes the United States, as the world's main superpower, look prejudiced and uncaring, which fosters resentment in the Muslim world

DIPLOMACY
Should the United States open up diplomatic relations with fundamentalist regimes such as Iran?

RESPONSIBILITY
Does the United States have a global responsibility as a superpower to engage with all the governments in the world?

NO: You only have to look at the failed peace talks of Israelis and Palestinians to realize that diplomacy does not work

NO: The United States should adopt a multilateral approach through the United Nations to challenge fundamentalist states

SHOULD THE UNITED STATES HAVE RELATIONS WITH FUNDAMENTALIST REGIMES?

KEY POINTS

YES: High-profile military campaigns, such as Iraq in 1991 and Afghanistan in 2001, prove that the United States consistently challenges hard-line fundamentalists. Economic sanctions are also consistently applied, although they get less media attention.

DOUBLE STANDARDS
Is U.S. foreign policy consistent toward all fundamentalist regimes?

NO: Saudi Arabia is a close ally of the United States even though it has a deplorable human rights record and is known to have funded extremist organizations

Topic 4

SHOULD THE UNITED STATES SHOW A STRONGER COMMITMENT TO THE UNITED NATIONS?

YES

FROM "CHOOSING ENGAGEMENT: UNITING THE UN WITH U.S. INTERESTS"
FOREIGN AFFAIRS, SEPTEMBER/OCTOBER 2000
WILLIAM H. LUERS

NO

FROM "PAVING THE ROAD TO HELL: THE FAILURE OF UN PEACEKEEPING"
FOREIGN AFFAIRS, MARCH/APRIL 2000
MAX BOOT

INTRODUCTION

Organized in 1945 at the end of World War II (1939-1945), the United Nations (UN) is a voluntary association of nearly every country in the world—in 2002 there were 190 member nations. Its aims are to keep peace in the world, to promote people's general welfare, and to support the rights of individuals to determine their own future.

The United States took an active role in the establishment of the UN—the headquarters of which were set up in New York—and for many years was regarded as the organization's leader. For example, the Korean War (1950-1953) was fought under the UN flag, although it was effectively a U.S. war against the spread of communism. The other main success of concerted U.S.-UN action was the 1991 Gulf War, in which the United States and its allies, again nominally under UN direction, expelled Iraqi troops from Kuwait.

On the face of it then, the United States should favor the UN not only because of its role in founding the organization but also because over the years the UN has largely supported—and indeed been an instrument of—U.S. foreign policy. However, by the end of the 20th century the United States' commitment to the organization appeared to be weakening. After the Gulf War the U.S. government's debts to the UN increased: By 1999 it owed more than $1 billion, although this figure needs to be set against the government's annual contributions to the UN of over $2 billion. In addition, the United States began to rely less on UN support for its actions and interventions overseas.

There were several reasons for this change in attitude. One was economic: For much of the 1990s the federal budget was in deficit, and in electoral terms at least, withholding payments to the UN was a relatively uncontroversial way to make savings. Another reason was criticism of the UN itself: Many people came to regard the organization as little more than a talking shop. Even when it did take action, they claimed, the UN was ineffectual. In 1994 UN forces were sent to keep the peace in Rwanda, but they found themselves powerless to prevent the majority Hutu population from slaughtering nearly one million Tutsi. In 1995 the UN set up "safe havens" for Muslims in Bosnia, but shortly afterward the very people who were supposed to have been protected by these refuges were massacred by Serbs at Srebrenica.

> "[The UN] brings nations closer together around basic principles of democracy, liberty, and law."
> —MADELEINE ALBRIGHT, SECRETARY OF STATE (1997–2001)

The third reason for the decline in commitment to the UN was that the organization lost its role as a balance between the rival superpowers after the breakup of the Soviet Union in 1991. From then on the United States was unchallenged as the preeminent world power, a situation that reduced its desire to engage in UN negotiations.

Yet many people regard the UN as a successful force for good in the world. They maintain that it was the UN that brought to an end the long civil wars in Central America, Mozambique, and Angola in the 1990s. Others credit the UN for arranging a peace agreement that halted the civil war in Cambodia in 1992 and for supervising an election there in 1993. Skeptics, however, point out that the loser in this ballot promptly seized power by force.

Clearly it is difficult to determine the success of UN actions, but the fact remains that there has been no major world war since the organization was set up. Although that fact may be mere coincidence, it is also possibly because the UN has provided a forum for constructive discussion among the world's major powers.

William H. Luers, in the first article, believes that the UN would have greater success if the United States showed a stronger commitment to it. The author argues that this increased commitment would benefit the United States since its own international interests are often at risk if trouble abroad is not nipped in the bud.

This view seems to have gained credence since September 11, 2001. Less than two weeks after the terrorist attacks on New York and Washington, D.C., the United States paid the UN $825 million in unpaid dues, some of which dated back to the Reagan era (1981–1988). UN Secretary-General Kofi Annan expressed the hope that September 11 might bring about a change in attitudes: "If we are going to win this war against terrorism … [i]t has to be through international law [and] cooperation; the sort of resolutions and convictions that this organization has passed." But some critics, including Max Boot in the second article, counter that foreign policy objectives are more likely to be achieved if America acts alone.

CHOOSING ENGAGEMENT: UNITING THE UN WITH U.S. INTERESTS
William H. Luers

In July 1893 a young professor of history, Frederick Jackson Turner, presented a statement on "American exceptionalism." He claimed that the settlement of the New World, especially that of the frontier, had helped shape exceptional Americans and a unique American intellect different from that found in Western Europeans.

Can you think of situations in which U.S. interests would be best served by acting alone?

The 1999 Lomé Peace Agreement between the Sierra Leone government and the Liberia-backed Revolutionary United Front (RUF) collapsed in May 2000. The RUF kidnapped 500 UN peacekeepers. Scarred by previous engagements in African disputes, the United States did not send forces in response, leaving other countries—such as Britain—to send troops to assist the UN.

YES

Since the end of the Cold War, the United States has pursued a successful international economic strategy through active engagement in the World Bank, the International Monetary Fund (IMF), and the World Trade Organization (WTO). Yet it has failed to make similar commitments in the areas of politics, security, and law. It remains deeply ambivalent about the United Nations and resistant to emerging international law for various reasons: its superpower status, its tradition of "American exceptionalism," and its long history of insular attitudes toward other cultures.

Reducing security challenges

Today, the United States considers itself the most powerful and the most democratic of states, committed to peace while standing ready to fight for what is right. As world powers go, it sees itself as the most benign in history. This self-image may be largely justified. Nevertheless, it is increasingly clear that U.S. interests are best served by working with other nations and international bodies to reduce the traditional security challenges. In addition, the United States must tackle the intensifying levels of brutalization against civilian populations, particularly women and children, due to ethnic conflict, mercenary leaders, and criminal gangs. Such civil strife creates millions of refugees and displaced persons and damages the health and economic well-being of many millions more. The gradual spread of these phenomena over ever larger regions will inevitably affect the United States, even if it does not directly seem to hurt American interests now.

The troubled peacekeeping efforts of recent years—from Kosovo to central Africa—signal an urgent need to improve our capacity for conflict management. A major obstacle is the current American posture. In most instances, such as Sierra Leone, the United States will not put its troops on the ground. Even worse, it wants to get by on the cheap— as amply illustrated by congressional resistance to paying the full American share of UN peacekeeping efforts. The next president and Congress must commit themselves to strengthening the United Nations system to handle these challenges. At the very least, they must stop scapegoating an institution that the United States is unwilling to support adequately.

Fixable flaws

First, however, the United Nations must honestly assess its own strengths and weaknesses. Limits on its efficiency partly stem from its multinational character. The 188 member states reduce General Assembly activities to interminable speech-making, while their demands for a quota of UN jobs hamper the secretary-general and other agency heads in selecting staff according to merit. But there are signs of genuine reform. A recent report from the U.S. General Accounting Office (GAO) gives high marks to Secretary-General Kofi Annan for improving the quality of staff and putting in place effective management practices.

The UN's financial weakness severely limits its capacity to respond to new challenges and prepare for unanticipated ones. At American congressional insistence, for example, the UN Secretariat's budget has been frozen at about $1.3 billion for the past four years. After accounting for inflation and delayed or defaulted payments by the United States and other nations, this means that the UN has far fewer funds to meet greatly expanded obligations.

Much of the financial weakness undermining the UN could be cured by a unilateral U.S. decision to pay its dues. Arrears in U.S. peacekeeping funds make up the lion's share of Washington's UN debt. These arrears largely result from the chronic skirmishes between the executive and the legislative branches. Both branches agree that a reduction in the U.S. assessment for peacekeeping must be achieved but differ on the strategy by which to achieve it....

Beyond the funding issue, the most obvious shortcoming of the United Nations is its lack of standby capacity—which Congress opposes—for peacekeeping, policing, and administration in troubled regions. This has been underscored during the past year by the UN experiences in Kosovo, East Timor, and Sierra Leone. The Security Council must reconsider the deployment of lightly armed UN peacekeeping forces into civil wars, a function not foreseen by the UN Charter. And the secretary-general should refuse certain tasks in war-torn countries unless he is empowered to raise—on short notice—adequately armed forces, trained police cadres, and a substantial body of civil administrators.

Go to http://www.un.org/ Pubs/chronicle/2001/ issue4/0104p60.html to find out more about the relationship between the UN and the United States.

Following the end of the Cold War in 1991, the UN expanded its role in dealing with regional conflicts and developed its peacekeeping objectives to include overseeing elections, monitoring human rights, and assisting civil governments.

The UN has no permanent army and relies on troops supplied by each member nation. It is at the mercy of nations choosing to reduce their troops at any time. The UN intervention in the Kosovo War (1999) relied on an international force of NATO (North Atlantic Treaty Organization) troops. And when violence erupted in East Timor after a vote in favor of independence in 1999, Australia led a UN force to help stabilize the region.

NATO is a military alliance of 17 European nations, Canada, and the United States. Since the Cold War its goals have been fostering links with former Soviet bloc countries and managing conflicts in Europe.

The five permanent members of the UN Security Council are China, France, Russia, the UK, and the United States.

For a chart showing the structure of the UN go to www.un.org/aboutun/chart.html. What are the pros and cons of separating the various UN agencies?

Such a refusal would force member states either to provide the UN with the increased capacity to respond or to acknowledge openly that they intend to do nothing to manage the snowballing crisis.

The Security Council is only as effective in conflict management as the permanent members want it to be. In the Gulf War, strong U.S. leadership led to resolute action. In Kosovo, deep divisions led NATO to avoid the Security Council altogether. In other cases, ambiguous resolutions led to confusion in execution. Without some agreed strategy among the five permanent members on how to improve the staffing, structure, and purpose of peacekeeping, the Security Council will continue to issue ambivalent or contradictory resolutions.

The various UN agencies that address health, food, development, and the plight of refugees and disadvantaged children are the unsung heroes of the UN system. Yet in the field, they have duplicated efforts and indulged in turf battles that inhibit the efficient delivery of assistance. This complication can confuse nongovernmental and governmental organizations and contribute to the reputation of UN ineffectiveness. In part, this competitive behavior stems from the independent mandates and separate funding of these agencies. Still, the GAO report noted progress resulting from the secretary-general's efforts to improve coordination among UN agencies and to establish a strategic framework for their field operations.

Public support

Another weakness of the UN stems from the often-cited lack of support for the institution by the American public. Yet public opinion surveys consistently show 60 to 70 percent support for the United Nations. To be sure, public affirmation is broad, not deep, leaving the congressional field of combat too often controlled by those with strongly negative views. And serious misunderstandings persist. For example, there is a widespread … belief that the UN environment is hostile to the United States, when in fact countries voted with the United States 86 percent of the time in the General Assembly last year.

Another supposed source of weakness is the Washington mythology about "UN failures." American legislative and executive officials employ Somalia, Rwanda, Srebrenica, and Kosovo as code words for UN incompetence. In most of these crises, there were UN management shortcomings, and the secretary-general has since published candid studies

See page 54 for more details on Rwanda and Srebrenica.

outlining some UN mistakes. But the Security Council's permanent members, who wrote and helped execute the resolutions calling for the peacekeeping actions, have failed to make similar revelations of their own severe shortcomings in supporting the authorized actions. Both the failures and the successes of UN operations need full airing so that the United Nations and its member states will be better prepared for future missions....

Starting afresh

The new president, unshackled from the burden of failed interventions and former political errors, can clear the air and address such issues as unsuccessful peacekeeping strategies and unpaid bills.... An early order of business will be to determine with other states what assignments the UN should undertake (peacekeeping and humanitarian relief) and those that should be handled by others (wars). The UN's peacekeeping capabilities should then be strengthened by such measures as the building of a command and control operation, standby police and military units, development of trained administrators and experts for nation-building, and training facilities.... The complexity of these tasks is daunting and unprecedented. It is little wonder that these issues have given rise to discord—all the more reason for strong American leadership....

Despite chronic woes that threaten the sustainability of some of the UN's most important work, the United States has a vital interest in strengthening the UN system. Acting alone is not a sustainable option. Political "realists" who oppose U.S. involvement in conflicts that do not directly affect American interests often fail to see the value in building the UN's capacity to manage strife around the world. In fact, a healthy and creative United Nations will diminish the pressures for direct American intervention and allow for a much broader sharing of the costs.

The UN is the central organization through which the United States can pursue its national interests; encourage others to take on the new challenges of peacekeeping, development, and humanitarian relief; share the burden in paying for those tasks; continue to exercise leadership in shaping decision-making on these key issues; and tap into the American proclivity for generosity and idealism. The American people are far ahead of recent U.S. administrations and congresses on these urgent matters. The next president should reconnect these American instincts with American interests by strengthening the UN system.

This article was published nine months before the election of President George W. Bush.

Why do you think it is important to make a distinction between roles for the UN and for sovereign countries?

Many people argue that the War Against Terrorism is an example of how the UN can help the United States achieve its aims. They maintain that independent action by the United States risks destroying the coalition developed after the September 11 terrorist attacks.

PAVING THE ROAD TO HELL: THE FAILURE OF UN PEACEKEEPING
Max Boot

NO

The United Nations started the 1990s with such high hopes. With the end of the Cold War, the U.S.-Soviet rivalry that had paralyzed the Security Council had become a thing of the past, supposedly freeing the UN to become more assertive. The Gulf War, the UN's second-ever military victory, seemed to vindicate those hopes—even though, as in the Korean War, the baby-blue banner was used as a mere flag of convenience for an American-led alliance. President Bush spoke of a "new world order." Candidate Clinton talked about giving the United Nations more power and even its own standing military force.

It is hard to find any U.S. officials making similar suggestions today, only a decade later. They have been chastened, presumably, by the UN's almost unrelieved record of failure in its peacekeeping missions.

"Worse than useless"

The United Nations itself has recently released reports documenting two of its worst stumbles. According to these confessions, UN peacekeepers in Rwanda stood by as Hutu slaughtered some 800,000 Tutsi. In Bosnia, the UN declared safe areas for Muslims but did nothing to secure them, letting the Serbs slaughter thousands in Srebrenica. The organization's meddling was worse than useless: its blue-helmeted troops were used as hostages by the Serbs to deter a military response from the West. Presumably, Secretary-General Kofi Annan—who was head of the UN's peacekeeping department at the time—hopes that an institutional mea culpa [acceptance of blame] now will wipe the slate clean and allow the organization to play a more vigorous role in the future.

The arrival of *Deliver Us From Evil*, a new book by British journalist William Shawcross, provides a good opportunity to ponder whether this is a realistic expectation. Shawcross presents a highly readable, if at times repetitive and scattershot, chronicle of UN diplomacy and humanitarian interventions in the past decade. Though predisposed to

This article is a review of Deliver Us from Evil *by William Shawcross, a book about the UN.*

In 1994 the UN overruled warnings that the Hutu militia were planning genocide against the Tutsi in Rwanda on the grounds that attempts to intervene militarily were beyond the "peacekeeping" nature of its mission. In 1995 the UN refused the request of Dutch peacekeeping forces for air support over Srebrenica. Some people blame this on ineffective leadership; others suggest it was part of a strategy to let the Serbs achieve limited goals so they would agree to a peace accord.

favor UN peacekeeping—much of this book is written from the view-point of Annan, with whom the author traveled the world—Shawcross is too honest a reporter to gloss over its failures. He even concedes that humanitarian aid may sometimes do more harm than good by prolonging a war.

For more on this issue see Topic 9 Should the United States give aid to developing countries irrespective of their politics? on pages 112–123.

Blame games

Despite the failures he chronicles, however, Shawcross' faith in UN peacekeeping—and in Annan—does not appear to have been seriously shaken. Although the book is generally sober, at points Shawcross gives in to giddiness, as when he describes the secretary-general as "the world's 'secular pope'" and "the repository of hope and the representative of such civilized standards of international behavior as we have been able to devise." At another point, Shawcross quotes (with no discernible irony) a UN official who describes the peacekeeping mission to Cambodia as "a model and shining example" because of the election staged there in 1993— never mind that Hun Sen promptly usurped power after losing at the ballot box.

Hun Sen, leader of the Cambodian People's Party, initially refused to give up power after the 1993 election, but was then persuaded by the UN to act as second prime minister in a coalition government. Do you think the author omits this information in order to strengthen his argument?

Wherever possible, Shawcross blames such messes on the permanent members of the Security Council, whom he indicts for blocking the expansion of these missions. He dutifully quotes UN bureaucrats who complain that they did the best they could with inadequate resources, and he suggests they be given more support in the future.

He's being too kind by half. The failures of the United Nations should not be blamed just on the great powers. They owe as much to the mindset of UN administrators, who think that no problem in the world is too intractable to be solved by negotiation. These mandarins fail to grasp that men with guns do not respect men with nothing but flapping gums. A good example of this incomprehension was Annan's opéra bouffe [absurd] negotiations with Saddam Hussein. In 1998, Annan undertook shuttle diplomacy to Baghdad, reached a deal with Saddam to continue weapons inspections, and declared him "a man I can do business with." Almost immediately Saddam flouted his agreement with Annan. But even then the secretary-general told Shawcross, "I'm not convinced that massive use of force is the answer. Bombing is a blunt instrument."

Iraq's defeat in the Gulf War left it subject to UN weapons inspections, but in 1997 it blocked access to U.S. weapons inspectors. Following Annan's deal with Saddam Hussein in 1998, Iraq wavered between cooperation and refusal, causing the UN to pull its inspectors out in December that year.

Annan has actually been more pragmatic than many of his predecessors. But his outlook is inevitable in anyone who has spent years working at Turtle Bay. Just as the U.S. Marine Corps breeds warriors, so the UN's culture breeds conciliators.

Turtle Bay is the site of the UN headquarters in New York City.

From 1992 to 1996 the UN imposed sanctions on the Federal Republic of Yugoslavia (FRY), made up of Serbia–Montenegro. The FRY has been unable to join the UN or other international organizations and the international community does not recognize it as the successor to the former Yugoslavia.

The previous article suggests that the UN's role is peacekeeping, not waging war. Do you agree with this? If so, do you think it is still important that UN troops are chosen for their "martial prowess"?

Many people argue that the UN does not seek to be an "independent force" but a world arbiter, weighing the potential consequences before deciding whether action is necessary. How do you see the role of the UN in today's world?

A large part of the problem is that Annan and his staff work not for the world's people but for their 188 (and counting) governments. Annan proclaimed last fall that sovereignty is on the decline—and so it is, everywhere except at the UN There, at least in the General Assembly, all regimes, whether democratic or despotic, have an equal vote. Annan and other employees must be careful not to unduly offend any member state, and so they wind up adopting a posture of neutrality among warring parties, even when one side (such as Serbia or Iraq) is clearly in the wrong.

When the United Nations does use force, the results are often pathetic. The various national contingents that make up UN peacekeeping operations—Bangladeshis, Bulgarians, Brazilians, and the like—are chosen not for martial prowess but because their governments are willing to send them, often for no better reason than to collect a daily stipend. The quality of these outfits varies widely: Shawcross writes, for instance, that the Bulgarians in Cambodia were "said to be more interested in searching for sex than for cease-fire violations." Trying to coordinate all these units, with their incompatible training, procedures, and equipment (to say nothing of languages), makes a mockery of the principle of "unity of command." Little wonder that blue helmets strike no fear in the hearts of evildoers.

Of course, as Shawcross repeatedly points out, this sorry state of affairs would change instantly if only the United States and its allies would commit more muscle to UN operations. But why should great powers limit their freedom of action by giving bureaucrats from not-so-great powers control over their military interventions?

Enter America

At the end of the 1990s, then, the United Nations remains what it has always been: a debating society, a humanitarian relief organization, and an occasionally useful adjunct to great-power diplomacy—but not an effective independent force. This does not mean we should kill the organization. But it should temper the high expectations of the UN's more idealistic supporters....

What Shawcross—and his views are reflective of a certain internationalist mindset—fails to fully grasp is how useless, and sometimes counterproductive, UN involvement has been. NATO won a victory in Kosovo but then unwisely turned over management of the province to the world body. The UN viceroy there, Bernard Kouchner, now faces an impossible task, having to coordinate myriad agencies while carrying out a contradictory mandate: to run Kosovo but to do nothing to prevent its eventual return to Serbian rule. As a result, his administration is in a shambles and reconstruction lags behind schedule. Although it may sometimes make sense to seek the UN's imprimatur for a mission, the organization should not be given operational control. Effective empires require strong proconsuls, not bureaucrats—Kitcheners, not Kouchners.

> UN Resolution 1244 states that Kosovo is part of Serbia.

Perhaps because he fails to grasp the problem, Shawcross doesn't explore alternatives to the United Nations. But others do. [The writer] David Rieff has forthrightly and courageously argued for the United States and its allies to undertake "liberal imperialism," while [the writers] William Kristol and Robert Kagan have called for the United States to assume a "benevolent global hegemony"—which will necessarily involve fighting some small wars in places like Kosovo.

> The author contrasts UN viceroy Bernard Kouchner with the British commander in chief Herbert Kitchener (1850–1916), who led the British to victory in the South African War (1899–1902). Is it fair to contrast an imperial commander with a UN official?

Contrary to received wisdom, this would not be a new role for the United States. Washington has been involved in other countries' internal affairs since at least 1805, when, during the Tripolitan War, the United States tried to topple the pasha [ruler] of Tripoli and replace him with his pro-American brother. Between 1800 and 1934, U.S. marines landed abroad 180 times. In the nineteenth century, they tended to stay for only a few days. Yet they helped open up the world to Western trade and influence, their most spectacular successes being Commodore Perry's mission to Japan and the defeat of the Barbary pirates. After 1898, U.S. involvements lasted longer: American forces remained behind to run such countries as the Philippines, Haiti, and Cuba. U.S. rule was not democratic, but it gave those countries the most honest and efficient governments they have ever enjoyed.

> The Tripolitan War (1801–1805) began when the United States cut off its payments to Tripoli (in modern-day Libya) that had secured protection of U.S. ships from the Barbary pirates of North Africa. The U.S. Navy's blockade of Tripoli's harbor led to a peace treaty with favorable terms for the United States.

There are significant obstacles, to be sure, in the path of reviving "liberal imperialism" today. But based on the record, I—unlike Shawcross—have more confidence in U.S. than in UN power.

Summary

In the first article William H. Luers contrasts the United States' enthusiastic involvement in some world organizations, such as the International Monetary Fund, with its aloofness and suspicion toward the United Nations. He outlines some of the possible reasons for this negative attitude, but believes that U.S. interests would be better served by increased commitment to the organization. The benefits of this would be reciprocal—the United States would strengthen the effectiveness of the UN, which in turn would help the United States protect its interests and further its own role in the quest for world peace. Although Luers acknowledges some of the UN's weaknesses, he argues that these are "fixable flaws," which could be cured if the United States paid its dues to the organization in both financial and political terms.

In the second article, a review of a book that is generally well-disposed toward the UN, Max Boot cites what he sees as the organization's "worse than useless" actions. He rejects the claims of UN officials who say that they have done their best with the limited resources at their disposal. In Boot's view the UN is institutionally ineffectual—for example, it recruits peacekeeping forces from countries that are more interested in payment than providing well-trained soldiers. Boot concludes that the UN is, and always has been, no more than a debating society. He proposes that if the United States is to achieve world peace and bring democracy to as many nations as possible, it is more likely to achieve these goals by acting alone than by going through the UN.

FURTHER INFORMATION:

Books:

Kristol, William, and Robert Kagan, *Present Dangers: Crisis and Opportunity in American Foreign and Defense Policy*. San Francisco, CA: Encounter Books, 2000.
Shawcross, William, *Deliver Us from Evil: Peacekeepers, Warlords, and a World of Endless Conflict*. New York: Simon & Schuster, 2000.

Useful websites:

http://www.betterworldfund.org/
Provides detailed information about the UN.
http://www.munfw.org/archive/50th/4th3.htm
"UN Role in Civil Conflict" by Karyn Becker.
http://www.rferl.org/nca/features/2000/07/F.RU.
000712152656.html
"Bosnia: UN Failure to Save Srebrenica Examined"
by Robert McMahon.
http://www.un.org/
Browse the UN's own wide-ranging site.

http://www.usinfo.state.gov/journals/itps/0300/ijpe/
pj51welc.htm
"The United Nations: An Arena for International
Leadership" by David Welch.

The following debates in the Pro/Con series may also be of interest:

In this volume:
   Topic 1 Does the United
   States have a duty to protect
democracy and freedom overseas?

   Topic 15 Should the
   United States use military
force against nations that
harbor terrorists?

SHOULD THE UNITED STATES SHOW A STRONGER COMMITMENT TO THE UNITED NATIONS?

YES: They succeeded when they acted together in the Korean and Gulf wars

YES: The world's nations should agree on policy through an international body with real power

RECIPROCITY
Can America and the UN help each other achieve their goals?

WORLD PEACE
Is the UN the best hope for global stability?

NO: Without U.S. leadership the UN has always been incapable of decisive action. The United States can achieve more on its own.

NO: The United States is the only political entity strong enough to act effectively as the world's police force

SHOULD THE UNITED STATES SHOW A STRONGER COMMITMENT TO THE UNITED NATIONS?

KEY POINTS

YES: The main obstacle to UN success is the lack of U.S. involvement and financial backing

YES: International consensus will bring peace sooner than the imposition of a policy by a single power, no matter how benign

EFFICIENCY
Does the UN provide a good return on member nations' investment?

NO: The United States should not pay an outside organization to carry out duties that it could perform better itself

NO: Time after time the UN's desire to be evenhanded has resulted in ineffectuality and disaster

PART 2
TRADE

The United States is the world's largest and most dominant economy. In 2000 its Gross Domestic Product (GDP)—the total value of goods and services a nation produces—was around $9.6 trillion, over twice that of its nearest competitor, Japan. The economy depends on trade. In 2000 U.S. exports were estimated at around $776 billion, including grain, aircraft, cars, military equipment, chemicals, and nonfuel minerals. U.S. imports—worth an estimated total of $1.223 trillion in 2000—include foods, machinery, industrial raw materials, crude oil, and refined petroleum products. Most of this trade takes place with Canada and Mexico; Japan, Germany, the United Kingdom, and China are also key trading partners.

The needs of trade have long influenced U.S. foreign policy. In 1794, only 11 years after the end of the American Revolution (1775–1783), the republic signed the Jay Treaty with Great Britain, guaranteeing British naval protection for U.S. shipping. In 1823 fears that the Spanish might try to reconquer the independent countries of Latin America—and thus close their lucrative markets to U.S. trade—was a major impulse behind the Monroe Doctrine. President James Monroe outlined foreign policy principles that excluded European intervention in the American hemisphere.

Throughout the 19th century trade interests continued to shape U.S.

relations with other powers. In 1853, for example, Commodore Matthew Perry led four warships into the harbor at Edo, Japan, to force that country to open its ports to foreign trade. In the 1890s the United States was instrumental in proposing a policy that allowed all nations the right to trade in China, in return committing itself to protect China's integrity.

Within the Americas, too, trade shaped U.S. activity. When it was decided in 1903 to build the Panama Canal to shorten the sea route between the east and west coasts, U.S. gunboats helped Panama achieve independence from Colombia. During the Mexican Revolution President Woodrow Wilson sent troops to Veracruz in 1914 to weaken the position of President Victoriano Huerta and bring to power Venustiano Carranza, whom Wilson believed would protect vast U.S. investments in Mexico. In 1944, when the Guatemalans overthrew their right-wing dictator and installed a democratic government, the U.S.-owned United Fruit Company (UFCO), which dominated Guatemala's economy, was threatened by proposed land redistribution. Under UFCO pressure the Central Intelligence Agency engineered a coup that brought to power another sympathetic dictator.

At home, meanwhile, the United States guarded its own economy by a policy of protectionism, or imposing tariffs and quotas to discourage foreign imports. Protectionism could not, however, prevent the Great Depression in the 1930s and probably exacerbated it by stifling international commerce.

After World War II (1939–1945) the United States continued to shape foreign policy at least partly in response to business interests. It was Fidel Castro's nationalization of U.S. assets that made America hostile toward Cuba, for example. The promise of vast markets led President Richard Nixon to open relations with China in the 1970s despite the Chinese communist government and its poor record on human rights. Since the 1980s the United States has supported free

In Topic 5 journalist Seth Gitell and academic I. M. Destler examine just how much direct influence big business has on the government. Topic 6 considers the effect of a specific international agreement—NAFTA—and asks whether it works. Opponents argue that it loses U.S. jobs to Mexico, where labor costs are cheaper, and that this is a form of U.S. exploitation of its neighbor. Supporters point to statistics showing a 78 percent increase in U.S. trade in the agreement's first six years and an improvement in environmental and labor conditions in Mexico. J. Bradford DeLong and Sarah Anderson et al. discuss this issue further. Mexico, however, remains a key route for

> *"I have never known much good done by those who affected to trade for the public good."*
> —ADAM SMITH (1723–1790), BRITISH ECONOMIST

trade—it signed the North American Free Trade Agreement (NAFTA) with Canada and Mexico in 1992—while periodically imposing tariffs and quotas on, for example, European steel imports.

Responsibility

With U.S. economic eminence come responsibilities for both protecting the domestic economy and preserving the international economy. The balance between national and international interests has long been the subject of controversy. To what extent should the United States act out of self-interest and to what extent out of paternalistic concern for others? The topics in this section examine aspects of this fundamental question.

smuggling drugs into the United States. Critics argue that the United States should use trade sanctions to influence the behavior of nations like Mexico. In 2002 President George W. Bush affirmed the role of trade in influencing foreign governments. Any nation, he said, that "respects human rights and the rule of law … will find in America a trading partner, an investor, and a friend." Kenneth Roth and Pradeep S. Mehta in Topic 7 discuss the value of using sanctions to promote human rights.

The final topic in this section considers whether the United States should be more open to imports from other countries. Jay Mandle and Patrick J. Buchanan look at the free trade versus protectionism debate.

Topic 5
DOES BIG BUSINESS HAVE TOO MUCH INFLUENCE ON FOREIGN POLICY?

YES
FROM "GET TOUGH"
BOSTON PHOENIX, APRIL 12, 2001
SETH GITELL

NO
"MANY CONSTITUENCIES INFLUENCE U.S. FOREIGN POLICY-MAKING"
U.S. FOREIGN POLICY AGENDA,
U.S. INFORMATION AGENCY ELECTRONIC JOURNALS, MAY 1996
I. M. DESTLER

INTRODUCTION

Do big corporations have too much say in the framing of the United States' foreign policy? In seeking influence over—or "lobbying"—the government, does business override less powerful, but equally legitimate, interests?

There is a long tradition in this country of lobbying government to protect or promote particular interests. The military, churches, labor unions, environmental and civil liberties organizations, and big business are just some of the interest groups—or "lobbies"—that have sought to exert influence in Washington. However, some people believe that the influence of big business—usually backed up with big money—is now too powerful.

Big business is interested in foreign policy because many corporations do not operate solely within the United States and are always looking overseas for new export markets, new sources of cheap labor, parts and raw materials,

new investment opportunities, and a higher percentage of international trade. If Congress sanctions an aid package to a developing country, business may be boosted in several ways: More U.S. goods may be imported into that country, the defense sector may win contracts to supply military hardware, and deals may be struck enabling companies to establish manufacturing bases there. In fact, the business lobby has argued that the United States should only increase aid to countries that allow U.S. business unlimited access to their markets.

The two most powerful business lobbies in the United States are the energy and arms industries. Critics claim that both have had a significant effect on foreign policy. After Iraq invaded Kuwait in 1990, for example, some people argued that the Gulf War had more to do with maintaining access to Middle Eastern oil supplies—crucial for U.S. industry—than with upholding international law or defending Kuwaitis. Would the United States have acted so decisively had valuable resources not been at stake? Other commentators maintain oil was a secondary benefit and not the primary motive.

> *"There is a perception of wealthy folks running the government and those who are not wealthy not participating in government."*
> —CHARLES LEWIS, CENTER FOR PUBLIC INTEGRITY, 2001

Observers who are suspicious of business influence on foreign policy claim it was the oil lobby that persuaded President George W. Bush to pull the United States out of the environmental Kyoto Agreement in 2001. The 1997 agreement sought to prevent global warming by limiting emissions from the burning of fossil fuels such as oil (see *Environment*, Volume 4, page 90). Critics of Bush's decision point to the industry's connections with his administration: The president himself, Vice-President Dick Cheney, Commerce Secretary Donald Evans, and National Security Adviser Condoleezza Rice have all held directorships of oil companies. Those who supported Bush's stance argued that there is no proof that fossil fuels cause global warming, and despite individuals' past links with the oil sector, the administration's policies are formed in the best interests of the United States as a whole.

What these interests are is not always easy to judge, however. In 2000 the United States sold $12.6 billion worth of arms to developing nations alone—a vital contribution to the American economy. However, critics point out that arms were often sold to undemocratic regimes that may one day use them against their own people or even against the United States.

Human rights is a crucial area in the debate. For example, trade between the United States and China has grown dramatically since diplomatic relations were reestablished in 1979 despite China's poor record on human rights. Many commentators believe that in the rush to gain access to this new market, U.S. businesses and government alike have turned a blind eye to human rights abuses. The business lobby, on the other hand, argues that integration into the world economy will bring material benefits to the Chinese people and accelerate China's democratic reforms. Yet in Cuba, where there have also been human rights abuses, the United States still applies sanctions. Some people say that is because there are no business opportunities in Cuba for U.S. companies. Cuba's leader Fidel Castro nationalized U.S. interests there in 1959 and opposes any attempts by U.S. businesses to regain a foothold.

In the following article Seth Gitell—political writer for the *Boston Phoenix*—argues that business has too much influence on U.S. foreign policy toward China, where human rights issues should come before business deals. In the second piece I. M. Destler—a foreign policy professor at the University of Maryland—argues that business exerts no decisive influence and is only one of many interests that affect the framing of U.S. foreign policy.

GET TOUGH
Seth Gitell

On April 1, 2001, a U.S. Navy plane was forced to land in Chinese territory after colliding with a Chinese fighter jet. The U.S. crew was held by the Chinese authorities for 11 days.

James "Whitey" Bulger was a Boston gangster.

For more on the events of June 4, 1989, in Tiananmen Square, Beijing, go to http://asia.cnn.com/SPECIALS/2001/tiananmen.

YES

☑ …China's 11-day refusal to release the 24 American crew members downed over the South China Sea after an overeager MiG pilot crashed into their surveillance plane suggests, if nothing else, that there's something deeply wrong with America's policy of nurturing China's business interests despite the tendency of that nation's leaders to govern their people the way Whitey Bulger ruled in South Boston. In the 12 years since the first President Bush averted his eyes when the Chinese leadership unleashed the legions of the 27th Army—jacked up on amphetamines to make them more aggressive—upon democracy activists in Tiananmen Square and their model of the Statue of Liberty, America's political relationship with China has gone from bad to worse. (The attack is now believed to have taken as many as 2600 lives.) And now, in the wake of Congress's decision late last year to grant China Permanent Normal Trade Relations (PNTR), Beijing seems to view America the way a heroin dealer sees an addict—as an easy mark.

Recent U.S. foreign policy toward China
[A] country that does not respect its own people can never be trusted to respect anyone else. And no American administration has done more than pay lip service to the cause of human rights in the People's Republic of China (PRC). After the Tiananmen massacre, former president Bush dispatched then-secretary of state James Baker to China to ease relations between the two countries—and though Bush the elder announced some mild sanctions in the direct wake of Tiananmen, he went out of his way to appease Beijing. For example, so as not to anger China, he vetoed a measure that would have extended the visas of Chinese students living in the U.S. Former president Bill Clinton, despite his charges during the 1992 campaign that his predecessor "coddled dictators," unlinked the causes of trade and human rights in China and pushed to grant Beijing PNTR. As for George W. Bush, even as he has hinted at selling warships to Taiwan, he has also indicated a willingness to push for China's entry into the World Trade Organization and to back the PRC's favored "One China" policy.…

China joined the World Trade Organization (WTO) on November 11, 2001. The "One China" policy refers to China's refusal to consider independence for the island of Taiwan.

Human rights in China

"The central issue is the human-rights issue," says Arthur Waldron, a professor of international relations at the University of Pennsylvania. "If China becomes a freer country, we're not going to have as many problems with them. If you have a humane, democratic regime, they're not going to be a problem internationally."

But American foreign policy toward China doesn't reflect this philosophy. Instead, policy is shaped by the debate between the business lobby, which looks longingly at China as a source of cheap labor, and the security hawks, who think Beijing should be treated as Moscow was during the Cold War. The status of China's human-rights activists on the information food chain mirrors that held by bicycling advocates within regional transportation planning—they're seen as well-meaning people who aren't, uh, exactly at the center of the debate. The movement to free Tibet, for example, is pigeonholed in foreign-policy circles as a … boutique issue rather than a serious fight for freedom.

Charles Kernaghan, the director of the National Labor Committee (NLC), experienced the sidelining of these issues firsthand when his group released a report in July 2000 detailing the complicity of American corporations in Chinese human-rights violations. (Unionizers in China, Kernaghan points out, find themselves fired, locked in psychiatric hospitals, and fed mind-altering drugs….) "When you're talking about human rights and worker rights in China and established US corporations, the world is a very lonely place," says Kernaghan…. "You're certainly not going to find a lot of support in the foreign-policy establishment."…

The 11-day diplomatic standoff vindicates what labor activists have been saying for some time. "Policies come back to bite the people who make them when they are shallow and they ignore worker rights and human rights and women's rights," says Kernaghan….

Political progress before economic development

America needs to inject concern about human rights into all of its dealings with China, suggests Harry Wu, a pro-democracy activist who spent two decades as a political prisoner in China. "Tell Chinese authorities no free lunch," he says. "We want to see political progress—human rights, not just economic development."

A naturalized American citizen, Wu received asylum in the United States in 1985 and founded the Laogai Research Foundation (laogai is the Chinese word for gulag). When Wu

Does China's poor record on human rights make it an international problem? Why does it matter what China does within its own borders?

In 1950 the Chinese invaded Tibet, claiming it was part of China. The following decades were marked by Tibetan guerilla warfare, Chinese repression of Tibetans, and the exile of many citizens. The "free Tibet" movement aims for Tibetan independence.

The NLC is an independent organization that defends human and worker rights. See www.nlcnet.org/report00/table_of_contents.htm for the NLC's 2000 report on China.

The Laogai Research Foundation collects data about Chinese labor camps. For more information visit its website at www.laogai.org.

The policy of engagement with China means increasing U.S.–Chinese diplomatic and trading links in the hope that stronger ties between the two countries will result, as well as an improvement in China's record on human rights. The author quotes Harry Wu to show some of the strong criticisms of engagement.

returned to China in 1995 to do research for his group, Chinese authorities held him for 66 days before sending him back to America. "If [the U.S.] is a country very concerned about democracy [and] human rights, our leaders would put this on the table all the time," says Wu, who scoffs at the idea that "money can change the authoritarian status of a repressive government." Economic ties between the countries won't help democratize China, he contends: "The engagement policy is only engaged with money."

"With human rights, they say China is different," Wu says of that policy's supporters, noting that some of them ironically are the same people who venerated Ronald Reagan for his anti-communism....If increased investment rather than direct confrontation leads to democracy, asks Wu, "why did Ronald Reagan call the Soviet Union the Evil Empire?... President John F. Kennedy also challenged the Soviets in Berlin, Wu points out; he didn't try to strike business deals with them.

Wu says his research suggests that American trade actually contributes to China's aggressiveness. The funds that China gleans doing business with U.S. corporate interests—including [the aerospace and defense manufacturer] Lockheed, which is helping China develop satellite rocket technology—end up financing missile and weapons development.... As for business advocates' contention that economic pressure can't change China's behavior, Wu points out that when American corporations were concerned about copyright infringement and convinced the US government to sanction China, Beijing quickly backed down....

Foreign policy alternatives

The Jackson–Vanik Amendment to the Trade Reform Act was passed in 1974. With the collapse of the Soviet Union in 1991 the amendment's importance has declined.

[W]e should re-evaluate the course America has taken since Tiananmen. For starters, we might want to consider some of the things that worked in the Cold War. During the early 1970s, the labor movement, neoconservatives, and human-rights advocates all united to advocate putting more pressure on the Soviet Union. Senator Henry Jackson, a Democrat from Washington, sponsored one particularly controversial measure. Jackson's bill tied the Soviet Union's treatment of refuseniks (Soviet citizens, usually Jewish, denied permission to emigrate) to the sale of American grain. The farm and business lobbies vehemently opposed this legislation. Eventually it passed, and Jackson-Vanik, as it came to be known, crystallized the moral element of America's policy toward the USSR.

Imprisoned by the Soviets in 1978, Anatoly Sharansky was released in 1986 and emigrated to Israel.

This pressure eventually convinced the Soviets to free Anatoly Sharansky, a prisoner of conscience whose televised release from prison became a symbol of the struggle for freedom.

By focusing on human rights, highlighting the work of Harry Wu and others, and tying business deals to democratic development, the U.S. can address some of the root causes of its conflict with China—and avoid the trap of simply militarizing the problem. Toward this end, says the AFL–CIO's [Thea] Lee, human-rights activists will begin raising shareholder resolutions that curtail corporate work in China. Labor sources say corporations such as Wal-Mart and Nike may face such actions....

The AFL–CIO (American Federation of Labor–Congress of Industrial Organizations) is the umbrella organization for U.S. labor unions. To find out more, visit www.aflcio.org. Can unions influence foreign policy too?

The future

If anything good comes out of the recent crisis, it will be a shift in American popular opinion that leads Congress and the administration to re-examine our relationship with China. The starting point lies with the American-based corporations so interested in doing business with Beijing.

As [the academic Arthur] Waldron says,

> *The business community is quite happy to have a place where not only are wages quite low, but if there's any business about unions, [the authorities] can go crack heads.*

But eventually "Nike and Reebok will learn that they'll pay some price from doing business over there," says Kernaghan of the NLC, which waged the public anti-sweatshop campaign that almost put Kathie Lee Gifford out of business several years ago.

In 1996 the NLC exposed how chat-show host Kathie Lee Gifford's line of sportswear (sold through Wal-Mart) was made using child labor. For more information go to www.nlcnet. org/Kathie.htm.

Perhaps a groundswell will rise from the universities, where the civil-rights and anti-war movements coalesced in the 1960s and the anti-apartheid movement took hold in the 1980s. But so far things don't look promising.

The Princeton student newspaper, the *Daily Princetonian*, reported on the plight of Li Shaomin, a Chinese-American alumnus of the university's graduate school who has been arrested by the Chinese police. When asked whether the university would help try to free Li, a spokeswoman for Princeton replied that the school did not have "an institutional role to play."

Dr. Li Shaomin was detained in February 2001 and convicted of "espionage" by the Chinese authorities. He was released on July 25, 2001. Why? See www. dailyprincetonian. com/archives/2001/ 09/18/news/3318. shtml for the story.

In the absence of a campus movement, the next stage in US–China relations may hinge on whether labor activists and public pressure can force American businesses and other institutions interested in the PRC to factor human rights into their business.

MANY CONSTITUENCIES INFLUENCE U.S. FOREIGN POLICY-MAKING
I. M. Destler

NO

X "Foreign relations begin at home." America's leading political scientist Richard Neustadt made this observation more than a quarter century ago, discussing events under Presidents Dwight D. Eisenhower (1953–61) and John F. Kennedy (1961–63). Even during the long Cold War with the Soviet Union, even before the virulent protests over U.S. involvement in Vietnam, American leaders knew that foreign policy required domestic support. For example, U.S. dealings with the People's Republic of China were minimal throughout the 1950s and 1960s because executive and congressional leaders feared a fierce political backlash to the United States "recognizing Red China." And the United States Congress, exercising its "power of the purse," regularly cut back presidential proposals for economic and military assistance to foreign nations.

See Volume 7, Constitution, especially Topic 3 Does the President have residual emergency powers? on pages 38–49.

Foreign policy and the Constitution

To understand why power over foreign policy is divided, the place to begin is our governing charter, the U.S. Constitution. Authorities sometimes state that it gives the President the predominant power over international issues. But it doesn't. He can draw from its direct language just a handful of powers of direct relevance: negotiating treaties, appointing and receiving ambassadors, commanding the armed forces. Congress has a longer specific list: ratifying treaties, confirming ambassadors, declaring war, maintaining armed forces, regulating foreign commerce. And if one moves to more general authorities, the legislative branch again appears to have the upper hand: the chief executive's right to sign or veto bills pales before its authority to control their content, particularly those bills which provide (or withhold) money. Had the Congress, skeptical about sending U.S. forces to Bosnia, employed all its powers in opposition, President Bill Clinton would not have been able to do so.

In December 1995 President Clinton sent troops to join an international peacekeeping force in Bosnia to stabilize the country following its civil war, which began in 1992.

Democratic Senator J.W. Fulbright of Arkansas, the most prominent legislative leader on foreign policy in the early Cold War years, called it conducting foreign policy "in the

20th century under an 18th century Constitution." He
saw U.S. international relations as hostage to "parochial
minded" legislators driven by narrow interests and local
constituencies. Yet this very fact—that senators and
representatives are driven by diverse concerns—gives the
President the opportunity to lead on most international
issues, most of the time. With congressional energies directed
mainly elsewhere, he and his key officials—the Secretary
of State, the Assistant to the President for National Security
Affairs—can use their control over the day-to-day conduct of
policy to maintain the initiative. The President is particularly
strong if he is pursuing causes for which there is broad
public support, for Americans expect the President to be
active in representing Americans' international concerns.

Foreign policy after the Cold War

This was more often than not the case on major strategic
issues in the half-century from the U.S. entry into World
War II in 1941 until the collapse of the Soviet Union in 1991.
Today, however, the President cannot count on broad support
so readily. The American public continues to favor U.S.
engagement in the world; despite the fears of many foreign
policy specialists, Americans have not turned isolationist. But
the public gives lower priority to foreign concerns than it
used to; there is less attention to matters international, and
more to problems within the United States. So it is less likely
that the President himself will give priority to expanding
or even maintaining international programs like foreign
assistance. And it is more likely that Congress will act to cut
funds for these programs. With both branches of government
under pressure to reduce the federal budget deficit, all
programs of "discretionary spending"—funded by year-to-
year congressional appropriations—are particularly
vulnerable to reductions.

With no single, central conflict to shape U.S. foreign policy,
there is also a higher probability that the President and/or
Congress will give priority to issues of particular concern
to ethnic or special-interest groups. Clinton has, for example,
concentrated personally on bringing democracy and law
to Haiti (an emphasis pressed by the Congressional Black
Caucus) and bringing peace to Northern Ireland (fervently
desired by Irish-Americans), as well as continuing his
predecessors' priority to the Middle East. And [he] has been
constrained in his approach to Cuba by the vocal (and
overwhelmingly anti-Castro) Cuban–American community
concentrated in the important electoral state of Florida.

Do you think that international relations are an important concern for U.S. politicians? What is your response to the view that politicians should concentrate more on domestic issues?

Do you think that the events of September 11, 2001, have made U.S. foreign policy more or less "isolationist," or inward looking, than in 1996, when this article was written?

For more on the Congressional Black Caucus Foundation go to www.house.gov/ebjohnson/cbcmain.htm.

In none of these cases is attention given solely for reasons of ethnic politics; for his actions to redound to his benefit over the longer term, the President must be pursuing goals which have support beyond narrow constituencies. Otherwise, he is vulnerable to the charge of "pandering" to special interests. But these groups can have disproportionate influence over the details of policy; because they care, their representatives take the time to "lobby" the responsible government officials. If they find the executive branch insufficiently responsive, they can work to get Congress to pass laws on their behalf. Indeed, the most effective lobbying groups, like the American Israel Public Affairs Committee (AIPAC), work continuously with both branches.

Find out more about the AIPAC at www.aipac.org and (for a different view) at www. palestinecampaign. org/news.asp?d= y&id=844. How much influence do you think lobbies like this can have on foreign policy?

Economic interests and foreign policy

Economic interests are another important influence, particularly on international trade and financial policies. When our government seeks to expand trade through negotiated reductions in import barriers, it needs the support of U.S. manufacturers whose sales will benefit from better access to foreign markets, in order to counter the predictable opposition of companies who compete with imports in the domestic market. If an industry seeking trade protection is large enough, and effective in building influence with Congress and the executive, it may win exceptions to the general U.S. policy of open trade. The textile-apparel industry is a case in point. Its persistent lobbying got members of Congress to threaten special legislation, and got successive Presidents to authorize negotiation of the Multi-Fiber Arrangement restricting textile and apparel imports. In the Uruguay Round negotiation concluded in 1993, the world's trading nations agreed to end this arrangement, but the industry was still powerful enough to win a slow, ten-year phase-out period.

See Topic 8 Should the United States be more open to exports from other nations? on pages 98–109.

Economic interests do not always win. Organized labor has had limited impact on U.S. trade policy, despite its campaigns against rising imports and movement of U.S.-owned factories to foreign nations. The major labor unions were important supporters of Clinton's election, but he overrode their passionate opposition in winning congressional approval of the North American Free Trade Agreement (NAFTA) in 1993. He also went against the wishes of a number of important environmental organizations whose support he had received before and would want again in the future.

See Topic 6 Does NAFTA work? on pages 74–85.

But while the President did not accede to these groups' strongest wishes, he did not ignore them either. Before presenting NAFTA (negotiated and signed by his predecessor, George Bush) to Congress for approval, Clinton negotiated "side agreements" with Mexico and Canada on labor and environmental issues. In seeking congressional authorization to negotiate future agreements reducing trade barriers, his administration asked specifically in 1994 that this include trade-related environmental issues and matters of international labor standards. When organized business and influential members of Congress resisted these labor and environmental provisions, the President accepted stalemate in U.S. trade policy rather than agreeing to proceed without them. This meant a delay in specific negotiations for free trade with other Western Hemisphere nations like Chile, as pledged in December 1994 at the Western Hemisphere summit in Miami. It has also limited U.S. steps to implement the November 1994 agreement by the nations of the Asia-Pacific Economic Cooperation forum (APEC) to achieve free trade among themselves by the year 2010.

The author points out that presidents are not necessarily swayed by big business interests. What do you think of this argument? Is the presidency too open to influence from rich corporations that can bankroll political campaigns?

Foreign policy as a branch of democratic politics

As these examples suggest, foreign policy-making is, when all is said and done, a branch of democratic politics. The President, Congress, the public, and special-interest groups all seek to influence decisions and actions in both the executive and legislative arenas. The President's influence remains greater on average, relative to Congress and special groups, than it is on most domestic matters; it is rare that a President suffers the sort of humiliating failure here that Clinton experienced in 1994 with his health care proposals. When the chief executive "goes to the mat" on a foreign policy issue, he will usually win. Clinton's initial proposals on aid to Russia were fully funded by Congress, notwithstanding a lot of criticism. But since the end of the Cold War, foreign policy-making has become less distinctive, less different from matters domestic. This means that Congress and special interests are likely to have greater impact than in 1941–1991. It means that the President must work more closely than ever with key groups if he is to carry out effective international policies.

Far-reaching health-care reforms were central to Clinton's 1992 election campaign, but he failed to win support in Congress and had to scrap his plans. Do presidents have a right to expect support from Congress in matters of foreign policy?

Summary

Seth Gitell claims that business exerts too much influence on U.S. foreign policy and cites China as an example. He argues that the detainment in China of U.S. servicemen and women after their plane was forced to land serves as a warning for the United States to rethink its policy toward that country. He says that the business lobby—which sees China as a golden economic opportunity and cares little about its human rights abuses—has steered U.S. policy toward appeasement. Gitell argues that economic relations with China should be tied to improvements in its human rights record and urges the public to challenge powerful business interests on this issue.

Although I. M. Destler accepts that economic interests are an influence, he believes that there are many factors—including Congress, special interest groups, and public opinion—that affect the making of foreign policy. In a democracy, he argues, foreign policy must go beyond the particular agendas of narrow constituencies, and he believes that in the United States it usually does. Although he thinks public interest in foreign policy—including toward China—has declined since the end of the Cold War, he does not think this means policy is therefore dictated by narrow business interests.

FURTHER INFORMATION:

Books:

Hertz, Noreena, *The Silent Takeover: Global Capitalism and the Death of Democracy*. New York: Simon & Schuster, 2002.

Lampton, David M., *Same Bed, Different Dreams: Managing U.S.–China Relations 1989–2000*. Berkeley, CA: University of California Press, 2001.

Mann, James H., *About Face: A History of America's Curious Relationship with China, from Nixon to Clinton*. New York: Random House, 2000.

Pilger, John, *The New Rulers of the World*. London: Verso, 2002.

Vogel, Ezra F. (ed.), *Living with China: U.S.–China Relations in the 21st Century*. New York: Norton, 1997.

Useful websites:

www.amnestyusa.org/business
Human rights group Amnesty International's site, with information on business and economics issues.
www.citizen.org/trade/china/index.cfm
Public Citizen site. Section opposing China's PNTR status.
www.hrw.org/asia/china.php
China section of Human Rights Watch site.

www.uschina.org/public/wto
U.S.–China Business Council site promoting U.S.–China trade relations.
www.wto.org/wto/english/news_e/pres01_e/pr243_e.htm
World Trade Organization (WTO) site. Press release about China's entry into the WTO.

The following debates in the Pro/Con series may also be of interest:

In this volume:
Topic 6 Does NAFTA work?

Topic 7 Should economic sanctions be used to promote human rights?

Topic 8 Should the United States be more open to exports from other nations?

DOES BIG BUSINESS HAVE TOO MUCH INFLUENCE ON FOREIGN POLICY?

YES: International arms sales can fuel tensions between warring groups or countries

YES: U.S. trade with China, for example, has boomed despite appalling human rights abuses

PEACE
Is global peace threatened by U.S. armaments corporations?

HUMAN RIGHTS
Do U.S. trading policies overlook human rights issues?

NO: By trading even with potential enemies, the United States is helping bring them onto its team

DOES BIG BUSINESS HAVE TOO MUCH INFLUENCE ON FOREIGN POLICY?

KEY POINTS

NO: The best way to encourage democracy is to integrate countries like China into the world economy, and U.S. business is doing just that

YES: The powerful oil lobby pressed the United States to pull out of the Kyoto Agreement on greenhouse gas emissions

YES: The business lobby has huge financial resources and many links with government

ENVIRONMENT
Is the global environment threatened by U.S. oil corporations?

BIG BUSINESS
Is the business lobby too powerful compared with other influences on foreign policy?

NO: It has not been conclusively proven that greenhouse gas emissions are responsible for global warming

NO: The business lobby is only one of many interest groups that influence policymaking, and in any case it is not always in agreement about what its interests are

73

NAFTA'S (QUALIFIED) SUCCESS
J. Bradford DeLong

J. Bradford DeLong served as President Clinton's deputy assistant secretary of the Treasury for economic policy between 1993 and 1995.

It is time to conclude that NAFTA—the North American Free Trade Agreement—is a success.

It is nearly seven years since the ratification of NAFTA, nearly seven years since then-Treasury Secretary Lloyd Bentsen argued and President Clinton decided that NAFTA should be the second major initiative of his administration. The major argument for NAFTA was that it was the best thing the United States could do to raise the chances for Mexico to become democratic and prosperous, and that the United States had both a strong interest and a neighborly duty to try to help Mexican political and economic development.

By that yardstick NAFTA has been a clear success.

Economic benefits for Mexico

Gross Domestic Product (GDP)—the total market value of all goods and services produced in a year—is a measure of an economy's size. Real GDP is GDP after inflation has been factored in.

NAFTA has helped Mexico economically. Over the past five years real GDP has grown at 5.5 percent per year. Even including the sharp shock of the 1995 peso crisis, Mexican real GDP has grown at 3.8 percent per year since the ratification of NAFTA. The urban unemployment rate that was 6 percent in 1992 and rose to 8.5 percent in 1995 is now less than 4 percent. The Mexican boom has been led by the manufacturing, construction, transportation, and communications sectors. Most of all, the Mexican boom has been led by exports: next year Mexico's real exports will be more than three times as large as they were at the ratification of NAFTA, and as a share of GDP exports have grown from a little more than 10 to 17 percent.

"Real exports" means the total value of exports after inflation has been factored in.

It is here—in the growing volume of exports and in the building-up of export industries—that NAFTA has made the difference. Four-fifths of Mexico's exports go to the United States. More than two-thirds of Mexico's imports come from the United States. NAFTA guarantees Mexican producers tariff- and quota-free access to the American market.

Quotas are limits on quantities of exports or imports.

Without this guarantee, a smaller number of Mexican exporters would dare try to develop the strong links with the market north of the Rio Grande that have enabled them to sell their exports. Without this guarantee, few—either in Mexico or from overseas—would have dared to invest in the manufacturing capacity that has allowed Mexico to satisfy United States demand.

Without NAFTA's guarantee of tariff- and quota-free access to the American market, we would not have seen the rise in trade within industries between Mexico and the U.S. over the past half decade. Rising intra-industry trade means that Mexico and the U.S. are moving toward a greater degree of specialization and a finer division of labor in important industries like autos—where labor-intensive portions are more and more done in Mexico—and textiles—where the U.S. increasingly does high-tech spinning and weaving and Mexico increasingly does lower-tech cutting and sewing. As economists Mary Burfisher, Sherman Robinson, and Karen Thierfelder put it, NAFTA has nurtured the growth of productivity through "Smithian" efficiency gains that result from "widen[ing] the extent of the market" and capturing "increasing returns to finer specialization."

Without NAFTA, would Mexican domestic savings have doubled as a share of GDP since the early 1990s? Surely not. Without NAFTA, would the number of telephone lines in Mexico have doubled in the 1990s? Probably not.

Moreover, Mexican exports are by no means low-tech labor- and primary product-intensive goods. More than 20 percent of all Mexican exports are capital goods. More than 70 percent of Mexican manufacturing exports are metal products. Without NAFTA, would [the] U.S. big three auto producers have invested in the Mexican auto industry, and would Mexican exports of autos and auto parts to the U.S. have grown from $10 to $30 billion a year? Surely not.

Political benefits for Mexico

More important, NAFTA has helped Mexico politically. Strong economic growth makes political reform much, much easier: reslicing a growing pie is possible under many circumstances where reslicing a static pie is not. Increasing economic integration brings with it pressures for increasing political integration as well: the liquidation of the statist-corporatist PRI order, and a shift toward democratic institutions that are more like those of the industrial democracies that Mexico hopes to join (and to which Mexico hopes that NAFTA will serve as a passport of admission). The result has been the first peaceful transfer of power in Mexico in more than a lifetime, with the election to the Mexican presidency of Vicente Fox Quesada. Economist Dani Rodrik describes political democracy as a powerful meta-institution for building the political and economic institutions needed

"Division of labor" is the breakdown of labor into specialized jobs— often done in separate places— for improved overall efficiency.

Scottish free-trade economist Adam Smith (1723–1790) argued against tariffs because restricted markets limit division of labor and hence limit efficiency.

Primary goods are agricultural products and raw materials. Capital goods are things like tools, components, and machinery— manufactured goods used to make other goods.

"Statist-corporatist" means inclined to economic and social intervention. The PRI (Institutional Revolutionary Party) ruled in Mexico (under different names) for 71 years until Vicente Fox Quesada (1942–), of the National Action Party (PAN), was elected president in 2000.

for success: thus Mexico's future looks much brighter now than it did back in the late 1980s when the dominant PRI regularly stole elections and held a hammerlock on Mexico's government.

The United States: unharmed by NAFTA?

But haven't all these good things for Mexico come at a substantial cost for Americans? In a word, no. Back during the debate over the ratification of NAFTA, commentators like Harley Shaiken predicted that NAFTA would send "high wage American jobs south," especially in the auto industry. Ross Perot and Pat Choate heard a "giant sucking sound" of American firms betraying their country by transferring up to five million American jobs to Mexico. Ralph Nader claimed that NAFTA would gut U.S. environmental regulation—that Americans would be poisoned by polluted Mexican strawberries—and that NAFTA would undermine the sovereign authority of the U.S. government.

Such claims were always incredible. The President and the Congress—not any committee established by NAFTA—continue to make and execute the laws: the U.S. government remains sovereign. The Mexican economy was always too small to have any significant macroeconomic effect on the American economy. Imports from Mexico rank way down on the list of factors affecting the distribution of income in America.

And in retrospect they have proved clearly false. You have to work really, really hard to find any significant effect—positive or negative—of increased economic integration with Mexico. American jobs that have been displaced because of increased imports from Mexico amount to less than two percent of all job elimination—the sum of those who lose their jobs and those who leave their jobs—in America. Far from shrinking, employment in autos and auto parts in America has grown by more than twenty percent since the beginning of NAFTA. Far from falling, hourly earnings of U.S. automotive workers have risen since the beginning of NAFTA.

But by the same token American jobs created by increased exports to Mexico are a very small fraction of job creation. NAFTA's effects are too small to materially influence the overall state of the American labor market for good or ill.

The future

All, however, is not rosy. Mexico's political and economic problems remain enormous. Mexico's destiny continues to hang in the balance.

Academic Harley Shaiken is an expert on globalization. Ross Perot is a businessman who ran as an independent presidential candidate in 1992. Pat Choate is an economic analyst and broadcaster. Consumer advocate Ralph Nader ran for the presidency in 1996 as the Green Party candidate.

Macroeconomics is about whole economic systems; microeconomics is about isolated parts.

Mexico's political democracy is very fragile. The Mexican banking system is still in crisis as a result of the collapse of the value of the peso in early 1995. Mexico's distribution of income is deteriorating—in part because of failures under the old regime to adequately finance education and infrastructure, in part because of demographic burdens, and in part because the initial benefits of economic integration with the United States flow to the well-educated and well-prepared.

Is there evidence that benefits from NAFTA will eventually be distributed more widely in Mexico?

Improving Mexico's distribution of income requires raising the incomes of the poorest—which means that Mexico's poorest families need to over time be shifted out of low-tech low-productivity near-subsistence corn-centered agriculture and into either fruit- and vegetable-based agriculture or into urban occupations. But will the government be able to fund the infrastructure to support such a potential mass migration? And will rural populations—extremely undereducated—do well in urban labor markets?

Moreover, Mexico's social welfare system is bureaucratically inept. Mexico's safety net is in shreds. Mexico has many problems—corruption, a legacy of past underinvestment, and a legacy of inefficient government-protected and -sponsored enterprises among them. NAFTA has not fixed these problems. NAFTA could not fix these problems: they would exist with or without NAFTA. NAFTA did not turn Mexico into Utopia. And NAFTA does not guarantee that Mexico's economic and political future would be bright.

Are enterprises protected or sponsored by governments always inefficient?

But NAFTA has done its job, has fulfilled its intended task: it has given some extra strength to the forces in favor of Mexican industrialization, modernization and democratization. It has loaded the dice somewhat in favor of a somewhat better outcome.

NORTH AMERICAN FREE TRADE AGREEMENT
Sarah Anderson, John Cavanagh, and Saul Landau

NO

… The North American Free Trade Agreement (NAFTA) sets guidelines for the elimination of most trade and investment barriers between Canada, the U.S., and Mexico over a 15-year period. In place since January 1, 1994, NAFTA is an experiment that builds upon a U.S.–Canadian Free Trade Agreement signed in 1988. Never before has an agreement gone so far to integrate the economies of nations that are so unequal. The gap between average U.S. and Mexican wages is about 8-to-1, which is twice as large as the wage gap between the European Union's richest and poorest members.…

Go to http:// canadian economy.gc.ca/ english/economy/ 1989economic.html for more about the Canada–U.S. Free Trade Agreement (CUSFTA).

The basic arguments
Supporters asserted that NAFTA would lead to a net increase of good U.S. jobs because trade liberalization would spur U.S. exports to Mexico and Canada in high-wage industries. Others argued that NAFTA would help Mexico build a stronger democracy and more modern economy.…

NAFTA opponents argued that the trade pact would undermine U.S. jobs and wages by providing extra incentive for U.S. corporations to move to Mexico to take advantage of high unemployment, low wages, and rising productivity. One factor behind these conditions, opponents claimed, was that the Mexican government denied basic worker rights and condoned lax environmental enforcement.

By increasing the power and mobility of U.S. corporations, NAFTA would increase the ability of U.S. firms to spread sweatshops and child labor in the U.S. and chip away at U.S. labor protections.…

Does it make sense to say that NAFTA could "spread sweatshops and child labor in the U.S."? Or is that more likely to happen in Mexico?

A rocky road to NAFTA expansion
To appease critics, Clinton promoted side agreements on labor and the environment. The side deals created a number of institutions to handle complaints regarding violations of labor and environmental laws and to arrange financing for environmental cleanup. Less than a year into the NAFTA

experiment, President Clinton proclaimed the trade pact a successful model for the Western Hemisphere and announced plans to expand NAFTA to include additional countries, beginning with Chile. However, progress on NAFTA expansion has been rocky. The Mexican government was forced to devalue the peso in December 1994, sending the U.S. trade deficit with Mexico soaring. Millions of Mexicans lost jobs, property, and savings.

Although NAFTA did not create the crisis, it contributed by creating a climate of investor optimism that kept short-term capital flowing into Mexico despite deep social and economic problems, including an overvalued peso. As the public sensed that NAFTA had played a role in the crisis, the trade pact's popularity plunged. Late 1995 polls showed that a majority of Mexicans and Americans felt that NAFTA had done more harm than good.

In early 1995 leaders of the new Republican-controlled U.S. Congress threw a monkey wrench into NAFTA expansion by vowing to exclude labor and environmental conditionality from future trade pacts. A fight about this issue derailed legislation to grant the administration the "fast-track" authority required to enter into official trade talks with Chile. Despite these setbacks, Canada and Chile negotiated a bilateral agreement, signed in November 1996 that is intended to serve as the basis for the accession of Chile to NAFTA.

NAFTA's harmful effects

… NAFTA did not create the problems related to increased trade and investment among three unequal nations. It accelerated them. Since the mid-1960s, corporations have pitted U.S. communities and workers against those in Mexico, pressuring those in the U.S. to accept lower wages and labor and environmental conditions. NAFTA simply made it easier for corporations to move jobs, plants, and money around North America, strengthening their power to drive down wages and environmental conditions in Canada and the U.S.

As of November 1, 1996, more than 90,000 workers have qualified for a NAFTA retraining program, which is available for U.S. workers who lose their jobs because their employer moved production to Canada or Mexico or lost revenues as a result of increased imports from those countries. The actual number of jobs lost is far greater, since many laid-off workers are unaware of the retraining program or do not qualify. There are also documented cases of corporations using threats to move to Mexico to bargain down U.S. and Canadian wages. NAFTA has forced workers to take these threats more seriously.

In December 1994 newly elected President Ernesto Zedillo devalued the peso in the hope that it would reduce the cost of Mexico's exports. That, it was thought, would improve Mexico's balance of trade and bolster foreign-trade reserves. It resulted, however, in a loss in investor confidence.

How significant are the findings about NAFTA's popularity in 1995?

Even though U.S. workers are hurt by the wage gap with Mexico, NAFTA has had a net negative impact on Mexican workers as well. Inasmuch as NAFTA exacerbated the late 1994 peso plunge, it contributed to lost jobs for millions of Mexicans in the past two years. And while it may be true that several hundred thousand new jobs have been created on the Mexican side of the border as a result of increased exports to the U.S. and Canada, wages are low, working conditions poor, and the environmental nightmare spreads.

NAFTA and the environment

NAFTA's North American Development Bank, designed to provide low-interest financing for environmental projects, did not approve a single project until September 1996, nearly three years into NAFTA, despite the Clinton administration's promise that the bank would inject up to $3 billion in the border region. NAFTA's environmental threats extend beyond the U.S.–Mexico border. The agreement locks in an unsustainable structural adjustment model that the World Bank and IMF began imposing on Mexico in the early 1980s, a model that measures success by increases in natural-resource extraction, such as several new mining ventures in Mexico.

The International Monetary Fund (IMF), an agency of the United Nations (UN), is linked to the World Bank (see www.imf.org and www.worldbank.org). They give financial help to economies in crisis, though this is often on condition that specific economic policies be put in place first.

NAFTA and workers' rights

Nor has NAFTA supported the efforts of Mexican workers who are struggling to increase their wages and improve working conditions. Complaints have been filed under the labor side pact regarding violations at four plants (three in Mexico and one in the U.S.), but not a single worker involved has benefited. A major flaw of the pact allows trade sanctions only in the case of violations related to minimum wage, health and safety, and child labor. Violations of core labor rights, including freedom of association, collective bargaining, and strikes, can only lead to consultation. Moreover, complaints can only be filed against a government for failing to enforce its own laws, while the corporate lawbreakers face no sanctions whatsoever.

"Freedom of association" is the right to form or join trade unions. "Collective bargaining" means negotiating with employers over pay and conditions collectively as a union.

NAFTA and the Mexican economy

NAFTA also served as a kind of "Good Housekeeping Seal of Approval" for the Mexican economy that further encouraged a flood of foreign money into the Mexican capital market. More than three-quarters of this capital was in portfolio investment, or "hot money," rather than productive investment. In this respect, again NAFTA built on a decade-old structure. Since the early-1980s, Mexico's shift toward a free-market, privatized model initiated the dangerous dependence on short-term, "hot money."

During the period of the NAFTA negotiations and since, the U.S. kept up the pressure on Mexico to free up any form of capital controls. Since NAFTA forbids investment controls, the Mexican government was helpless to prevent the rapid capital flight that occurred after the December 1994 peso devaluation....

"Capital controls" are government restrictions on the withdrawal of investments in domestic assets by foreign investors.

Toward a new foreign policy

The North American economies have been undergoing a process of integration for decades. Rather than trying to stop integration by erecting walls or other barriers, a practical approach would focus on reshaping the process so that workers and communities—not the Fortune 500— become the primary beneficiaries. A wide range of citizen groups in all three countries are calling for a new, improved agreement to replace NAFTA that would be specifically designed to serve as a tool for equitable development.

Fortune *magazine publishes an annual list of the 500 highest-earning U.S. companies. See* www.fortune. com/lists/F500/ index.html *for the latest list.*

... Given the gaping disparity in incomes and environmental enforcement, our countries need a set of rules for economic integration that will help create a more level playing field for workers and communities across North America. Unless we narrow these gaps, there will be no way to reduce the incentives for U.S. corporations to move to Mexico to exploit the country's workers and environment.

Any serious effort to reduce inequalities in North America must also address the issue of Mexico's debt. In 1995 Mexico paid an estimated $57.8 billion to foreigners just to meet its external and internal debt obligations. This staggering drain places the Mexican government in the desperate position of attracting foreign investment by any means necessary. Unless a realistic debt-reduction plan is developed, the Mexican government will most likely continue to rely on the strategy of attracting foreign investment by offering a system of labor repression and lax environmental enforcement.

Go to www.jubileeusa. org *for more information about the campaign to cancel the debts of developing nations like Mexico. See also* Topic 12 Should rich countries cancel the "Third World Debt"? *in Volume 3* Economics.

Environmental and labor agreements

In addition, both the environmental- and labor-side agreements need serious revision. First, they must become part of the main body of a new trade agreement rather than tacked on as weak side pacts. Second, penalties for violations of labor and environmental laws need to be much more severe and designed so that both the negligent governments and the corporate violators feel the pain....

Summary

For J. Bradford DeLong NAFTA has succeeded in its aims: increasing North American trade and helping Mexico's economic and political development. He cites figures showing the growth in the Mexican economy since 1993 and claims exports have risen as a result of NAFTA's guarantee of access to the U.S. market. He says NAFTA has created efficiency savings for Mexico and the United States, with companies locating different parts of their production process in the countries best suited to them. He thinks NAFTA is responsible for improved democracy in Mexico and argues that all NAFTA's benefits have come at little cost to U.S. jobs. Finally, he warns that despite NAFTA, Mexico still needs to undergo further political and economic modernization.

Sarah Anderson, John Cavanagh, and Saul Landau claim NAFTA has accentuated problems caused by existing inequalities between its signatories. They argue that by making it easier for U.S. companies to relocate to Mexico—with its low pay and lax labor standards—NAFTA has created more sweatshops there as well as job losses and lower wages in the United States. They claim NAFTA contributed to the 1994 peso crisis by encouraging mainly short-term investment in Mexico and argue that NAFTA's side agreements to protect labor rights and the environment are ineffectual. They advocate a more equitable and environmentally sustainable form of economic integration that would reduce Mexico's debt and bring benefits to wider communities.

FURTHER INFORMATION:

Books:

Baer, M.Delal, and Sidney Weintraub (eds.), *The NAFTA Debate: Grappling with Unconventional Trade Issues.* Boulder, CO: Lynne Rienner Publishers, 1994.
Hogenboom, Barbara, *Mexico and the NAFTA Environment Debate: The Transnational Politics of Economic Integration.* Utrecht, Netherlands: International Books, 1998.
Kingsolver, Annie E., *NAFTA Stories: Fears and Hopes in Mexico and the United States.* Boulder, CO: Lynne Rienner Publishers, 2001.
Nader, Ralph (ed.), *The Case against Free Trade: GATT, NAFTA, and the Globalization of Corporate Power.* Berkeley, CA: North Atlantic Books, 1993.

Useful websites:

www.heritage.org/research/tradeandforeignaid/bg1462.cfm
"The Effects of NAFTA on Exports, Jobs, and the Environment: Myth vs. Reality" by Sara J. Fitzgerald.

www.citizen.org/trade/nafta/index.cfm
Site of Ralph Nader's consumer advocacy group Public Citizen. Section outlining campaign against NAFTA.
www.epinet.org/briefingpapers/nafta01
Economic Policy Institute site. Includes the 2001 "NAFTA at Seven" report.
www.ustr.gov/regions/whemisphere/nafta.shtml
United States Trade Representative site. Big section on NAFTA, including 2002 "NAFTA at Eight" report.

The following debates in the Pro/Con series may also be of interest:

In this volume:
Topic 8 Should the United States be more open to exports from other nations?

DOES NAFTA WORK?

YES: NAFTA has increased the trading potential of North America and has led to increased exports between each of the three member countries

YES: National employment levels have risen in the United States and Mexico since the implementation of NAFTA

ECONOMY
Does NAFTA equally benefit its member nations' economies?

JOBS
Has NAFTA created new jobs?

NO: It has made Canada and Mexico much more dependent on the unstable U.S. consumer market

NO: Employment levels have not risen in Canada. NAFTA has meant the loss of U.S. manufacturing jobs because firms have relocated to Mexico.

DOES NAFTA WORK?

KEY POINTS

YES: By allowing firms to relocate to countries where environmental standards are lower, NAFTA has increased levels of industrial pollution

YES: By helping improve Mexico's economy, NAFTA has contributed to the process of democratic reform in that country

ENVIRONMENT
Has NAFTA contributed to environmental decline?

DEMOCRACY
Is NAFTA good for democracy?

NO: NAFTA has created a number of new agencies to protect the environment. It has led to more cooperation and funding to solve environmental problems.

NO: Increasing corporations' power to challenge country's laws—with the threat of withholding investment—is profoundly undemocratic

Topic 7
SHOULD ECONOMIC SANCTIONS BE USED TO PROMOTE HUMAN RIGHTS?

YES
"THE ROLE OF SANCTIONS IN PROMOTING HUMAN RIGHTS"
TESTIMONY BY KENNETH ROTH, DIRECTOR OF HUMAN RIGHTS WATCH, TO THE
SENATE TASK FORCE ON ECONOMIC SANCTIONS, SEPTEMBER 8, 1998
KENNETH ROTH

NO
"HUMAN RIGHTS AND INTERNATIONAL TRADE: RIGHT CAUSE WITH WRONG INTENTIONS"
CONSUMER UNITY AND TRUST SOCIETY'S CENTRE FOR INTERNATIONAL
TRADE, ECONOMICS, AND ENVIRONMENT
PRADEEP S. MEHTA

INTRODUCTION

Many people in the Western world are concerned that some governments abuse or deny the human rights of their citizens. Many of the same people, however, also condemn Western military intervention in other countries. How, then, is it possible to get nations to change their policies? The answer, many people argue, is economic sanctions—withholding aid or restricting trade until governments stop practices such as detention without trial, torture, disenfranchisement, and the persecution of minorities.

Advocates of the use of sanctions to bring about political change claim that such measures have been successful in many cases. Trade embargoes are said to have put an end to the corrupt regime of Jean-Claude Duvalier in Haiti (1986), to martial law in Poland (1990), and to apartheid in South Africa (1994). Yet other people argue that sanctions are ineffective for this purpose; they did not work in the 1960s against Rhodesia or Cuba, and they failed to undermine Saddam Hussein in Iraq. These people claim that although sanctions may play a minor part, bad governments tend to fall for other reasons, such as armed opposition or inherent weaknesses in their economic and social infrastructure.

Regardless of whether human rights sanctions are effective, their use raises many questions. For example, what goods should be withheld? It is easy to see the benefits of banning the supply of armaments to regimes that torture their citizens or of not selling helicopters to dictatorships that use them as tools of repression. But withholding food and medical supplies may cause greater suffering to the very people the sanctions are intended to help.

Another difficulty is that there is no universal standard of human rights. Many people may agree that it is unacceptable for a nation to carry out ethnic cleansing or genocide on its population, but other human rights issues are less clear-cut. Should the West impose sanctions on countries that have a lower age of consent, for example? The West may see arranged marriages and the denial of job opportunities to women as subjugating women, but they are foundations on which many Eastern societies are based.

"Sanctions must not punish or ostracize, but rather they must encourage a change of policy that leads to compliance with standards of international law."

—JAMES A. PAUL,

GLOBAL POLICY FORUM

Again, some people believe that the West should refuse to trade with nations that are undemocratic. Although democracy may be right for the United States and other developed nations, that does not necessarily mean that it is the best, or even a sustainable, form of government for every country. In fact, some staunch allies of the United States are undemocratic countries, such as Saudi Arabia and Pakistan.

Another objection against sanctions is that in practice, they are imposed not against cruel or totalitarian governments, but against those with which the West has failed to forge beneficial trading relationships. In other words, the

decision to stop trading with a country is reached less because of its human rights record and more for economic reasons. Some people said that the "moral" foreign policy adopted by President Jimmy Carter's administration (1977–1980), for example, was merely a disguised instrument of self-serving imperialism. Others, however, point to the sanctions imposed against martial law in Poland by President Ronald Reagan's administration (1981–1989) as being well administered and inspired by principle, not politics. Sanctions were lifted gradually in response to the Polish government's taking specific positive steps, such as releasing political prisoners and finally lifting martial law.

In response, critics of sanctions argue that the effects are not always so predictable. For example, the West opposes the use of child labor, but would ending it through sanctions actually improve those children's lives?

Kenneth Roth, the author of the first of the following articles, argues that sanctions promote a global environment of respect for human rights and help prevent a worsening of civilian repression and suffering. He claims that sanctions tied to clear, realistic, and principled criteria can serve as a carrot as well as a stick and are capable of achieving positive results.

However, in the second article Pradeep S. Mehta claims that many young people who have lost their jobs in the developing world because of Western sanctions or threats of sanctions have been forced onto the streets and into crime. He argues that if sanctions were imposed to reduce the children's suffering, they failed. If, on the other hand, they were intended to stop nations from producing cheap goods, then they were used merely for protectionism.

THE ROLE OF U.S. SANCTIONS IN PROMOTING HUMAN RIGHTS
Kenneth Roth

In 1971 Haitian Jean-Claude Duvalier (1951–) was declared "president for life" on the death of his father, President François Duvalier. Jean-Claude Duvalier's government soon came to be viewed as tyrannical. He was overthrown in 1986 and lives in exile in France. Idi Amin (1925–) ousted Ugandan President Milton Obote from power in 1971 in a military coup. He expelled 50,000–90,000 South Asians and is thought to have murdered at least 300,000 Ugandans. The international community subsequently imposed sanctions on Uganda. In 1978 Amin invaded Tanzania, which in turn invaded Uganda. Amin fled abroad first to Libya, then onto Saudi Arabia, where he still resides.

YES

... While we agree that the commercial impact of sanctions should be considered, so too the U.S. must consider the human rights impact of imposing—or not imposing—these measures. Just to cite a few examples of their usefulness, the multilateral imposition of sanctions contributed to the end of the apartheid regime in South Africa, while unilateral U.S. sanctions helped build pressure on and hasten the downfall of the Argentine military junta, Jean-Claude Duvalier and Idi Amin. And only this summer, in a different context, we saw the threat of sanctions help to resolve the negotiations involving Holocaust-era assets held in Switzerland.

I would like to begin today with a brief discussion of sanctions policies generally, followed by a number of comments relating to approaches currently under consideration.

I. Sanctions as an important tool of foreign policy

Human Rights Watch believes that, as set out in the Foreign Assistance Act, a principal goal of United States foreign policy should be to promote the increased observance of human rights by all countries. To this end, the United States government should, on the one hand, seek sustainable long-term improvements through assistance programs which promote human rights, the rule of law and democratic development, and, on the other hand, use active diplomacy—including frank exchanges with the government concerned, and unilateral and multilateral public criticism—to address human rights violations. When diplomatic pressure fails to curb egregious abuses, however, the U.S. and other nations claiming to uphold human rights must retain the ability to employ limited and targeted sanctions to express their condemnation of violations, press for a change in abusive government policies, and avoid complicity in abuses.

Sometimes even the threat of sanctions, if consistently and credibly applied, can avoid the need for their imposition. At times, however, the actual application of sanctions is necessary. Their prompt imposition in such cases can serve the interests of the U.S. and the international community by promoting an environment of respect for human rights, and by helping to prevent a worsening of repression and resulting disorder which can create destabilizing refugee flows or in which military or other extreme measures may become necessary.

Multilateral sanctions are generally more effective than unilateral sanctions, so efforts should always be made to join forces with like-minded nations to address human rights abuses. The European Union has officially linked its aid programs to human rights practices, as have most other western donors. We have regularly faulted the U.S. government for making insufficient efforts to enlist multilateral support for sanctions. At the same time, the U.S. government should be able to resort to unilateral sanctions when multilateral sanctions are not possible or urgent action is required—as it did this spring in response to events in Kosovo when the Contact Group and Security Council were deadlocked.

Foreign policies that promote human rights, good governance, income security and the rule of law, including through the use of conditionality and sanctions, are also consistent with U.S. trade interests, because they can help foster truly stable societies that, in the long run, offer greater opportunities for economic growth and development. They also help create the level playing field in terms of respect for basic labor rights on which Americans are more likely to support enhanced global trade.

II. Considerations for effective sanctions policies

The term "sanctions" covers a multitude of penalties that can be imposed on an abusive regime, including conditions on aid or trade benefits and restrictions on trade. Our experience has taught us that certain types of sanctions, under certain conditions, offer the greatest promise of success in countering abusive human rights practices. A number of policy prescriptions flow from this experience:

Sanctions supported by domestic constituency in targeted country

When human rights activists seeking freedoms in their own countries ask the international community to impose sanctions, the choice is clearest. The United States must listen to Burmese voices today, as it listened to South African voices in 1986 and Polish voices in 1981. Sanctions imposed in

"Multilateral sanctions" are measures adopted by two or more nations; "unilateral sanctions" are those imposed by only one nation.

Roth made this testimony in 1998. On March 9 the Contact Group (Britain, France, Germany, Russia, Italy, and the United States) agreed to impose an arms embargo on the Federal Republic of Yugoslavia through the Security Council in response to a Serbian crackdown on ethnic Albanians. The European Union subsequently agreed to impose similar measures. It then emerged that in December 1997 Russia and Yugoslavia had negotiated a military-technical assistance agreement. The Security Council eventually won Russia's agreement to the embargo.

response to their pleas reinforce and legitimize their efforts. Domestic support also undermines any effort by the targeted regime to blame the U.S. or the international community for the negative economic impact of sanctions. However, we must recognize that severe repression can prevent a population from expressing its approval for sanctions, and in those cases it may be necessary to act without a manifestation of local support.

Is it right for Western governments to try to guess whether or not a country's population would approve of sanctions if it could?

Targeted sanctions

We advocate sanctions that are targeted, and designed to have the greatest impact on an abusive regime by depriving it of the tools and means of repression, while avoiding or minimizing any negative impact on the general civilian population.

First in the hierarchy of sanctions are arms embargoes and restrictions on military assistance that a brutal regime would likely use to perpetrate further abuses. In the case of systematically abusive governments, these sanctions are mandated under section 502B of the Foreign Assistance Act, which also requires that security assistance be administered in a manner which promotes human rights and avoids identifying the U.S. with repressive foreign governments. Unfortunately, the U.S. government routinely ignores section 502B, and thus contributes to the suffering of the victims of abuses perpetrated with U.S. military equipment and aid. In addition, the U.S., together with the wider international community, has not provided the means and the resources to effectively implement existing arms embargoes which are often thus reduced to mere pronouncements.

Go to http://usinfo.state. gov/usa/infousa/ facts/democrac/ 54.htm for the full text of Section 502B of the Foreign Assistance Act.

Turkey provides an example of the power of potential arms sanctions. Objections were raised to the sale of attack helicopters to Turkey in 1996, when it was shown that the Turkish military was using these in its highly abusive counterinsurgency campaign against Kurdish rebels; facing this criticism, Turkey withdrew its tender for the U.S. equipment. This year, as once again Turkey seeks to purchase U.S.-manufactured helicopters, Prime Minister Yilmaz and members of the Turkish military have promised President Clinton and senior administration officials concrete human rights improvements in exchange for marketing licenses. It remains to be seen, of course, whether Turkey will live up to its commitments and get the U.S. equipment....

Mesut Yilmaz (1947–), chairman of the Motherland Party (ANAP), became prime minister of Turkey in 1997 in a coalition government with the Islamist Welfare Party (RP) and the True Path Party (DYP). He was forced to resign in 1998 due to allegations of corruption.

Sanctions consistent with human rights

We oppose sanctions that themselves violate norms of international human rights or humanitarian law. Therefore, we oppose restrictions of aid or trade that is essential to meet basic human needs for food, shelter, clothing, sanitation or medical care, particularly when such measures would violate fundamental economic rights or prohibitions against the use of starvation and related deprivation as a method of warfare. As President Clinton recently reiterated, "food should not be used as a weapon to influence other nations." Generalized sanctions are a notoriously blunt instrument susceptible of causing severe adverse humanitarian consequences. If they are ever imposed, their implementation must be carefully monitored for these consequences and provisions must always be made to meet the basic needs of the civilian population, as is being attempted in the case of the "oil-for-food" sales in Iraq....

Sanctions tied to clear benchmarks

We have found that sanctions that are tied to clearly defined benchmarks are most effective. The sanctions should be inspired by principle, not political expedience, and this should be reflected in benchmarks rooted in international norms and standards, which, if reached, would trigger a lifting of sanctions. The often-cited example of such graduated sanctions was the Reagan Administration's response to martial law in Poland; tough sanctions were gradually lifted in return for various positive steps by the Polish government, from the release of political prisoners to the formal lifting of martial law....

By contrast, we have objected to the form of sanctions currently imposed on Cuba because they reflect an all-or-nothing approach, with no promise of loosening until the government changes, rather than rewarding concrete steps toward democratization and respect for human rights. In the case of Burma, we have linked our opposition to private foreign investment to a specific human rights abuse: the egregious use of forced labor by Burma's military government on a wide scale, including for infrastructure development and to attract tourism and investment. We do not believe that U.S. or other foreign companies should directly or indirectly contribute to or benefit from forced labor.

When thus tied to clear, realistic, and principled criteria, sanctions serve as a carrot as well as a stick and are more likely to achieve the desired results. For this approach to work, all institutions and agencies of the U.S. and other sanctioning governments must consistently press for implementation of the stated conditions for removal of sanctions. Mixed signals or waffling greatly dilute the effectiveness of sanctions....

For an in-depth report on the Reagan administration's imposition and lifting of sanctions on Poland go to www.tnr.com/052900/michnik052900.html.

The United States trade sanctions on Cuba have been in place since 1960. For more information see Cuba–U.S. Relations, pages 148–149.

The United States imposed sanctions on Burma in 1997 for human rights violations, especially the systematic use of forced labor. For arguments on their effectiveness go to www.cato.org/pubs/trade/tpa-001.html and http://news.bbc.co.uk/1/hi/world/asia-pacific/1847227.stm.

HUMAN RIGHTS AND INTERNATIONAL TRADE: RIGHT CAUSE WITH WRONG INTENTIONS
Pradeep S. Mehta

NO

The demand to link human rights with trade sounds innocent enough, but it is not. The intentions with which these demands are being raised are highly ambiguous and, in most of the cases, motivated by economic reasons.... The developed countries are following double standards on the issue, ignoring violations in their own countries in spite of having the resources and capacity to deal with them. For example, European trade unions have opposed health warnings on cigarette packets and limits on tar and nicotine levels for cigarettes destined for foreign markets.

The OECD was founded in 1948 as an economic cartel to foster good economic and political relations between countries. In 2002 it had 30 democratic member countries.

Developed countries could do more to protect human rights by linking trade and poverty reduction. Organisation for Economic Co-operation and Development (OECD) countries are committed to reducing the level of global poverty by half by 2015, yet there has been little progress in this regard. Developed countries could help by bringing down barriers to developing countries' exports and reducing the debt burdens on these countries and allowing the free movement of labour between countries. If the real motivation for trade–human rights linkages was concern for people's welfare, developed countries would have taken action on these real issues.

Do you think debt relief should be linked with human rights for developing countries?

Not only is the tie-up of human rights and trade undesirable, in practice also, it is inappropriate and inequitable to link human rights with trade. Some of the practical problems with the sanction-based system in the international trading rules are:

1. Genesis of human rights is different
Different parts of the world having different cultures, traditions and lifestyles have different definitions of human rights as well. Universalising human rights ... is practically not possible and lead[s] to universality of the privileged only.

Objections have been raised against the specific rights which reflect western cultural bias, for instance, the right to political pluralism, the right to paid vacation and most troublesome of all, the rights of women.

It is next to impossible to have universal women's rights in the face of widespread divergences of cultural practice. In some societies, for instance, marriage is not a contract between two individuals but an alliance between families and the behaviour of the womenfolk is central to a society's perception of its honour.

Similar is the argument with the values and moral preferences, which cannot be the same in different parts of the world. Moreover, powerful countries will be able to impose their values but weaker ones are less likely to do so.

2. Trade protectionism

In many cases, developed country governments adopt these positions in response to lobbying by powerful domestic interests. Trade unions in developed countries, for example, have been vociferous in calling for the introduction of labour standards at the WTO. They argue that the poor working conditions in developing countries allow these countries to produce goods more cheaply and, therefore, constitute an unfair competitive advantage for their exports. However, most research that has been conducted on this topic suggests that poor working conditions are not correlated with competitive advantage in production.

The World Trade Organization (WTO) was founded on January 1, 1995, as a global forum for trade negotiations and assistance to developing countries. It currently includes 144 member countries and is based in Geneva, Switzerland.

Allowing human rights in the WTO would give … countries greater opportunities to protect their industries unfairly against foreign competition. Just like environmental clauses, under the pretext of human rights concerns, some countries might penalise others nations that do not import certain goods from their domestic industry by enacting new regulations.

3. Labour rights flaws are everywhere

Developed countries think that everything at their end is right and everything in developing countries is wrong. Nonetheless, in many cases, their own policies or actions have led to deterioration of human rights. New Zealand, the staunch Welfare State, for instance, has introduced the Employment Contracts Act, 1991, which promotes individual employment contracts at the expense of collective bargaining. It does not require to be publicised under secrecy clauses either. Even the ILO has found New Zealand's legislation contrary to ILO conventions.

The Employment Relations Act, 2000, replaced the Employment Contracts Act, 1991. For more information on the new act see www.ers.dol.govt. nz/act/changes. html.

The US labour laws have a provision that allows employers to replace striking workers and displace permanent workers, which clearly nullifies workers right to strike. Similarly, the UK introduced eight pieces of legislation between 1980 and 1993, which have piecemeal taken away the rights and

The International Labor Organization (ILO) is a UN agency founded in 1919 to promote social and labor rights.

functions of trade unions. Under these legislations, sympathy strikes or solidarity strikes are prohibited, trade union members may be denied wage increase for refusing to sign individual employment contracts and workers could be black listed by employer organisations for further recruitment.

Nonetheless, even if sanction-based mechanisms are incorporated in the WTO, it is very unlikely that smaller and poorer countries will be able to use them against powerful economies and also expect them to be effective.

4. Sanctions do backfire

Sanctions always have a … potential to backfire and are in no way a better mechanism to achieve social objectives. Consider, for example, just one aspect of human rights: Child labour.

There is a big hue and cry about South [Asia's] child labour in rich countries, but none of them have ever tried to go to the root of the problem. Sometime back, import sanctions were imposed on the carpet industry employing child labour in some South Asian countries. As a result, children abruptly were thrown out of the industry and the North was happy to note that they have removed child labour. However, the children, working earlier in the relatively safe carpet industry ended up working in more hazardous units. Some …who couldn't manage to get jobs turned into beggars, thieves or prostitutes.

The author presents a specific and vivid example of how sanctions can cause more harm than good. Using good examples or anecdotes can strengthen an argument.

5. Different priorities

There is also a North-South argument on the issue. Human rights are seen only as a cover for western interventionism in the developing world. Developing countries, as some argue, cannot afford human rights (what western countries define as human rights), since nation building is still unfinished and suspending or limiting human rights is, thus, the sacrifice of the few for the benefit of the many.

Can you think of recent examples in which the West has been accused of using human rights as a cover for interventionism in the developing world?

6. Trade rules cannot guarantee human rights

Export production in developing countries comprises only 4.5 percent of the total production and so trade rules … have a very limited influence. Therefore, even if social clauses are inserted in the WTO, only a miniscule part of the problem will be addressed. Moreover, it is practically impossible to measure and relate human rights conditions in a country to trade.

Conclusions

The campaigners for human rights can be broadly divided into two camps: 1) those who want governments to write a clause for human rights into international laws, especially trade laws, and 2) those who argue for creating the real material conditions essential for freedom. This freedom … includes … freedom from debt, restrictions on capital and curtailing trade laws that divest the people of their sovereign rights.

There are already allegations that WTO's policies are promoting corporate interests of rich countries. Up to some extent this is correct also, as the developing countries … are not getting proper market access in the developed world. The new issues added in the Uruguay Round are already resulting in benefits for fewer and fewer people around the world, and in negative impacts on the human rights of others.…

Most of the WTO's agreements are the result of the 1986–1994 Uruguay Round of trade negotiations.

The demand for non-trade issues like human rights, environment and labour standards … further attempts to keep developing countries at a disadvantage. The fact of the matter is that when the conditions for the exercise of freedom and, therefore, of human rights exist, the freedom will be real and enduring. And, hence, before talking about linking trade and human rights, we should focus our energies on eradicating poverty from the world and gradually empowering the people.

Moreover those (mainly a small-westernised minority) interested in linking human rights with trade laws are in fact motivated more by economic reasons rather than concern for humanity. Ironically, the origin of the debate on trade and human rights itself was motivated by protectionism within the rich countries, on the assumption that lax standards in developing countries need to be off-set by appropriate trade policy measures in order to snatch their competitive advantage.

It is evident that human rights cost money and resources to make them real possibilities and these hold little water for impoverished third world countries, which are struggling hard to get out of the vicious circle of poverty. It is the need of the hour that the rich countries stop raising unnecessary issues, which have a great potential for being misused to deny market access to products from developing countries and to disrupt international trade. They, rather, need to show greater sensitivity to the concerns of the developing countries and take positive actions through development programmes, aid and other means to rectify problems of child labour, forced labour and other human rights rather than trade sanctions.

What is important … is that trade should be used as a means of eradicating poverty, which ultimately leads to improved human rights. However, imposing trade sanctions on economies to try to achieve social objectives is likely to backfire. Sanctions are likely to inhibit development and prevent poor people from coming out of the vicious circle of poverty, which itself is a serious violation of human rights.

The author concludes with a strong statement that sums up his argument and leaves the reader in no doubt as to his opinion on sanctions.

Summary

Kenneth Roth begins the first article by listing some of the countries against which, he says, sanctions have been used successfully to bring about a change in government or the abandonment of a policy that violates human rights. The author states that sanctions should be used only after conventional diplomacy has failed, and that threatening them can sometimes be as effective as a real trade embargo. Although the United States is strong enough to act alone against most countries in the world, Roth thinks it desirable for sanctions to be multilaterally imposed by "like-minded nations." He stresses that to achieve the desired effect, sanctions must be aimed carefully at a regime, rather than at the victims of its persecution. Thus it may be beneficial to ban the sale of arms but to maintain supplies of humanitarian aid.

In the second article Pradeep S. Mehta doubts the effectiveness of sanctions as a method of ending human rights abuses. He also questions the motives of those who try to impose such trade restrictions. Mehta makes the point that different cultures have different customs, and that one nation's traditional practice may be another nation's human rights violation. He also detects a double standard—the West criticizes developing countries' labor laws on humanitarian grounds, but workers in developed nations including Britain, New Zealand, and the United States now have fewer rights than they had 50 years ago. Mehta claims that the real purpose of sanctions is to enable strong nations to maintain their economic and political advantage over weaker competitors. Human rights are generally unimproved and may even be worsened by the imposition of sanctions.

FURTHER INFORMATION:

Books:

Haass, Richard (ed.), *Economic Sanctions and American Diplomacy*. New York: Council on Foreign Relations Press, 1998.

Articles:

Hufbauer, Gary Clyde, "The Snake Oil Diplomacy: When Tensions Rise, the US Peddles Sanctions." *The Washington Post*, July 12, 1998.

Useful websites:

www.dfait-maeci.gc.ca/english/foreignp/dfait/
policy_papers/1994/94_17_e/94_17_e.html#s3
"Pro-active Sanctions: A New/Old Approach to Nonviolent Measures" by Dr. Nicholas Tracy.
www.state.gov/www/issues/economic/econ_sanctions.html
Dept. of State Economic and Business Affairs website.

The following debates in the Pro/Con series may also be of interest:

In this volume:

Topic 1 Does the United States have a duty to protect democracy and freedom overseas?

Topic 2 Is U.S. foreign policy too interventionist?

Topic 11 Should the United States normalize relations with Cuba?

SHOULD ECONOMIC SANCTIONS BE USED TO PROMOTE HUMAN RIGHTS?

YES: If Hitler had met foreign opposition sooner, World War II might have been averted

YES: Western democracies have a moral duty to oppose persecution, and sanctions can express their disapproval

MORAL ASPECT
Is it right to interfere in the domestic policy of a foreign power?

ULTERIOR MOTIVES
Are we using sanctions for human rights purposes?

NO: Cultural differences are too easily mistaken for, or depicted as, abuses of human rights

NO: Sanctions are imposed for commercial reasons—the human rights issue is a red herring

SHOULD ECONOMIC SANCTIONS BE USED TO PROMOTE HUMAN RIGHTS?

KEY POINTS

YES: They brought down abusive regimes in Argentina, Haiti, Poland, South Africa, and Uganda

YES: As long as we embargo the right goods, banning, for example, the supply of arms while maintaining humanitarian aid

PRACTICAL CONSIDERATIONS
Do sanctions work?

NO: They were ineffective against Rhodesia (modern Zimbabwe) and Cuba, and they have failed to end human rights violations in Iraq

NO: In times of economic hardship the poor people who are meant to benefit from the sanctions imposed on their governments will suffer even more

Topic 8
SHOULD THE UNITED STATES BE MORE OPEN TO EXPORTS FROM OTHER NATIONS?

YES
FROM "THE WRONG ENEMY: WHY WE SHOULDN'T FEAR LOW-WAGE IMPORTS"
THE AMERICAN PROSPECT, VOL. 9, NO. 37, MARCH 1, 1998
JAY MANDLE

NO
FROM "ADDRESS TO THE CHICAGO COUNCIL ON FOREIGN RELATIONS"
NOVEMBER 18, 1998
HTTP://WWW.BUCHANAN.ORG/PA-98-1118-CFR.HTML
PATRICK J. BUCHANAN

INTRODUCTION

Should the United States be open to exports from foreign countries, or should it try to restrict them?

The economic livelihood of the world's nations depends to a great extent on their ability to sell their goods abroad: Every economy can grow through increased exports. But there is much debate over the nature of world trade. Should countries think first and foremost of their own industries and restrict foreign trade in order to promote home businesses? Or should countries export and import goods freely without trade restrictions?

Many people favor the "protectionist" approach in which restrictions on imports, usually in the form of "tariffs" (taxes), are adopted in order to shield domestic industries from the possibly damaging competition of foreign goods. Other people, however, argue that the best way to increase prosperity for everyone is to allow the unrestricted flow of goods between nations in what is often called a "global economy." This policy—which derives partly from the ideas of the Scottish political economist Adam Smith (1723–1790) —is known as "free trade."

There is a growing lobby of people who believe that free-trade policies are in the best interests of the United States since they benefit consumers, allowing them a wider range of products, help keep the market competitive, and also create better and closer relationships with other countries.

Protectionists, however, believe that if the United States does not guard its industries through import restrictions, the domestic economy will suffer. Imports from countries where workers are low paid will lead to a reduction in the demand for unskilled labor in the developed world. The more goods the United States allows in from these countries, the greater will be the job losses in industries that cannot compete. Trade protection can offset the competitive advantages of foreign producers, such as lower wages, and enhance labor welfare in protected industries. It can also generate tax revenue and increase national economic self-sufficiency.

> *"The path toward freer and freer trade has been littered along the way with squalid little protectionist deals to make progress possible."*
> —BRINK LINDSEY,
> THE CATO INSTITUTE

Free traders, on the other hand, argue that if the United States helps emergent countries develop by being open to their exports, that will increase U.S. prosperity as well. As people in poorer countries become richer, they will be better able to afford U.S. products, and the resulting rise in exports will in the end maximize employment for Americans. As world markets grow, the United States will have a bigger and more profitable share of them.

Free traders accept that in the short-term there may be job losses as a result of competition from low-wage economies, but they believe that the U.S. labor market—relatively flexible compared to others—can cope with this. Unskilled workers who have

become redundant in one industry, they argue, find it easy to retrain or relocate in order to find work. For free-traders this is better than the artificial protection of inefficient domestic industries and the higher consumer prices that result from import taxes.

Historically, the United States was protectionist from independence until 1934, when tariffs were cut to stimulate trade and end the Depression. Faith in free trade has since led the United States to back the United Nations Monetary and Financial "Bretton Woods" Conference in 1944—at which the World Bank and International Monetary Fund (see page 82) were set up—and the 1947 General Agreement on Tariffs and Trade (GATT). Recently, free trade has been the conventional wisdom in America (see Topic 6). In practice, however, selective restrictions are often imposed to protect some sectors, such as the steel industry, which was protected by tariffs in 2002.

The huge expansion of global trade in recent years has led to calls from some quarters for more protection of U.S. companies and workers whose products face particularly intense competition from imports. Such calls grow louder when the dollar is highly valued in international exchange markets, since a strong dollar makes imports cheaper. Recessions may also increase pressures for tariffs, as foreign trade is blamed for economic troubles.

In the first of the following articles Jay Mandle—an economics professor at Colgate University—puts the case for free trade. In the second Patrick J. Buchanan—a former adviser to presidents Nixon, Ford, and Reagan, who ran for the Republican presidential nomination in 1992 and 1996—argues for a return to protectionism.

THE WRONG ENEMY: WHY WE SHOULDN'T FEAR LOW-WAGE IMPORTS
Jay Mandle

YES

The economic development of poor countries is heavily dependent on their ability to export. But many American liberals are troubled, wrongly in my view, that commerce with low-wage countries will infect our own body politic. Rather than worrying so much about Third World export growth, we should be addressing how to attain full domestic employment and mobility. We need to concentrate on formulating policies that make trade the mutual opportunity promised in the textbooks. If we fail to do this, trade will still provide an economic gain on average, but will also represent a costly burden for the victims of the abrupt dislocations it causes.

The Third World is growing. Almost half of the world's population resides in China, India, Indonesia, Pakistan, Turkey, and Thailand, poor countries where, even in the richest of them (Thailand), adjusted per capita income is only about one-fourth of ours. Yet in these countries recent growth rates of manufactured goods have been phenomenal. Between 1990 and 1995, the annual growth in manufacturing output has ranged from a "low" of 4.7 percent in Turkey to a high of 17.2 percent in China.

International trade has played a critical role in this growth. In four of these countries, export growth exceeded 10 percent per year between 1990 and 1995, and in the other two it was nearly as great. Furthermore, the countries' economic modernization is most dramatically revealed in the composition of their exports. As recently as 1980, manufactures as a share of exports exceeded 50 percent only in the case of India, and was as low as 2 percent in Indonesia. Thirteen years later, manufactures exceeded 70 percent of exports in all cases except that of Indonesia, where it had grown to 53 percent.

What is clear is that the economic success of these large countries has been heavily based upon their ability to produce and sell manufactured goods overseas.

Despite these impressive accomplishments, export-led growth in the Third World is seen as a threat by many

"Adjusted per capita income" means annual income per person after inflation has been factored in.

Mandle groups his statistics together so that they support his argument without interrupting his flow.

American liberals. A number of progressive legislators, commentators, and activists, who otherwise express great concern for poverty, sincerely believe that expanded exports from poor countries to the United States threaten American wages and environmental protections. Some even suggest that contemporary modernization benefits only small elites.

The Sierra Club was established in May 28, 1892, with John Muir as its president, to deal with conservation issues. See www.sierraclub.org for more information on their activities.

For example, in the recent Sierra Club publication *The Case Against the Global Economy*, critic Jerry Mander writes that "even at its optimum performance level, the long-term benefits [of global development] go only to a tiny minority of people who sit at the hub of the process and to a slightly larger minority that can retain an economic connection to it."

But Mander's assessment of the benefits of growth is almost certainly wrong. The development in South and East Asia has, with the likely exception of China, been accompanied by an increasingly equal distribution of income. In China the share of income received by the poorest 20 percent of households is quite low—only 5.5 percent. Nevertheless, that country's economic growth was associated with what the United Nations Development Program (UNDP) described as a "dramatic" decline in poverty through the mid-1980s. Though this favorable trend stalled during the last half of that decade, the UNDP reports that in recent years poverty is once again falling, with the number of rural poverty-stricken people in China dropping from 94 million to 65 million between 1991 and mid-1995. In Asia the benefits of growth have in fact raised the region's standard of living....

See www.undp.org for more about UNDP, the United Nations' global development network, which gives advice, advocacy, and grant support to developing nations.

Trading with the Third World

International trade has obviously benefited the rapidly growing Asian countries. But it has also benefited the countries to which these countries have exported, including the United States. On one hand, developing countries' growing income and growing market size have allowed the United States to increase its own exports. On the other hand, and too often overlooked in discussions of international trade, we gain from our ability to import, since purchasing goods from abroad allows us to buy at relatively low prices. Thus the fact that the share of our exports going to Asia between 1990 and 1995 increased from 18.2 percent to 22.7 percent, while our share of imports from that continent grew from 23.8 percent to 26.6 percent, meant that Asia's growth contributed in two ways to our welfare. Increased exports raised our incomes. But so too did increased imports. In this latter connection, economist Adrian Wood estimates that if imports from the South—his designation for the poor

Adrian Wood is chief economist at the UK's Department of International Development.

countries of the world including but not confined to Asia—had not been available, those goods typically would have "cost about three times as much if they were made in the North."

Benefits vs. concerns

Despite the benefits of trade, there are also concerns.... A ... major concern of critics is that United States trade with the Third World has had a negative impact on our labor market.... There is validity to this concern. There is a body of analytic work linking deteriorating labor market conditions for the unskilled to increased imports. Adrian Wood, for example, has produced estimates suggesting that imports from low-wage countries have caused a 5 percent fall in the demand for unskilled labor in the developed world. In the United States, where wages are more flexible than in Europe, this decline in demand has shown up mainly as an increase in the gap between the wages of the unskilled relative to the skilled. In Europe, in contrast, where wages are less flexible, the result of trade with developing nations has been to increase unemployment among the unskilled. Is the best solution, then, to curtail the purchase of goods from poor countries?

> *The author claims that U.S. wages are more flexible than those in Europe. Is that a good thing for workers?*

Wood says no, observing that protectionism "is clearly the least desirable of the possible alternatives." Tariff protection, he writes, "would help unskilled workers in the North, but would be more costly than other ways of doing so" and in the process "would hurt much poorer workers in the South." If implemented, Wood concludes, protectionism "would rob many millions of people in the South of the chance to work their way out of much more serious poverty."

> *Do you believe that the United States has a moral obligation to help poorer nations?*

Yet the temptation to curb imports remains powerful....

There are two fallacies in this view...[however]. The first is that it scapegoats the efforts of people in poor countries to achieve higher standards of living. The second is that it overlooks better remedies, such as domestic full employment and investment in worker retraining and mobility.

Trade can benefit everyone

> *A "zero-sum game" is one in which whatever is gained by one "player" is lost by the other. Since gains cannot be shared, this represents a situation of pure competition.*

The protectionist impulse falsely implies that a zero-sum game is necessarily at work in trade among nations. It implicitly accepts the view that the interests of workers in poor countries can only be advanced when the interests of the labor force in rich countries are harmed. That this is a false dilemma is precisely the lesson that international trade theory—and practice—teaches. With supportive policies in place in both sets of countries, advancing the interests of one group will promote the well-being of the other. Therefore, the response of choice, I believe, is not to attack trade, but to implement domestic policies that will allow the gains from increasing trade to be widely dispersed throughout the population.

It is relatively easy to outline the domestic policies that should be adopted in light of the increased integration of the world economy. Our fundamental objective should be to ensure that the industries that come to dominate the American economy are sufficiently productive to be competitive internationally even though they offer high wages. The only way successfully to protect the standard of living in this country is for our industries to be at the technological frontier. Government policy must actively promote that objective.

Apart from improving the public education system, how might the government keep U.S. industries "at the technological frontier"?

It is critical, for example, that our educational system produce graduates capable of being highly productive in a technologically sophisticated workplace. Seen in this light, the poor performance of our urban public schools harms not only their students, but the nation as a whole. Poorly educated young people retard productivity growth when they become members of the labor force.

Conversely, we should not attempt to preserve the life of those industries whose survival is dependent upon the use of low-cost labor. These are industries that can compete successfully only if they are engaged in a race to the bottom in wages. Tariff protection for them will slow the process of adjustment necessary to ensure that we remain a high-wage country. We should be aiming at an economy that is increasingly composed of high-productivity sectors rather than low-productivity ones.

To be sure, the latter will continue to exist, especially in sectors not subject to overseas competition, but it should not be the objective of public policy to defend low-wage industries from imports. Doing so has the perverse effect of increasing the numbers of the working poor....

Globalization is often criticized for its negative effects. Why do you think Mandle believes that it can be positive?

We should endorse globalization as an effective way to allow people throughout the world to escape poverty. Rather than oppose the spread of development and the growth of international trade, we should work politically for domestic policies that can ensure that the benefits of increased international economic integration are widely and fairly shared. In this way complementarity, rather than conflict, can come to characterize the relationship between the labor forces of both the developed and the underdeveloped world.

ADDRESS TO THE CHICAGO COUNCIL ON FOREIGN RELATIONS
Patrick J. Buchanan

The Chicago Council on Foreign Relations (CCFR)— see www.ccfr.org— is an independent forum for the discussion of international affairs and U.S. foreign policy.

NO

… This is a prestigious forum; and I appreciate the opportunity to address it. As my subject, I have chosen what I believe is the coming and irrepressible conflict between the claims of a new American nationalism and the commands of the Global Economy.

The myth of the global economy

As you may have heard in my last campaign, I am called by many names. "Protectionist" is one of the nicer ones; but it is inexact. I am an economic nationalist. To me, the country comes before the economy; and the economy exists for the people. I believe in free markets, but I do not worship them. In the proper hierarchy of things, it is the market that must be harnessed to work for man—and not the other way around.

As for the Global Economy, like the unicorn, it is a mythical beast that exists only in the imagination. In the real world, there are only national economies….

In these unique national economies, critical decisions are based on what is best for the nation. Only in America do leaders sacrifice the interests of their own country on the altar of that golden calf, the Global Economy.

George Washington (1732–1799), Alexander Hamilton (1755–1804), and James Madison (1751–1836) were all important in framing the Constitution. Go to Volume 7 Constitution, pages 24–25, for more information.

"Economic nationalism" in the United States

What is Economic Nationalism? Is it some right-wing or radical idea? By no means. Economic nationalism was the idea and cause that brought Washington, Hamilton and Madison to Philadelphia. These men dreamed of creating here in America the greatest free market on earth, by eliminating all internal barriers to trade among the 13 states, and taxing imports to finance the turnpikes and canals of the new nation and end America's dependence on Europe. It was called the American System.

The "American System" was advocated by politician Henry Clay (1777–1852). He called for a protective tariff in support of home manufacturers and a strong national bank.

The ideology of free trade is the alien import, an invention of European academics and scribblers, not one of whom ever built a great nation, and all of whom were repudiated by America's greatest statesmen, including all four presidents on Mount Rushmore.

In 2000 Pat Buchanan was presidential candidate of the Reform Party. He ran against his former colleagues in the Republican Party on an ultraconservative, protectionist ticket.

The second bill that Washington signed into law was the Tariff Act of 1789. Madison saved the nation's infant industries from being buried by the dumping of British manufactures, with the first truly protective tariff, the Tariff Act of 1816. "Give me a tariff and I will give you the greatest nation on earth," said Lincoln. "I thank God I am not a free trader," Theodore Roosevelt wrote to Henry Cabot Lodge.

See www.econlib. org/library/Taussig/ tsgEnc1.html for more on these tariffs.

Under economic nationalism, there was no income tax in the United States, except during the Civil War and Reconstruction. Tariffs produced fifty to ninety percent of federal revenue. And how did America prosper? From 1865 to 1913, U.S. growth averaged 4% a year. We began the era with half Britain's production, but ended with twice Britain's production....

Buchanan cites a series of renowned politicians. How do these quotations help his argument?

Not only did America rise to greatness through economic nationalism, so did every other first-rank power in history—

105

Otto von Bismarck (1815–1898) was the Prussian statesman who brought about the unification of Germany in the 19th century and became Germany's first chancellor.

from Britain in the 18th century, to Bismarck's Germany in the 19th, to post-war Japan. Economic nationalism has been the policy of rising nations, free trade the practice of nations that have commenced their historic decline. Today, this idea may be mocked by the talking heads, but it is going to prevail again in America, for it alone comports with the national interests of the United States. And this is the subject of my remarks....

The costs of free trade

Karl Marx (1818–1883) was the German economist and social thinker who founded communism. Why does Buchanan bring Marx into his argument?

Back in 1848, another economist wrote that if free trade were ever adopted, societies would be torn apart. His name was Karl Marx, and he wrote: "... the Free Trade system works destructively. It breaks up old nationalities and carries antagonism of proletariat and bourgeoisie to the uttermost point ... the Free trade system hastens the Social Revolution. In this revolutionary sense alone ... I am in favor of Free Trade."

Marx was right. Here, then, is the first cost of open-borders free trade. It exacerbates the divisions between capital and labor. It separates societies into contending classes, and deepens the division between rich and poor. Under free trade, economic and social elites, whose jobs and incomes are not adversely impacted by imports or immigration, do well. For them, these have been the best of times.

Since 1990, the stock market has tripled in value; corporate profits have doubled since 1992; there has been a population explosion among millionaires. America's richest one percent controlled 21 percent of the national wealth in 1949; in 1997 it was 40 percent. Top CEO salaries were 44 times the average wage of their workers in 1965; by 1996 they were 212 times an average worker's pay.

How has Middle America fared?

"Real wages" are wages adjusted for inflation.

Between 1972 and 1994, the real wages of working Americans fell 19 percent. In 1970, the price of a new house was twice a young couple's income; it is now four times.

In 1960, 18 percent of women with children under six were in the work force; by 1995 it had risen 63 percent. The U.S. has a larger percentage of women in its work force than any industrial nation, yet median family income fell 6 percent in the first six years of the 1990s....

A second cost of global free trade is a loss of independence and national sovereignty. America was once a self-reliant nation; trade amounted to only 10 percent of GNP; imports only 4 percent. Now, trade is equal to 25% of GNP; and the trade surpluses we ran every year from 1900-1970 have turned into trade deficits for all of the last 27 years....

U.S. sovereignty

And American sovereignty is being eroded. In 1994, for the first time, the U.S. joined a global institution, the World Trade Organization [WTO], where America has no veto power and the one-nation, one-vote rule applies. Where are we headed? Look at the nations of Europe that are today surrendering control of their money, their immigration policy, their environmental policy, even defense policy—to a giant socialist superstate called the EU [European Union].

For America to continue down this road of global interdependence is a betrayal of our history and our heritage of liberty. What does it profit a man if he gain the whole world, and suffer the loss of his own country?

A third cost of the Global Economy is America's vulnerability to a financial collapse caused by events beyond our control. Never has this country been so exposed. When Mexico, with an economy no larger than Illinois', threatened a default in 1994, the U.S. cobbled together a $50 billion bailout, lest Mexico's default bring on what Michel Camdessus of the IMF called "global financial catastrophe."

When tiny Asian dominoes began to fall last year, the IMF had to put together $117 billion in bailouts of Thailand, Indonesia, South Korea, lest the Asian crisis bring down all of Latin America and the rest of the world with it.

In the Global Economy, the world is always just one default away from disaster. What in heaven's name does the vaunted Global Economy give us—besides all that made-in-China junk down at the mall—to justify having the U.S. financial system at permanent risk of collapse if some incompetent foreign regime decides to walk on its debts?...

There is another reason the free trade era is coming to a close. One day soon, Americans will wake up and discover that other nations do not believe in free trade, and do not practice our particular faith. China and Japan each run $60 billion in annual trade surpluses at America's expense, but each cordons off its own market to U.S. goods. We must start looking out for America first. As Andrew Jackson once declared: "We have been too long subject to the policy of [foreign] merchants. We need to become more Americanized, and instead of feeding the paupers and laborers of Europe ... feed our own...."

America First, and not only first, but second and third as well.

The World Trade Organization (WTO) deals with the rules of trade between nations. Buchanan protests that the United States has no veto. Why should it have one? Find out about the European Union (EU) on www.google.com. Is it fair to call it a "socialist superstate"?

See page 82 for more information about the IMF (International Monetary Fund).

What effect does the author's tone in this paragraph have on his overall argument?

PART 3
THE DEVELOPING WORLD

The United States is the world's richest country, and its citizens are among the best-off people in the world. In 2000 Americans had a GDP per capita—an economic indicator of spending power based on the amount of revenue generated per each individual—of $36,200. In Mexico the figure is $9,100. In the world's poorest countries, such as Burkina Faso or Chad in Africa, the figure is as low as $1,000. The problems of poor countries are in many cases also worsened by debt. Some have to pay huge amounts of interest to service loans they received from richer nations or international financing organizations.

Many people believe that successful countries such as the United States have an obligation to try to improve conditions in poorer nations. Some argue that there is a moral reason to make the global distribution of wealth more fair. They argue that successful trading nations have largely achieved their success by exploiting smaller, less powerful states, particularly during the colonial era in the 18th, 19th, and early 20th centuries. Others argue that helping poorer nations is a purely practical decision. They believe that stimulating developing economies will create new markets for the rich industrial nations.

Other people, however, question why the United States should become involved in the affairs of the developing world. Just because the United States is

rich, does it really have a duty to share its wealth, technology, and knowledge with less successful countries? And if the United States does provide overseas aid, should its assistance come with certain stipulations? This section deals with four issues on the subject of U.S. policy toward the developing world.

A common goal

In June 2000 the Washington, D.C.-based U.S. Agency for International Development (USAID) published a report on U.S. government initiatives to help build the economies of poorer nations. The report argued that the evolution of a successful global economy depends on how much developing countries can participate in a "multilateral trading system." It concluded that industrialized nations share a common interest with developing economies in helping create a market that will contribute to the well-being of people everywhere.

In recent years the United States has increased its efforts to help developing countries increase their trade. From 1998 to 2000 the U.S. government committed over $600 million to strengthening trade-related industries and providing a wide range of technical assistance in developing countries. Advocates of decreased U.S. assistance argue that most aid does not reach the places where it is most needed, and that bureaucracy and corruption often

United States' foreign aid is donated by private individuals. In 2001 Americans gave over $34 billion in charity to foreign countries.

Individual donations differ significantly from government aid packages. Private donations are made in the hope that they will alleviate the suffering of people and are often paid out during periods of crisis, such as famines and war.

> *"Our foreign assistance programs are vital to the achievement of our foreign policy goals."*
> —GEORGE SHULTZ, SECRETARY OF STATE (1982–1989)

This money usually goes to nongovernmental organizations, such as Save the Children or the Red Cross, which spend the money in trouble spots around the world. In contrast, U.S. government aid, for example, is either paid directly to a foreign government or distributed as loans through the International Monetary Fund (IMF) or the World Bank. Government aid packages generally come with several conditions attached, stipulating for what purpose the money should be spent, for instance, to improve infrastructure or encourage economic growth.

Many people believe that undemocratic and corrupt foreign governments should not receive aid. They argue this for several reasons. First, granting aid to such regimes serves to legitimize policies that members of the donor nation might find abhorrent. Second, even when conditions are imposed on aid packages, money can be stolen by political elites in the recipient country. Third, some foreign governments might use aid to develop their military capability in a manner that would threaten international security.

Other people reject these arguments, maintaining that all countries should be entitled to foreign aid. Again, there are a number of reasons to support this position. One reason is that on humanitarian grounds, help should be given to people regardless of their country's politics. Another reason is that aid can help reduce the instability of poor countries, which, if unchecked, could pose a threat to international security. And when conditions such as democratic reforms are attached to aid packages, many people believe they can move countries toward less corrupt forms of government.

Furthermore, aid can help the donor nation gain leverage over a foreign power. An example of how foreign aid can be a useful diplomatic tool was the creation of the worldwide coalition against Iraq's Saddam Hussein in 1990, prior to the Gulf War in 1991. Key Arab states were asked to join the coalition against Iraq or risk losing U.S. aid. All but one country, Yemen, agreed to join.

In the first of the following articles Carol Lancaster argues that aid should be granted to countries irrespective of their politics both for humanitarian reasons and to promote international peace and stability. William Easterly, however, believes that corrupt governments will squander whatever money is granted them and therefore should not receive any assistance.

REDESIGNING FOREIGN AID
Carol Lancaster

This article was published one year before the terrorist attacks on September 11, 2001. Do you think those attacks changed the "basic challenge" facing the United States?

The Democratic Republic of the Congo (DROC) has been torn apart by civil war since 1994, sparked by a massive influx of refugees from the civil wars in Rwanda and Burundi. In the late 1990s interventions by neighboring African nations fueled tensions within the DROC.

The author argues that foreign aid should be available to different factions to encourage peace. By doing this, she implies that politics should not be a barrier to granting aid.

YES

✓ The most basic challenge facing the United States today is helping to preserve peace. The end of the Cold War eliminated a potential threat to American security, but it did not eliminate conflict. In 1998 alone there were 27 significant conflicts in the world, 25 of which involved violence within states. Nine of those intrastate conflicts were in sub-Saharan Africa, where poor governance has aggravated ethnic and social tensions. The ongoing war in the Democratic Republic of the Congo has been particularly nightmarish, combining intrastate and interstate conflict with another troubling element: military intervention driven by the commercial motives of several neighboring states. Such motives could fuel future conflicts in other weak states with valuable resources. Meanwhile, a number of other wars—in Colombia, the former Yugoslavia, Cambodia, Angola, Sudan, Rwanda, and Burundi—have reflected historic enmities or poorly resolved hostilities of the past. Intrastate conflicts are likely to continue in weakly integrated, poorly governed states, destroying lives and property, creating large numbers of refugees and displaced persons, and threatening regional security. The two interstate clashes in 1998—between India and Pakistan and Eritrea and Ethiopia—involved disputes over land and other natural resources. Such contests show no sign of disappearing. Indeed, with the spread of weapons of mass destruction, these wars could prove more dangerous than ever.

The role of aid in peacemaking
Peacemaking will therefore be an important focus of U.S. diplomacy in the twenty-first century. As in the past, the United States is likely to take a lead in conflict prevention and peacemaking in regions that have high priority but lack effective alternatives to U.S. leadership: parts of Europe, the Middle East, countries near U.S. borders, and the Pacific Rim, especially Korea and Taiwan. Foreign aid will become more important to peacemaking diplomacy than before—as a symbol of U.S. engagement, an incentive for warring parties to negotiate peace, and a source of resources to help countries recover from the legacies of war. For example, a

promise of half a billion dollars of U.S. aid was a key element in efforts by the Clinton administration to negotiate an end to the Bosnian war. The growing importance of peace aid is already evident in increases in foreign aid appropriations in 1999 and 2000, much of which was slated for peacemaking in Kosovo and the Middle East. Congress has also recently passed a large supplemental appropriation of more than $1 billion to fund such a policy in Colombia....

From wealth to soft power

This ... diplomacy is fundamentally driven by U.S. interests in preserving world peace and prosperity and protecting the quality of life for Americans. However, American foreign policy has never been based on interests alone. It reflects deep-seated humanitarian values as well. If anything, the role of values in U.S. foreign policy is likely to grow as Americans become increasingly aware of the world beyond their borders, thanks to CNN and the Internet, and demand action by their government to ease human suffering. A U.S. diplomacy of values is also important in fortifying America's "soft power"—the credibility and trust that the United States can command in the world—and ensuring effective American leadership in other areas.

Do you agree that U.S. foreign policy reflects humanitarian values?

Following September 11, 2001, the Bush administration used aid, particularly in Pakistan, to secure the support of its allies for the War on Terror.

Four principal elements make up a U.S. diplomacy of values: providing relief in humanitarian crises; helping to promote development and reduce poverty in the poorest countries; advancing "humane concerns" by improving the quality of life for the neediest and most vulnerable abroad; and supporting the expansion of democracy and human rights. Foreign aid will be essential in each area.

Humanitarian relief will likely make increasing demands on U.S. aid as disasters, both human and natural, continue to proliferate. Natural disasters have been on the rise in recent years, in both number and severity. They could become even more numerous in the future as a result of climatic changes and more severe as a result of the pressure of growing populations on fragile environments....

Problems in Africa

A number of countries—largely in Africa—have not fared ... well over the past four decades. Although they have made some progress in literacy and life expectancy (until the devastating impact of AIDS), many still lack the capacity and access to international capital to address their deepening problems of poverty. U.S. foreign aid still has a role to play there, but several difficult dilemmas have complicated the

Research the issues affecting African nations by going to http://www.cia.gov/ cia/publications/ factbook/.

The "Transparency International Corruption Perceptions Index" was first published in 1995 in order to monitor countries with the worst records of corruption. The 2002 Index showed that Indonesia, Kenya, Angola, Madagascar, Paraguay, Nigeria, and Bangladesh were among the worst offenders. Go to http://www. transparency.org/ pressreleases_ archive/2002/2002. 08.28.cpi.en.html for more information.

provision of effective aid for African development. The first involves the issue of when to provide aid and when to withhold it. For much of Africa, the core development problem has been not a lack of resources but bad politics. In many countries, policy and regulatory environments continue to discourage investors, while government institutions remain weak and often corrupt. It is noteworthy that in the 1999 Transparency International Corruption Perceptions Index, five of the ten worst offenders were in Africa. Until the political leaderships of African countries come to value the long-term betterment of their populations over their own personal and political interests, policies will remain faulty, institutions weak, investment and growth low, and aid ineffective.

But the problem of weak institutions in Africa is also in part the responsibility of aid donors themselves. With 40 or more poorly coordinated aid agencies working in numerous African countries, pursuing their own priorities, and expecting their own separate administrative and procurement requirements to be met, the burdens of aid have overwhelmed African officials and disrupted government budgets. These multiple aid agencies urgently need far better coordination and discipline.

Utilizing the World Bank

Another criticism of the World Bank relates to the demands it can make for economic reform in return for aid (known as structural adjustment programs). Critics argue that these reforms—such as the privatization of national companies and the removal of trade barriers— increase the First World's ability to exploit the Third World.

The primary responsibility for international leadership on development must lie with the World Bank. To its credit, it has been trying to better coordinate the different mechanisms for delivering aid. It is the one international institution with the expertise, coordination, and potential aid resources that can work for governments committed to economic and social progress. True, some critics of the Bank argue that it needs to be more focused. Others, including a number of nongovernmental organizations, argue that the Bank needs to be more accountable, especially to those it is trying to benefit. Both are right. But with appropriate reforms the World Bank can effectively serve as the primary channel for U.S. development aid in the future.

If promoting development in poor countries will have less priority in U.S. aid policy, helping disadvantaged and vulnerable groups and communities abroad to better their lives will assume a more prominent place. Indeed, it already has. But an important difference distinguishes these two goals. Development policy seeks to bring about broad-based economic and social changes on a national level; this kind of foreign aid takes a strategic approach, removing obstacles to development and helping spur national economic and social progress. Most major aid donors produce periodic assessments of the overall development needs of particular countries and shape their interventions to fit those needs. In contrast, aid for humane concerns—directly helping vulnerable groups to improve their lives—may also help development, but its principal goal and impulse is humanitarian: to help those in need who cannot easily help themselves....

Do you think that helping "those in need" is an adequate goal for governments? Do you think this help should be linked to development strategies to overcome long-term problems?

Aid, human rights, and democracy

Finally, future American administrations must continue to support human rights and democracy in the world to reflect the broadly shared values of the U.S. population. Foreign aid can play a role in furthering democracy through funding elections and providing training for legislators, judges, and police forces. Assuming the trend of democratization continues, however, aid for this purpose is likely to decline as the basic building blocks of democracy fall into place throughout the world.

Do you think that the attacks and consequences of September 11, 2001, suggest that the "trend of democratization" might not be as smooth as the author believed it to be in 2000?

In sum, foreign aid will continue to be an essential foreign policy tool to promote U.S. interests and values abroad. Its major purposes will include peacemaking, addressing transnational issues and other challenges arising from globalization, providing humanitarian relief, and promoting "humane concerns" abroad. The first two purposes relate primarily to U.S. interests; the second two reflect U.S. values. Support for development and democracy abroad will not disappear, but they will not be among the major priorities for foreign aid spending in the decades to come....

THINK AGAIN: DEBT RELIEF
William Easterly

In the 1970s many developing nations borrowed heavily from foreign governments. When the price of these nations' exports (such as oil, coffee, and cocoa) fell in the 1980s, they were unable to meet their debt repayments. The debt-relief movement argues that First World governments should cancel this debt because it is crippling poor countries, was loaned irresponsibly in the first place, and was often accepted by unelected regimes that are no longer in power.

NO

☒ Debt relief has become the feel-good economic policy of the new millennium, trumpeted by Irish rock star Bono, Pope John Paul II, and virtually everyone in between. But despite its overwhelming popularity among policymakers and the public, debt relief is a bad deal for the world's poor. By transferring scarce resources to corrupt governments with proven track records of misusing aid, debt forgiveness might only aggravate poverty among the world's most vulnerable populations....

"Crushing debts worsen third world poverty"

Wrong in more ways than one. Yes, the total long-term debt of the 41 HIPC [Highly Indebted Poor Countries] nations grew from $47 billion in 1980 to $159 billion in 1990 to $169 billion in 1999, but in reality the foreign debt of poor countries has always been partly fictional. Whenever debt service became too onerous, the poor nations simply received new loans to repay old ones. Recent studies have found that new World Bank adjustment loans to poor countries in the 1980s and 1990s increased in lock step with mounting debt service. Likewise, another study found that official lenders tend to match increases in the payment obligations of highly indebted African countries with an increase in new loans. Indeed, over the past two decades, new lending to African countries more than covered debt service payments on old loans.

Second, debt relief advocates should remember that poor people don't owe foreign debt—their governments do. Poor nations suffer poverty not because of high debt burdens but because spendthrift governments constantly seek to redistribute the existing economic pie to privileged political elites rather than try to make the pie grow larger through sound economic policies. The debt-burdened government of Kenya managed to find enough money to reward President Moi's home region with the Eldoret International Airport in 1996, a facility that almost nobody uses.

Left to themselves, bad governments are likely to engage in new borrowing to replace the forgiven loans, so the debt burden wouldn't fall in the end anyway. And even if

The previous article argues that the United States has a duty to "help those in need." Do you think that the government should refuse to help poor countries if their leaders are corrupt or attempt to ensure aid goes to those who need it?

irresponsible governments do not run up new debts, they could always finance their redistributive ways by running down government assets (like oil and minerals), leaving future generations condemned to the same overall debt burden. Ultimately, debt relief will only help reduce debt burdens if government policies make a true shift away from redistributive politics and toward a focus on economic development.

"Debt relief allows poor nations to spend more on health and education"

No. In 1999, Jubilee 2000 enthused that with debt relief "the year 2000 could signal the beginning of dramatic improvements in health care, education, employment and development for countries crippled by debt." Unfortunately, such statements fail to recognize some harsh realities about government spending.

First, the iron law of public finance states that money is fungible: Debt relief goes into the same government account that rains money on good and bad uses alike. Debt relief enables governments to spend more on weapons, for example. Debt relief clients such as Angola, Ethiopia, and Rwanda all have heavy military spending (although some are promising to make cuts). To assess whether debt relief increases health and education spending, one must ask what such spending would have been in the absence of debt relief—a difficult question. However, if governments didn't spend the original loans on helping the poor, it's a stretch to expect them to devote new fiscal resources toward helping the poor.

Second, such claims assume that the central government knows where its money is going. A recent IMF and World Bank study found that only two out of 25 debt relief recipients will have satisfactory capacity to track where government spending goes within a year. At the national level, an additional study found that only 13 percent of central government grants for non-salary education spending in Uganda (another recipient of debt relief) actually made it to the local schools that were the intended beneficiaries.

Finally, the very idea that the proceeds of debt relief should be spent on health and education contains a logical flaw. If debt relief proceeds are spent on social programs rather than used to pay down the debt, then the debt burden will remain just as crushing as it was before. A government can't use the same money twice—first to pay down foreign debt and second to expand health and education services for the poor.

Jubilee 2000 was an international campaign that in the run-up to the millennium, gathered 24 million signatures demanding that the leaders of the seven richest nations (G7) cancel Third World debt by 2000. As a result, the G7 countries agreed to write off $100 billion in debt.

The author argues that granting aid/debt relief to certain countries ignores the lessons of history. However, other people maintain that the governments that received the original loans are often not the same as the ones now in power. Which argument do you feel is more valid?

The debt relief the author has in mind is the reduction of poor countries' debt payments. Most debt campaigners want all debts to be canceled.

119

Over the long term do you think that spending on health and education can reap economic benefits?

This magic could only work if health and education spending boosted economic growth and thus generated future tax revenues to service the debt. Unfortunately, there is little evidence that higher health and education spending is associated with faster economic growth.

"Debt relief will empower poor countries to make their own choices"

See page 116 for some of the criticisms of "rich nations telling poor countries what to do." Then read more about this issue at www. globalexchange.org /wbimf/faq.html.

Not really. Pro-debt relief advocacy groups face a paradox: On one hand, they want debt relief to reach the poor; on the other, they don't want rich nations telling poor countries what to do. "For debt relief to work, let the conditions be set by civil society in our countries, not by big world institutions using it as a political tool," argued Kennedy Tumutegyereize of the Uganda Debt Network. Unfortunately, debt relief advocates can't have it both ways. Civil society remains weak in most highly indebted poor countries, so it would be hard to ensure that debt relief will truly benefit the poor unless there are conditions on the debt relief package.

Attempting to square this circle, the World Bank and IMF have made a lot of noise about consulting civil society while at the same time dictating incredibly detailed conditions on debt relief. The result is unlikely to please anyone. Debt relief under the World Bank and IMF's current HIPC initiative, for example, requires that countries prepare Poverty Reduction Strategy Papers. The World Bank's online handbook advising countries on how to prepare such documents runs well over 1,000 pages and covers such varied topics as macroeconomics, gender, the environment, water management, mining, and information technology. It would be hard for even the most skilled policymakers in the advanced economies to follow such complex (no matter how salutary) advice, much less a government in a poor country suffering from scarcity of qualified managers. In reality, this morass of requirements emerged as the multilateral financial institutions sought to hit on all the politically correct themes while at the same time trying hard to make the money reach the poor. If the conditions don't work—and of course they won't—the World Bank and IMF can simply fault the countries for not following their advice....

Find out more about Poverty Reduction Strategy Papers at www.worldbank. org/poverty/ strategies/ overview.htm.

"Debt relief will promote economic reform"

Don't hold your breath. During the last two decades, the multilateral financial institutions granted "structural adjustment" loans to developing nations, with the understanding that governments in poor countries would cut their fiscal deficits and enact reforms—including privatization of state-owned enterprises and trade liberalization—that would promote economic growth. The World Bank and IMF made 1,055 separate adjustment loans to 119 poor countries from 1980 to 1999. Had such lending succeeded, poor countries would have experienced more rapid growth, which in turn would have permitted them to service their foreign debts more easily. Thirty-six poor countries received 10 or more adjustment loans in the 1980s and 1990s, and their average percentage growth of per capita income during those two decades was a grand total of zero. Moreover, such loans failed to produce meaningful reforms, and developing countries now cite this failure as justification for debt relief. Yet why should anyone expect that conditions on debt forgiveness would be any more effective in changing government policies and behavior than conditions on the original loans?

Partial and conditional debt forgiveness is a fait accompli. Expanding it to full and unconditional debt forgiveness— as some groups now advocate—would simply transfer more resources from poor countries that have used aid effectively to those that have wasted it in the past. The challenge for civil society, the World Bank, IMF, and other agencies is to ensure that conditional debt forgiveness really does lead to government reforms that enhance the prospects of poor countries.

Do you think "debt forgiveness" would be beneficial to developing countries?

Conclusion

How can we promote economic reform in the poorest nations without repeating past failures? The lesson of structural adjustment programs is that reforms imposed from the outside don't change behavior. Indeed, they only succeed in creating an easy scapegoat: Insincere governments can simply blame their woes on the World Bank and IMF's "harsh" adjustment programs while not doing anything to fundamentally change economic incentives and ignite economic growth. It would be better for the international financial institutions to simply offer advice to governments that ask for it and wait for individual countries to come forward with homegrown reform programs, financing only the most promising ones and disengaging from the rest. This approach has worked in promoting economic reform in countries such as China, India, and Uganda. Rushing through debt forgiveness and imposing complex reforms from the outside is as doomed to failure as earlier rounds of debt relief and adjustment loans.

For a related debate on the question of engagement versus disengagement see Topic 2 Is U.S. foreign policy too interventionist? on pages 22–33.

Summary

Writing before the events of September 11, 2001, Carol Lancaster believes that the most important task facing the United States is to preserve peace around the world. She believes that foreign aid has a role to play in this task. Aid, she argues, can help diplomatic efforts "as an incentive for warring parties to negotiate peace." She cites how the Clinton administration used aid during its efforts to conclude the Bosnian conflict. Moreover, Lancaster believes that aid reflects people's desire to help those in need all over the world. For these reasons she suggests that aid should be given to developing countries irrespective of their politics. She acknowledges that there are corrupt regimes where aid can be "ineffective" in achieving goals, but even here she feels that the responsibility lies also with the aid donors themselves, who need to be more unified and coherent in their efforts.

William Easterly focuses on developing countries' debt and argues that the bad politics of some debtor nations is the very reason why campaigns to cancel this debt are wrong. He contends that the poverty of people in developing nations is largely due to their corrupt governments, which, instead of using loans and aid to promote economic growth, parcel out funding among the privileged few or spend it on military hardware. He further argues that governments that have already run up huge debts will continue to borrow more once these current debts are removed. Easterly concludes that institutions such as the World Bank and the IMF should only finance debt-relief plans for countries with "promising" reform plans. The latter institutions should, he believes, disengage from other developing countries.

FURTHER INFORMATION:

Books:

Anderson, Mary B., *Do No Harm: How Aid Can Support Peace—Or War.* Boulder, CO: Lynne Riener Publishers, 1999.

Moran, Michael, *Road to Hell: The Ravaging Effects of Foreign Aid and International Charity.* New York: Free Press, 1997.

Useful websites:

http://www.cato.org/pubs/pas/pa-273es.html
"Help or Hindrance: Can Foreign Aid Prevent International Crises"? by Doug Bandow.
http://www.jubileeusa.org/
Jubilee USA site, with background information on the debt-relief campaign.
http://www.usaid.gov/
Site for the U.S. Agency for International Development.

The following debates in the Pro/Con series may also be of interest:

In this volume:
Topic 1 Does the United States have a duty to protect democracy and freedom overseas?

Topic 7 Should economic sanctions be used to promote human rights?

In *Economics*:
Topic 11 Should rich countries cancel "Third World debt"?

SHOULD THE UNITED STATES GIVE AID TO DEVELOPING COUNTRIES IRRESPECTIVE OF THEIR POLITICS?

YES: It is important for the government to provide help to others around world

YES: Donated funds need to be properly controlled so they reach where they are needed

GOVERNMENT AID
Is it the job of the government to give aid to foreign countries?

STRINGS ATTACHED
Should the government apply conditions to its aid packages?

NO: Foreign aid should be made up of private charitable donations that can be spent by nongovernmental organizations

NO: The conditions usually benefit the aid giver rather than the receiver

SHOULD THE UNITED STATES GIVE AID TO DEVELOPING COUNTRIES IRRESPECTIVE OF THEIR POLITICS?

KEY POINTS

YES: The United States needs allies around the world. Aid is a good way to maintain friendly diplomatic relations.

YES: Aid with conditions attached can help bring about democratic reform in countries

ALLIES
Should the United States use its aid to influence undemocratic countries?

NO: An undemocratic, unaccountable government may use aid to enrich its elite or even develop its military capability

NO: Only by withholding aid can undemocratic regimes be encouraged to become more democratic

Topic 10
HAS THE UNITED STATES EXPLOITED LATIN AMERICA?

YES
FROM "A 'KILLING FIELD' IN THE AMERICAS: U.S. POLICY IN GUATEMALA"
WWW.THIRDWORLDTRAVELER.COM/US_THIRDWORLD/US_GUAT.HTML
THIRD WORLD TRAVELER

NO
FROM "THE PROSPECT FOR U.S.–LATIN AMERICAN RELATIONS"
AMERICAN ENTERPRISE INSTITUTE, DECEMBER 2000
MARK FALCOFF

INTRODUCTION

Some people believe that the United States' long history of economic and military involvement in Latin America has been driven by a need to exploit the region's labor and commodities: The countries of Central and South America have been plundered for their primary products and cheap labor and have not received their just rewards. But defenders of the U.S. role in the region argue that without the involvement of American companies, living standards would be even lower, and there would be fewer employment opportunities.

This debate is well illustrated by the "maquiladora" industries in Mexico—foreign-owned assembly plants—close to the U.S. border. There are around 3,800 mainly U.S.-owned factories, employing almost one million Mexican workers and producing electronic equipment, clothing, plastic products, furniture, and auto parts. While the hourly rate for an American production line worker averages $10, a rate of $2 an hour is considered above average in a maquiladora.

Critics claim that the maquiladora system exploits cheap Mexican labor, but supporters of the system respond that it has created many jobs in a region of underemployment.

Coffee exports, meanwhile, have long represented the prime source of foreign exchange for many Central American countries. But as long ago as 1949 Andres Uribe of the Colombian Federation of National Coffee Growers explained that while American consumers paid more than $2 billion for their coffee, most of that money went to U.S. businesses rather than the growers in Latin America.

After 1962 an International Coffee Agreement was signed to guarantee fair prices to the producers, but in 1989 the United States withdrew from the agreement. Prices fluctuated then fell dramatically. The effects on many parts of Latin America were severe: Since many coffee growers could not get a decent price, they did not harvest their crop. Some abandoned their plantations, while others started growing coca, the plant from which the drug cocaine is derived. The World Bank estimated that about half a million jobs in the coffee industry were lost in Cental America in 2000–2001. Coffee drinkers spent $66 billion in 2001, while producers received just $5.5 billion. The leading marketing firms— 33 percent of world coffee sales are accounted for by just three U.S. companies—are making enormous profits at the expense of the growers in Latin America.

"If coffee cannot receive an equitable price, then you cast these millions of persons loose to drift in a perilous sea of poverty and privation."

—ANDRES URIBE, COLOMBIAN FEDERATION OF NATIONAL COFFEE GROWERS

The counterargument is simple: Without the U.S. coffee market the industry would be a fraction of its size, and Latin America would be worse off. The fall in price on the world markets simply suggests that there is a surplus.

Bananas represent another key Latin American commodity. The history of U.S.-owned banana companies, such as United Fruit, is steeped in controversy.

When a land reform program introduced in Guatemala in 1954 threatened United Fruit's plantations, the company won government backing to stop the reforms. When the governments of Costa Rica, Honduras, and Panama imposed a tax on banana exports in 1973, they met opposition from the United Fruit Corporation. In retaliation, United Fruit refused to export bananas from Panama, and overnight the country's exports fell 45 percent.

More controversial, some people argue, was the alleged involvement of the United States in the internal affairs of various Latin American countries.

In 1973 the CIA was implicated in overthrowing the democratically elected government of Salvador Allende in Chile. The government had embarked on a program of nationalization that jeopardized U.S. business interests, worth more than $1 billion at the time. After Allende was elected, U.S. nonmilitary aid to Chile was reduced, while military aid doubled between 1970 and 1974. Following the bloody coup of 1973, General Pinochet took power, and Chile once again became a safe place for U.S. business investment.

A decade later, after the Sandanista regime came to power in Nicaragua, the United States funded Contra rebels to destabilize the new government. Critics question whether the measures taken in Chile and Nicaragua were justified since they protected U.S. interests. Others claimed that they were an unwarranted infringement on the affairs of foreign nations.

In following articles Third World Traveler examines the 1954 coup in Guatemala, while Mark Falcoff argues that without U.S. involvement Latin America would be in a worse position.

of elite-corporate-Army control. Those on the lists were hunted down and killed.

The U.S. mission and its advisors prodded the military to take measures to establish a U.S. base for counter-insurgency (counter-revolutionary) actions, in order to maintain cheap labor for the landowners and U.S. corporations, and to preserve the System. Terror was the weapon, and the American CIA was the agent. Targeting guerrillas, peasants, students, labor leaders, and professionals, the Guatemalan military jailed thousands. And thousands more, struggling to overcome poverty and injustice, were murdered or disappeared by the police, the Army, and the death squads, all armed and trained by the CIA.... By the end of 1968, the guerrillas had been wiped out. For the Pentagon it had been a limited war; for the Guatemalans the war had been total.

Short, pithy statements are a memorable way to summarize an argument.

The CIA, the Guatemalan G-2, and Israel

But, the war did not end with victory over the guerrillas. Since the 1960s, the CIA has had links with a Guatemalan Army unit—the G-2—that maintains a network of torture centers and body dumps throughout Guatemala. Operating out of the U.S. Embassy, CIA undercover agents, secretly working with the G-2—a group of 2,000 elite Guatemalan Army Intelligence officers—have trained, advised, armed, and equipped these officers to torture, assassinate and disappear thousands of Guatemalan dissidents. Some G-2 bases have crematoriums where the tortured and murdered are disposed of.

What is the role of the CIA as you understand it? Do you think America is justified to use the CIA to intervene in another country's affairs?

In the 1970s, international publicity revealed the pattern of torture and killing, and public reports exposed the Guatemalan Army as the most repressive in Latin America. This series of events resulted in a change in human rights sentiment in the U.S. In 1977, U.S. President Jimmy Carter cut off overt military aid. However, money and arms still got to there—through the CIA. When President Lucas Garcia began his fearsome regime in 1978, and set out to eliminate all the new popular leaders by either murdering or coopting them, and when death squads roamed the land and murdered at will, the CIA was there to help. In addition to U.S. and CIA support, Argentina, and Chile provided expertise and aid to Guatemala's military. And, Israel has played a very important role in Guatemala since 1977, supplying weapons, building munitions factories, and training soldiers....

The author introduces the subject of Israel. How relevant is this to his argument? Does it make it more or less effective?

The Reagan administration

Before his administration took office in 1980, President Reagan courted the Guatemalan right, whose views he shared. He promised then-president of Guatemala General Romeo Lucas Garcia and leaders of the right, a 180 degree turn in U.S. policy toward their country. The agreement provided for the restoration of U.S. weapons sales, the curtailment of State Department criticism of human rights violations, and the promise that the U.S. would intervene militarily in the event of a popular uprising. The assurances by Reagan may have led the Guatemalan government officials who ran the death squads to feel confident that the U.S. would support their activities. The death squads were staffed and directed by the Guatemalan Army and Police under the command of President Lucas. Private businessmen paid the salaries and often assisted in compiling lists of potential victims—usually student, labor, professional, and political leaders….

The author uses language carefully in suggesting a possible link between President Reagan's attitude to Guatemala and the operation of death squads.

The "New World Order" and Guatemala

The war against Guatemalans still involves guns, bombs and human rights abuses, but the war of the 1990s is also an economic war against the poor. It is an international system of social, economic, and political control which works to separate the largest portion of the population of the world— those who are poor, people of color, and women, especially within the developing world—from the smallest portion of the population who are wealthy….

Do you think the United States is engaged in an "economic war against the poor"? If so, what does it stand to gain from such a war?

In Guatemala, in the 90s, the Cold War has been replaced by the "war against drugs" and NAFTA. The war on drugs has given the enemies of democracy in Guatemala an excuse to bomb the indigenous population in the countryside. The real narcotraffickers are not in the countryside; they are in the cities where the seats of power are. And NAFTA, is attempting to ensure that the landed elite and the agri-corporations will control the country for some time to come.

But, there are signs of hope…. Guatemala today stands on the brink of a long-awaited peace agreement—the government and representatives of all sectors of society have been negotiating conditions for peace. The peace process represents much more than a cease fire. After more than 35 years of armed conflict and staggering injustice, Guatemalans want a transformed society—democratic leadership, rights for indigenous people, demilitarization, constitutional reforms, an end to impunity, a Truth Commission to examine human rights abuses, political participation, and attention to socio-economic issues such as land reform. Americans can help this process by demanding that the U.S. government stop the death squads, support political and economic reform, and end the decades-old war against the Guatemalan people.

The Cold War was a period of East–West tension and hostility that lasted from the 1940s to the early 1990s. The main participants were the United States, the Soviet Union, and Britain. The North American Free Trade Agreement (NAFTA) was signed in 1994 and removed trade and investment barriers between the United States, Canada, and Mexico.

To read more about the peace process, go to www.workablepeace. org/pdfs/Guat.pdf.

THE PROSPECT FOR U.S.–LATIN AMERICAN RELATIONS
Mark Falcoff

NO

X After a decade during which the Latin American environment was relatively benevolent and which allowed policymakers to concentrate on more constructive issues like market reforms and democratic development, many indicators have signaled that the first decade of the new century will be considerably more nettlesome—for Latin America and for the United States.

To give the Clinton administration its due, it courageously brought to a successful conclusion the free-trade treaty with Mexico negotiated by its Republican predecessor, paying a remarkably high political price with some of its core constituencies. In spite of a strong antimilitary bias and a decided reluctance to intervene in civil conflicts in Latin America, it brought itself to support Plan Colombia, a program of civil and military assistance developed by the government in Bogotá to counteract the growing strength of the narcoguerrilla movement in that country. And although there are strong undercurrents of sympathy for the Cuban dictatorship in some key constituencies of the Democratic Party and in Congress, it somehow managed (helped along, no doubt, by the Helms–Burton Law) to hold fast to the notion that some sort of democratic opening on the island was a precondition to serious improvement of relations.

For the past year, however, U.S.–Latin American relations have been in something of a holding pattern. This often happens in the last days of a waning administration, when the temptation is strong to pass on unpleasant decisions to its successor—all the more if it appears that the latter will represent a different political party…. Unfortunately, the next occupant of the White House will have no choice but to grapple with some very difficult issues.

Expanding commerce and maintaining security
The first of these is the extension of NAFTA to comprehend the entire Western Hemisphere. This idea—now known as the Free Trade Area of the Americas—was first proposed by former president George Bush…. However, two rather

This is a reference to the North American Free Trade Agreement (NAFTA). For more information see Topic 6 Does NAFTA work? on pages 74–85.

Fidel Castro (1927–) has ruled Cuba since the revolution of 1959. The Helms–Burton Law of 1996 sought international sanctions against Castro's government and is named for its primary sponsors, Senator Jesse Helms and Representative Dan Burton.

For more detail on the Free Trade of the Americas proposal go to www.ftaa-alca.org/alca_e.asp and www.stopftaa.org/.

contradictory developments have emerged. Fearful of further alienating its core constituencies, the Clinton administration has been reluctant to request fast-track authority from Congress to negotiate with Chile an agreement similar to the one reached with Mexico. Meanwhile, however, the process of trade liberalization for the hemisphere as a whole proceeds with all deliberate speed at various ministerial and subministerial conclaves. Sometime around 2004 a new trade treaty covering a wide range of signatories—not just Chile—may land in the lap of a deeply divided Congress....

In the best of cases, one can expect that Democrats in Congress will try to load down the document with as many reservations dealing with environment and labor rights as they can; if they have become a majority by then—a distinct possibility—they may manage to sink the project altogether. The potential impact on hemispheric relations is obvious: If the United States cannot offer Latin America anything positive—that is, if all we talk about is drugs and illegal immigration—it is difficult to see why Latins should be particularly solicitous to other, less attractive (to them) aspects of Washington's agenda.

Then the president must grapple with security issues. To be sure, with the demise of the Soviet empire, in a strict geopolitical sense the hemisphere has become a far safer place. In fact, the past decade has been the first since the end of World War II in which no extrahemispheric power had the capacity to seriously intervene in the internal affairs of the region. But we and our neighbors are increasingly faced with important issues of international criminality. Most of these center around the vigorous drug traffic that proceeds from the Andean countries and Mexico to the United States, though in the case of Colombia an entire state is at risk....

The situation in Columbia

The complaint most often heard these days is that by agreeing to provide military assistance to the Colombian army in its pursuit of narcotraffickers, Washington is "escalating" a conflict that should be resolved purely by political means. In fact, however, only a fraction of the $1.3 billion going to Colombia under the plan will be devoted to military purposes; the rest will be spent on social and political reforms. These may, of course, prove incapable of counteracting the drug scourge. But so far negotiations between the Colombian government and the FARC guerrillas have gone nowhere, and the latter seem in no particular hurry to reach a political solution....

This article was published in December 2000.

Do you think that U.S.–Latin American relations focus too much on the issues of drug trafficking and illegal immigration?

Does the United States have to become involved militarily in Colombia if it is to fight a drug war that directly involves the American people?

The Revolutionary Armed Forces of Colombia (FARC), formed in 1964, is an antigovernment organization. It asks the U.S. government to legalize the narcotics trade, among other things.

Democracy issues

Falcoff's central argument is that democracy has driven U.S.–Latin American policy, not exploitation.

During the 1980s the great agenda of U.S. Latin American policy was democracy and free elections, and in fact by 1989 considerable progress had been made in this direction.... While the old-fashioned military coup is a thing of the past, and so—except in Colombia—is Marxist-inspired guerrilla warfare, all is not well in the civic culture of the nascent democracies. Perhaps the most positive examples are the ABC countries (Argentina, Brazil, and Chile), as well as the perennially praise-worthy Costa Rica; the most troubled—in different ways—are Venezuela, Ecuador, Bolivia, and Peru. All, however, suffer from a kind of disillusionment with the democratic process and also with economic reform (or "neoliberalism," as its critics call it)—except possibly for Mexico, a special case given the recent election for the first time of an opposition presidential candidate.

For a discussion of the definition of neoliberalism go to web.inter.nl.net/users/Paul.Treanor/neoliberalism.html.

In 2000 the National Action Party's Vicente Fox became president of Mexico, thus breaking the Institutional Revolutionary Party's (PRI) 71-year-old hold on Mexican political power.

Unfortunately, elections alone have not solved the region's problems. Nor have they effectively canceled out some of the less salutary features of its traditional political culture, such as cronyism [the appointment of friends to positions of influence], misuse of government resources, strong-arming opponents, or attempts to extend presidential terms beyond their legal limits. Meanwhile, new constituencies—women, along with ethnic and even sexual minorities—are demanding their place in the sun. New demands are emerging to improve the quality of democratic life.... Unfortunately, the discourse of Latin American electoral politics is still somewhat antique; there is still a tendency for contending parties to regard political competition as a zero-sum game, and increasingly, young people regard politics as a frivolous pursuit meaningless to anyone except the congenitally corrupt and insanely ambitious.

Do you agree that most young Americans see politics in this way?

In the past, the United States has utilized passive instruments—nonrecognition or sanctions—to discipline nondemocratic Latin American regimes. Neither have proven successful. Apart from the fact that the U.S. is not the only source of arms and credit in the world, the Latin American states themselves reject the use of nonrecognition as an instrument of statecraft. This is true not only for Cuba, but for other noncommunist Latin American countries as well. During the Bush administration Latin allies were nowhere to be found when General Noriega seized power in Panama....

Does the United States have the right to "discipline" other countries in its hemisphere? If you believe this, why is that so?

One might argue that a minimalist democratic agenda is enough for U.S. policy and is probably also the only one that has any chance of success. And one might add as well that corruption and judicial reform are matters best left to the countries themselves. This is not, however, the view of the broad Latin American public, which continues to believe the United States could easily improve the quality of democratic governance in Latin America *if it only wanted to*. This is an example of the "hegemonic presumption" that we Americans were counseled some years ago to abandon, but which the Latins themselves continue to hug tightly to their bosoms.

If the United States benefits economically from its neighbors, is it obliged to open up economic opportunities to immigrants from Latin America?

The Latins among us

A final word about immigration. Some time ago Mexico's President Vicente Fox provoked quite a stir in the United States by urging a policy of "open borders," which would allow his countrymen to move freely back and forth in search of work. The response in Washington was so emphatically negative that Fox himself was forced to clarify his original suggestion, which he subsequently said was merely an idea for the longer term.

The fact is that the border between the United States and Latin America—not just Mexico—is already extremely porous.... These people are brought here by both push and pull factors. On one hand, the burgeoning U.S. economy has an apparently inexhaustible appetite for abundant, cheap unskilled or semiskilled labor (as well as for skilled professionals in many fields). On the other, low wages, limited opportunities for social advancement, the high cost of housing, and the mediocrity of available consumer goods— not to mention deteriorating physical security—are driving industrious people northward. To which might be added the seductive force of American popular culture, upon which Latin American youth has seized with a particular vengeance. The increasing use of the Spanish language in many places in the United States, including nontraditional locales, has cushioned the cultural trauma of immigration....

Do the author's comments about immigration surprise you? How do they compare to the usual arguments made about immigration? To read an article on U.S.–Mexican immigration, go to www.ailf.org/ pubed/mexico/ overview.htm.

The impact of this immigration on the United States has yet to be fully felt. But in Latin America, its effects have been immediate and unambiguous: It has provided a flow of remittances that have stabilized many Latin American economies, and it has also removed from these societies people whose thwarted ambitions might prove politically destabilizing. The case of Mexico is the most obvious, since the amounts run into billions of dollars each year. But every Central American republic depends upon these transfers, as does—in a curious way—the Castro dictatorship in Cuba and the thuggish regime of Aristide in Haiti. Soon the same may be true for Peru, Bolivia, and Ecuador, if not indeed for countries further south....

Summary

Third World Traveler, a website providing alternative views from the mainstream media, examines the 20th-century history of Guatemala, providing examples of U.S. interference in the country's affairs. From the 1930s land ownership and trade were dominated by one U.S.-owned company; and when the government of Arbenz Guzmán began a land reform program in the 1950s threatening the corporation's interests, the Eisenhower administration sponsored a coup in Guatemala. U.S. aid has also strengthened its army, which organizes death squads. In the 1980s Ronald Reagan backed the Guatemalan leader General Garcia in a civil war against the country's rural communities. Third World Traveler argues that U.S. support for undemocratic policies in Guatemala persists today. The government's "war on drugs" is an excuse to continue repression of the indigenous people, while the North American Free Trade Agreement is in effect a war on the poor of the nation.

Mark Falcoff maintains that the influence of the United States on Latin America has been mostly positive. Answering critics of Plan Colombia, he argues that only a small part of U.S. aid to that country will be spent on the military, with the majority directed to social and political reforms. The United States has long worked to encourage democracy in the region, writes Falcoff, and if anything, Latin Americans expect the United States to be more involved in the region. Falcoff also argues that the money earned by migrants to the United States, which is sent back to home countries, is essential for helping stablilize those domestic economies.

FURTHER INFORMATION:

Books:

Chomsky, Noam, *Latin America: From Colonization to Globalization*. Melbourne, Australia: Ocean Press, 1999.

Gleijeses, Piero, *Shattered Hope: The Guatemalan Revolution and the United States 1944–1954*. Princeton, NJ: Princeton University Press, 1992.

Useful websites:

www.thirdworldtraveler.com/South_America/ColombiaPlan_Chomsky.html
June 2000 magazine article by Noam Chomsky on the Colombia Plan.
www.fas.org/irp/threat/terro_95/terlat.htm
State Department on terrorism in Latin America.
www.gwu.edu/~nsarchiv/NSAEBB/NSAEBB11/docs/me
Archive of information on U.S. policy in Guatemala from 1966 to 1996.

The following debates in the Pro/Con series may also be of interest:

In this volume:
Topic 1 Does the United States have a duty to protect democracy and freedom overseas?

Topic 2 Is U.S. foreign policy too interventionist?

Topic 12 Does the war on drugs give the United States the right to intervene in other countries' affairs?

HAS THE UNITED STATES EXPLOITED LATIN AMERICA?

YES: U.S. companies pay much lower wages to workers in Latin America than they would to those in the United States

YES: If the price of Latin American commodities such as coffee fall on the world market, the industries in question suffer too

WAGES
Does U.S. business activity in Latin America keep wages low?

EMPLOYMENT
Has U.S. control of markets destroyed Latin American jobs?

NO: U.S.-owned companies pay higher wages than other employers in the Latin American economy

NO: The jobs would not be there in the first place had it not been for the United States

HAS THE UNITED STATES EXPLOITED LATIN AMERICA?

KEY POINTS

YES: Many Latin American dictators who have committed human rights abuses have been installed with the assistance of the United States

YES: In the region's civil wars thousands have been killed by U.S.-provided weapons used by U.S.-trained soldiers

HUMAN RIGHTS
Has the United States undermined human rights in Latin America?

PEACE
Has U.S. involvement in Latin America helped foment civil war?

NO: Aid and advice have been given only when there has been a risk of countries sliding into anarchy, as in Chile in 1973

NO: The United States has only given assistance to regimes fighting communist insurgents, such as Guatemala and El Salvador

Topic 11
SHOULD THE UNITED STATES NORMALIZE RELATIONS WITH CUBA?

YES
"NO SANCTIONS, NO CASTRO"
AMERICAN ENTERPRISE INSTITUTE, MARCH 1998
JAMES K. GLASSMAN

NO
"SHOULD AMERICA LIFT SANCTIONS ON CUBA?"
THE HERITAGE FOUNDATION
STEPHEN JOHNSON

INTRODUCTION

For over 40 years the United States has imposed a full trade embargo against its communist neighbor Cuba. Sanctions include a ban on trade between the two countries and general restrictions on travel to Cuba by American citizens. While the official line urges Cuban President Fidel Castro to adopt a democratic system of government and put an end to serious human rights abuses, it is widely recognized that the United States has sought to isolate and undermine Castro in a broader attempt to overthrow his communist regime.

Living for so long under both Castro's regime and the embargo, Cuba is now a very poor country. Many Cubans suffer from malnutrition, and thousands have fled to the United States in search of a better life. While many Cubans voice their opposition to the regime—at risk of imprisonment—many others toe Castro's line and blame the United States for their country's problems.

Cuba has a long history of conflict and repression. Spain took control of the island in 1511, and for over 300 years Cuba's history was characterized by failed revolts against Spain's harsh rule. After a long struggle the United States brokered a deal that gave Cuba its independence from Spain in December 1898.

The United States continued to forge close relations with Cuba up until the 1960s, establishing many businesses and building on the island. With such a large stake in Cuba the United States reserved the right to intervene in Cuba's affairs.

During most of the period between the 1930s and 1950s Cuba was ruled by Fulgencio Batista y Zaldivar—a dictator whose regime was marked by years of corruption and terrorism. In 1952 Batista successfully blocked an attempt at a democratic election. However, after several years of unrest Fidel Castro, a young lawyer who had run in the abortive elections, led a revolution that overthrew Batista's dictatorship in 1959.

Castro's communist ideals alarmed the Eisenhower administration (1953–1960), which did not like a regime allied to the Soviet Union being so close to its shores. The worries were soon substantiated. Shortly after taking control of Cuba, Castro nationalized most of the island's industries, many of which were owned by U.S. companies. Castro then signed a trade agreement with the Soviet Union in 1960, and relations between Cuba and the United States reached boiling point.

"Condemn me. It does not matter. History will absolve me."

—FIDEL CASTRO (1927–),

PRESIDENT OF CUBA

When the United States refused to process Soviet petroleum supplies in its oil refineries on Cuba, Castro seized control of all U.S. and foreign assets on the island. In response an outraged Eisenhower canceled an agreement to buy Cuban sugar, marking the start of a series of trade sanctions that are still in force today.

Successive administrations maintained the hostility. In 1961 President John F. Kennedy introduced a total embargo against Cuba in an attempt to undermine Castro's regime. A few months later Kennedy launched an invasion of Cuba. A force of Cuban exiles armed by the CIA landed at the Bay of Pigs, but they were crushed by Castro's army.

In 1962 the island was the focus of perhaps the most critical episode in the Cold War. Castro had agreed to house Soviet nuclear missiles in Cuba. That was unacceptable to the United States, which could not hope to defend itself against missiles launched so close to its shores. Kennedy demanded that the missiles be removed, and for several days the world stood on the brink of nuclear war. The Soviet Union eventually took the missiles back after Kennedy agreed never to invade Cuba.

Economic sanctions were the only weapon left to tackle the Cuban crisis. Few other nations imposed similar sanctions, however, and Cuba was supported financially with subsidies from the Soviet Union. The collapse of the Soviet Union in 1991 precipitated a drastic slump in Cuba's economy. To raise money, Castro was forced to open Cuba to more foreign trade through tourism and limited private enterprise. Although Castro seemed to take steps toward democratic reform, Cuba has remained a thorny issue in the United States, not least because of Castro's poor human rights record.

The two articles that follow discuss the relationship between the United States and Cuba. In the first article James K. Glassman argues that the only way to encourage democratic reform is to lift the sanctions. He suggests that it is the economic sanctions themselves that have kept Fidel Castro in power for so long.

However, Stephen Johnson in the second article thinks that the sanctions are beginning to have an effect. The collapse of the Soviet Union means that Cuba must now rely on foreign investment. The United States can use the sanctions as a bargaining tool to enact democratic reform.

NO SANCTIONS, NO CASTRO
James K. Glassman

The author sums up the main point of his argument in the first paragraph. This makes his position clear from the start.

✓ *Unilateral economic sanctions are invariably ineffective, and the U.S. embargo of Cuba is no exception. Lifting the embargo would remove Fidel Castro's principal excuse for his failures and would quickly undermine his regime.*

As a political leader, Pope John Paul II has no equal in the world. In 1979, eight months after becoming pope, he visited his native Poland, drew crowds of 2 million, and helped establish the Solidarity movement. In 1983, he traveled to Nicaragua, criticized the liberation theology of its priests, and helped end the Sandinista regime.

The pope—even more than Ronald Reagan, Margaret Thatcher, or Mikhail Gorbachev—was responsible for the near-bloodless revolution that routed communism and replaced it in Europe and Latin America with imperfect but largely humane and democratic capitalism.

The only holdout is Cuba, a country of 11 million, frozen in time (1959 or thereabouts), morally and economically bankrupt, ruled by an aging, preening dictator who can't shut up. That is why John Paul II's journey to Cuba [in] January 21–25, [1998,] the first ever by a pope, was so important. His major aim was to spread the Gospel to a nation that has been spiritually starved for four decades. When Fidel Castro took power, there were 723 priests in the country; today, there are 269. The pope also talked about violations of human rights, and, after his departure, Castro released about 200 political prisoners.

Collectivists believe that people should sacrifice their individual rights for the common good. This idea conflicts with capitalism, which is based on the principle of individual rights. Capitalist neoliberalism is a revived belief in free trade with no restrictions.

On the economy, the church has moved away from collectivism. Even the U.S. Conference of Catholic Bishops now admits that "the economy exists for the person, not the person for the economy." Yet, in a speech in José Martí Square in Havana, the pope criticized "the resurgence of a certain capitalist neo-liberalism, which subordinates the human person to blind market forces and conditions the development of people on those forces. From its centers of power, such neo-liberalism often places unbearable burdens upon less favored countries.… As a result, the wealthy grow ever wealthier, while the poor grow ever poorer."

COMMENTARY: Strained relations

Relations between the United States and Cuba deteriorated in 1960 following Fidel Castro's decision to take under state control two U.S. oil refineries. An outraged President Eisenhower canceled an agreement to buy sugar from Cuba and initiated a plan to overthrow the Cuban leader. Castro then nationalized all U.S. real estate and businesses in Cuba, a move that prompted a partial economic embargo on shipments of goods to Cuba.

The Kennedy administration (1961–1963) extended the scope of the embargo. A total trade ban was imposed on February 7, 1962. Steps were then taken to restrict the importation of Cuban goods and materials—even if they came through other countries. A year later the United States imposed a travel ban and made trade relations with Castro's regime illegal.

President Jimmy Carter broke the stalemate in U.S.–Cuban relations in 1977 by dropping the travel ban and relaxing certain trade restrictions. The reprieve was short-lived, however. Ronald Reagan's presidency (1981–1989) marked the beginning of another period of hostility, with tighter economic sanctions and a new ban on travel. The Bush administration (1989–1993) also pursued a hostile foreign policy. In 1992 Congress passed the Cuban Democracy Act, calling for sanctions against countries "assisting" Cuba and increased restrictions on humanitarian aid.

The next major piece of legislation came in 1996, when President Clinton signed into law the Cuban Liberty and Democratic Solidarity Act. This act met with international criticism since it made it possible for the United States to impose penalties on foreign investors in Cuba and sue investors using Cuban property formerly owned by American citizens.

Perhaps in the face of this criticism, the tide once again began to turn in favor of lifting the sanctions. While Cuba's human rights record remains a thorny issue (see page 144), many people now feel that lifting the sanctions would open the door to democracy. Others believe that continuing the economic embargo is the only way to force Castro into democratic change.

Ending the embargo

Oh, well. Nobody's infallible. While the pope's understanding of economics needs work, in one area he proved he was far ahead of most American politicians. He forcefully preached ending the embargo that the United States has imposed on Cuba. The embargo limits the rights of Americans to travel there and forbids us to sell things to Cubans or to buy things from them. These sanctions have been in place for forty years— with absolutely no beneficial results. That's hardly surprising. In a recent United Nations vote, we were supported in our effort by only two countries: Afghanistan and Israel. The truth is that multilateral sanctions work rarely, unilateral ones never.

In 2001 the General Assembly of the United Nations again voted to adopt a resolution to end the economic, commercial, and financial embargo imposed by the United States on Cuba. This was the tenth resolution the Assembly had passed in as many years.

You can find out more information about the 1962 Cuban missile crisis at the U.S. National Security Agency website at www. nsa.gov. Click on the "NSA's Cryptologic History" link and then "Cuban Missile Crisis Archives."

The Cuban–American community forms a powerful and highly organized lobby group in Florida. Can you think of other politically powerful ethnic groups in other parts of the United States?

"Economic embargoes," said the pope on January 23, "are always deplorable because they hurt the most needy." But there are other reasons that this one is especially deplorable. It has not only failed to bring down Castro's regime, but has, on the contrary, reinforced it by providing a scapegoat at which he can rail. If Americans truly believe in economic freedom, how can we perpetuate a policy that not only flouts that principle but hasn't worked anyway?

Trade, in fact, is a human right. We should all have the liberty to exchange our work, the products and services that we create, with anyone in the world—from the corner dry cleaner to the Balinese artist to the Havana cigar maker. The only exception is war, and we are not at war with Cuba.

Some thirty-five years have passed since the Cuban missile crisis In the rest of Latin America, with its 400 million Catholics, Castro can no longer subvert or agitate. Without Soviet aid, he is a pathetic old man. What are Bill Clinton and Congress so afraid of?

The Cuban exiles of Miami? Maybe, but over the years they have shed their insularity and paranoia. Their uncompromising leader, Jorge Mas Canosa, recently died without a forceful successor. And, more important, most exiles understand that they would be beneficiaries of a lifted embargo and a Cuba open to two-way trade. Take a trip to Miami, as I did recently, and you'll find one of the two or three most exciting cities in the United States—its buildings painted joyfully pink and ocher and turquoise, its port jammed with container ships and cruise ships, its banks and restaurants bustling.

Undermining Castro

No, the politician who has the most to fear from a lifting of the embargo is Fidel Castro. "There is no surer way to undermine the Castro regime," said the *Economist* in January, "than to flood his streets with American tourists, academics, and businessmen, with their notions of liberty and enterprise."

If we lifted the embargo, not only would Castro be denied a scapegoat, but if he still tried to keep out U.S. investment (and films and soft drinks and computers), then he himself would have to shoulder the blame. It would be a heavy burden, and, like the Berlin Wall, he might fall of his own weight.

"In her social doctrine," Pope John Paul II said in Cuba, "the church does not propose a concrete political or economic model, but indicates the way." The way is clear. The last Communist leader in the Western Hemisphere—

and, some would say, the world—overplayed a weak hand in allowing the pope to visit his country. In a six-hour speech that stretched from one day to another, he praised John Paul II and insisted the pope had much in common with Cuba's leaders. "He's done all his criticisms of communism," said Castro. "Now, he's criticizing capitalism."

Not really. Despite his unkind words about neo-liberalism (this means us), the pope clearly prefers a system that stresses economic choice, not government command. His most pressing complaint about capitalism involves a country that professes to practice it but that enforces an embargo that mocks it. That country's president—who, by coincidence, found himself facing the biggest scandal of his tenure on the very day the pope landed in Havana— could add to his legacy by taking advantage of the papal visit to declare that he will end all sanctions immediately, no matter what the anachronistic old man in the beard and the fatigues does.

In the wake of John Paul II's visit, Bill Clinton should call Fidel's bluff. The result, before very long, would be a thriving, Castro-less Cuba, a diamond crescent glistening in the blue Caribbean Sea. As the pope said on his arrival, "May Cuba, with all its magnificent potential, open itself up to the world, and may the world open itself up to Cuba."

News of Clinton's sexual liaisons with Monica Lewinsky— a White House intern—broke during the pope's visit to Cuba.

The pope's visit to Cuba prompted a proposal by the Miami-based Cuban American National Foundation to send food and medical aid to Cuba while keeping the U.S. embargo intact. Castro rejected the proposal.

SHOULD AMERICA LIFT SANCTIONS ON CUBA?
Stephen Johnson

NO

Former U.S. President Jimmy Carter gave a mixed message when he spoke directly to the Cuban people on May 14 [2002].

Speaking live and uncensored on Cuban state television, Carter urged Cuba to join "the community of democracies," explained human rights as defined by the United Nations Universal Declaration of Human Rights, and revealed the existence of a petition signed by more than 11,000 Cubans that calls for a national referendum on guarantees of human rights and civil liberties.

Yet Mr. Carter also suggested the United States lift its principled embargo on trade with the regime of dictator Fidel Castro as a goodwill gesture to restore relations.

He qualified the plea by saying the embargo has not caused Cuba's economic woes, but he stopped short of identifying the real culprit-communism. He also stopped short of condemning Cuba as a sponsor of terrorism that facilitates links between this hemisphere's subversive groups and international terror organizations such as the Irish Republican Army (IRA).

Security forces who arrested three IRA agents in Colombia in August 2001 revealed an international web of terrorism that linked one of the IRA agents, Niall Connolly, with Cuban-led terrorist training camps in Nicaragua, Panama, and Venezuela.

And he naively accepted Castro's assurances that the regime has not engaged in biological weapons research or transferred such technology, despite statements by a former Cuban biotechnology expert that it had sold its expertise to Iran.

Leaving those issues aside, the embargo remains one of the few instruments the United States has that can promote change on the island. Critics claim it has produced no results, but then, 43 years of commercial relations between the regime and other nations around the world hasn't produced much change either. That's because commerce is possible only with the state, since private enterprise is illegal in Cuba.

More to the point, now is not the time to lift sanctions. Castro's Cuba-low on cash-finally seems to be running out of lenders as well. Soviet subsidies to the island nation dried up in 1991 with the fall of the Soviet Union. Since then, Castro has survived by purchasing on credit wherever he could. But

Reports indicate that Cuba received an annual subsidy of $5 billion from the Soviet Union before its collapse.

The communist leader Fidel Castro (with beard) pictured shortly after the 1959 revolution that toppled Cuba's right-wing dictator Fulgencio Batista.

last September, France reportedly halted $175 million in trade when Cuba failed to pay for commodities purchased in 2000, and other governments and foreign companies have frozen accounts as well.

His economy, lacking a market and free enterprise to generate income, is unable to make good on the arrears. The government's main export is sugar, but inefficient cultivation and distribution policies keep it from competing in the world market. Last year, Cuba's central bank reported a balance of payments deficit of $687 million and an overall foreign debt of $11 billion.

The U.S. embargo limits commerce with Cuba's unelected leaders, who confiscated property owned by U.S. citizens now worth about $7 billion. Those limits should remain in place until the regime enacts democratic reforms, agrees to respect human rights and releases its political prisoners. If

Analysts blamed the stall in Cuba's economy in 2001 on the downturn in tourism in the aftermath of the September 11 terrorist attacks and on the damage caused by Hurricane Michelle in November.

COMMENTARY: Cuba and human rights

The General Assembly of the United Nations adopted the Universal Declaration of Human Rights (UDHR) in 1948. This international agreement guarantees certain fundamental rights to all human beings. As a member state of the United Nations, Cuba is bound by the provisions of the UDHR. However, many independent human rights organizations have condemned Cuba's repressive regime. They argue that Castro's Cuba is characterized by repression, harassment, and torture.

The denial of basic civil and political rights is written into Cuban law. In the name of legality, armed security forces, aided by state-controlled mass organizations, silence dissent with heavy prison terms, threats of prosecution, harrassment, or exile.

—Human Rights Watch, 1999

Legal experts argue that Cuban legislation—with its emphasis on state-security interests—tightly restricts fundamental rights to free assembly, association, movement, press, and speech. So nonviolent activities such as criticizing the government, discussing the economy, or reporting political or economic developments are treated as criminal offenses. Cuban authorities have prosecuted dissidents for defamation, resisting authority, association to commit criminal acts, and the universal charge of "acts against state security." Cuban Justice Minister Roberto Díaz Sotolongo justified the restrictions on dissent in a statement in 1998: "As Spain has instituted laws to protect the monarch from criticism, Cuba is justified in protecting Fidel Castro from criticism."

Cubans who speak out against the state face the full force of Cuba's repressive legislation. Cuban courts often deny defendants internationally recognized due-process guarantees, such as the immediate right to an attorney, and Castro's supreme ruling body—the Council of State—has overall control of the courts, raising doubts about the impartiality of trials.

In 2002 an estimate by the dissident organization the Cuban Commission for Human Rights and National Reconciliation alleged at least 230 political prisoners in Cuba's prisons. Human rights groups report degrading and inhuman conditions under which prisoners endure malnourishment, isolation, and physical and sexual abuse. Castro occasionally releases political prisoners in response to international criticism, but there are many more waiting to take their place.

In April 2002 the United Nations adopted a resolution that called on Cuba to accept a visit by an expert human rights monitor. The resolution also demanded progress in civil, human, and political reforms. But the Cuban authorities prefer to strengthen their repressive legislation rather than bow to pressure from the international community. The result is a stalemate.

the United States eases the sanctions, such changes definitely won't take place.

If Castro wants money, he should do the right thing: Enact democratic reforms and agree to respect human rights. Meanwhile, the United States can encourage an eventual Cuban transformation by expanding contact with Castro's captives and offering a combination of carrots and sticks to nudge the regime toward freedom of choice. To that end, the Bush Administration should:

The carrot-and-stick approach means rewarding Castro if he complies with American demands (the carrot) and penalizing him if he ignores or disobeys them (the stick).

- Support legislation that will allow U.S. citizens to give money to Cuban victims of repression, self-employed Cubans and the island's independent non-governmental organizations.
- Authorize scholarships for Cuban students to attend universities in democracies throughout the hemisphere.
- Promote U.S. and multilateral microenterprise credits for independent, self-employed Cubans and independent Cuban businesses when they are allowed.
- Maintain "cash and carry" sales policies for food and medicine until the state permits independent enterprise and adopts free-market reforms, but expand the list of exportable goods to include farm machinery and soft goods, such as clothing and household products.
- Permit joint U.S.-Cuban ventures, and ease U.S. travel restrictions when Cuba provides market access, ends state monopolies and enacts labor reforms. U.S. companies should be able to employ whoever they wish, and Cubans should be able to work for anyone they please, receive fair market compensation, form their own unions and purchase the goods and services their employers provide.

While the general economic embargo remains intact, legislation does allow for the sale of food and medicine to Cuba. However, the legislation restricts U.S. financing of the sales. Most Cuban purchasers could not afford to buy the products in any case.

Former President Carter was right to tell Cubans their country is isolated without true democracy and human rights. But lifting the trade embargo will remove the only incentive Castro has to reform. Instead, the United States should cultivate closer relations with ordinary Cubans, support those struggling for freedom and prod the dictatorship to loosen its grip.

Summary

With his communist ideology and repressive regime, Fidel Castro and his rise
to power in 1959 marked the start of 40 years of hostility between the United
States and Cuba. The United States officially broke off diplomatic relations with
Cuba in 1961. Since then Congress has enacted a series of tough economic
sanctions against Cuba in an attempt to subvert Castro's regime and promote
Western democratic ideals. While the U.S. embargo has undoubtedly crippled
the Cuban economy, Castro has kept a tight grip on power. Many people now
feel that it is time to rethink the current policy toward Cuba.

In the first article James K. Glassman argues that unilateral economic
sanctions will never bring about Castro's demise; rather, the embargo reinforces
Castro's position as the nation's protector against its old enemy. Lifting the
embargo would no longer allow Castro to blame the United States for Cuba's
own economic failures. Glassman believes that the sanctions were originally
adopted to control the threat of communism. The collapse of the Soviet
Union—Cuba's former sponsor—means that sanctions are no longer necessary.

In the second article Stephen Johnson suggests that by lifting the embargo,
the United States would be removing the only incentive Castro has to reform.
Johnson believes that the embargo remains the most effective way to deal
with Castro's regime. Now that Cuba's Soviet subsidy has dried up, Castro is
increasingly unable to sustain the country's failing economy—the sanctions
are beginning to work. If Castro wants money to pay for commodities, he will
have to enact democratic reforms, respect human rights, and allow private
enterprise to rebuild his country.

FURTHER INFORMATION:

Books:

Franklin, Jane, *Cuba and the United
States: A Chronological History.* New York:
Ocean Press, 1997.

Kaplowitz, Donna Rich, *Anatomy of a Failed Embargo:
U.S. Sanctions against Cuba.* Boulder, CO: Lynne Rienner
Publishers, 1998.

Schwab, Peter, *Cuba: Confronting the U.S. Embargo.*
New York: Palgrave Macmillan, 1999.

Useful websites:

www.ciponline.org
The Center for International Policy site on foreign policy
issues in the United States.
www.heritage.org
The Heritage Foundation site analyzes domestic and
foreign policy in the United States.

www.cato.org/dailys/12-12-96.html
"Trade Embargo In and Castro Out" by Ian Vásquez
and L. Jacobo Rodríguez.
www.hrw.org/reports/1999/cuba/Cuba996-01.htm
"Cuba's Repressive Machinery: Human Rights Forty
Years after the Revolution" in Human Rights Watch,
June 26, 2002.

> **The following debates in the
> Pro/Con series may also be
> of interest:**
>
> In this volume:
> Topic 7 Should economic
> sanctions be used to promote
> human rights?

SHOULD THE UNITED STATES NORMALIZE RELATIONS WITH CUBA?

YES: Many competitors invest heavily in the Cuban economy. Easing the sanctions will allow businesses in the United States to compete for a share in the profits.

YES: The trade embargo and political hostility have failed to stop Castro's human rights abuses. The United States can encourage reform by relaxing its hostile foreign policy.

TRADE RELATIONS
Should the United States open up trade relations with Cuba?

HUMAN RIGHTS
Can the United States influence Cuba's position on human rights?

NO: Cuba is a risky place to do business. With no legislation to protect contracts, many countries have lost millions of dollars in failed business ventures.

SHOULD THE UNITED STATES NORMALIZE RELATIONS WITH CUBA?

KEY POINTS

NO: Many countries invest in Cuba's economy, but the human rights abuses continue. If the United States relaxed the embargo, would it really make a difference?

YES: Sanctions harm the very people that they are meant to help, not those in positions of power

YES: Trade with the United States would bolster Castro's weakened economy and delay efforts at democratization

POVERTY
Is the United States to blame for Cuba's poor standard of living?

CASTRO'S POSITION
Does Castro want an end to the economic embargo?

NO: Castro's communist regime is the real reason behind Cuba's failing economy

NO: Castro would rather blame the embargo for Cuba's problems than his own failings as president

CUBA–U.S. RELATIONS IN THE 20TH CENTURY

"I am a Marxist-Leninist, and I shall remain one until the end of my life."

—FIDEL CASTRO (1927–), CUBAN LEADER

1902 Tomás Estrada Palma is elected president of an independent Cuba. The Platt Amendment keeps the island under the protection of the United States and gives it the right to intervene in Cuban affairs.

1906 Estrada Palma invokes the Platt Amendment and invites the U.S. military to Cuba. He then resigns.

1909 José Miguel Gómez becomes president. The U.S. military occupation ends.

1924 Gerado Machado is elected president and receives diplomatic and financial support from the United States.

1925 Cuban Communist Party is founded.

1933 August: Machado resigns after a general strike. **September**: In an uprising known as the "Revolt of the Sergeants" Fulgencio Batista takes control of the island.

1934 Cuba and the United States sign the "Treaty on Relations," which ends the Platt Amendment but allows the United States to continue using the base at Guantanamo Bay.

1944 Batista retires and is succeeded by the civilian Ramón Gray San Martín.

1952 Batista seizes power again and presides over an oppressive and corrupt regime.

1953 Fidel Castro leads an unsuccessful revolt against the Batista regime.

1956 Castro lands in eastern Cuba from Mexico and takes to the Sierra Maestra Mountains where, aided by Ernesto "Che" Guevara, he wages a guerrilla war.

1959 Batista is forced to flee, and Castro leads a 9,000-strong guerrilla army into Havana. Castro becomes president.

1960 All American businesses in Cuba are nationalized. The United States begins a partial economic embargo.

1961 U.S.–Cuban diplomatic relations are officially ended. America sponsors an abortive invasion by Cuban exiles at the Bay of Pigs with the covert support of the CIA. Castro proclaims Cuba a "socialist country." President Kennedy authorizes Operation Mongoose, which aims to assasinate Castro.

1962 Cuban Missile Crisis: after a 13-day standoff the USSR agrees to withdraw missiles from Cuba in exchange for America taking nuclear missiles out of Turkey. The United States imposes a full trade embargo on Cuba.

1963 The United States prohibits travel to Cuba and makes financial and commercial transactions with Cuba illegal for U.S.

citizens. All Cuban-owned assets in the United States are frozen.

1976 The Cuban Communist Party approves a new socialist constitution; Castro is elected president of the State Council.

1976–81 Cuba sends troops first to help Angola's left-wing MPLA withstand a joint onslaught by South Africa, UNITA, and the FNLA and, later, to help the Ethiopian regime defeat the Eritreans and Somalis.

1977 President Jimmy Carter drops the ban on travel to Cuba and on U.S. citizens spending dollars in Cuba.

1982 The Reagan administration reestablishes the travel ban and prohibits U.S. citizens from spending money in Cuba.

1983 The United States invades Grenada with 8,800 troops to topple the Cuban-supported leftist government,. It captures 642 Cubans, killing 24 and wounding 57.

1984 A Cuba–U.S. agreement returns 2,746 refugees (Marielitos) to Cuba. The United States permits the immigration of 20,000 Cubans annually.

1988 Cuba agrees to withdraw its troops from Angola following an agreement with South Africa.

1990 The House of Representatives condemns Cuba for human-rights violations.

1991 Soviet military advisers leave Cuba following the collapse of the USSR.

1992 Congress passes the Cuba Democracy Act, which prohibits transactions between U.S. subsidiaries overseas and Cuba, travel to Cuba by U.S. citizens, and family remittances to Cuba. Critics claim it is in violation of

International law. The UN issues a resolution condemning the U.S embargo.

1993 Cuba holds its first direct elections since the revolution. Dollar ownership is legalized.

1994 The United States agrees to allow a minimum of 20,000 Cuban immigrants a year in return for Cuba stopping the exodus of illegal refugees.

1996 The U.S. trade embargo on Cuba is made permanent after Cuba shoots down two U.S. aircraft operated by Miami-based Cuban exiles. President Clinton signs the Helms–Burton law, allowing U.S. penalties for foreign companies investing in Cuba.

1999 Cuban child Elián Gonzalez is rescued off the Florida coast after a boat capsizes, killing his mother, his step-father, and nine other people.

2000 June: Elián Gonzalez rejoins his father in Cuba after a prolonged court battle.

2001 The United States exports food to Cuba for the first time in more than 40 years, following a request from the Cuban government to help it cope with the devastation caused by Hurricane Michelle.

2002 January: Prisoners taken during the United States-led action in Afghanistan are flown into Guantanamo Bay for interrogation as Al Qaeda suspects. Russia's last military base in Cuba, at Lourdes, is closed down. **May**: Under Secretary of State for Arms Control and International Security John R. Bolton accuses Cuba of trying to develop biological weapons, adding the country to Washington's list of "axis of evil" countries. **June**: The National Assembly amends the country's constitution to make Cuba's socialist system of government permanent and untouchable.

Topic 12

DOES THE WAR ON DRUGS GIVE THE UNITED STATES THE RIGHT TO INTERVENE IN OTHER COUNTRIES' AFFAIRS?

YES

FROM "NARCO-TERROR: THE INTERNATIONAL CONNECTION BETWEEN DRUGS AND TERROR"
SPEECH TO INSTITUTE FOR INTERNATIONAL STUDIES, APRIL 2, 2002
ASA HUTCHINSON

NO

FROM "MILITARIZATION OF THE U.S. DRUG CONTROL PROGRAM"
FOREIGN POLICY IN FOCUS POLICY BRIEFS, SEPTEMBER 1998, VOL. 3, NO. 27
PETER ZIRNITE (EDITED BY TOM BARRY AND MARTHA HONEY)

INTRODUCTION

The use of narcotics is nothing new. For example, native people in parts of the Andes in South America have used the coca plant, the source of cocaine, for leisure and medicinal purposes for nearly 4,000 years. However, in recent decades coca and opium (derived from poppies and the source of heroin) have become major cash crops in parts of South America and Asia. Most of the drugs produced in these regions are trafficked to North America and Europe, where they are sold for huge profits. The economies of some countries are, or have been, very dependent on this trade. For example, in 2000 Afghanistan produced 3,656 metric tons of illicit opium, which sold at $333 per kilogram.

No one knows the value of the narcotics industry for certain, but the Drug Enforcement Administration (DEA) estimates a value of $300–400 billion a year, larger than most national economies. Huge drug-producing and -exporting groups, such as the Medellín and Cali cartels in Colombia and the Arellano-Felix organization in Mexico, employ thousands of people and handle cocaine, heroin, methamphetamines, and other drugs worth billions of dollars. Despite spending vast sums of money on protecting its borders, U.S. law-enforcement agencies cannot stem the flow of drugs into America.

The human cost of the drug trade in the United States is enormous. Drug dependency has created a huge volume of related crime, billions of dollars of lost working days, and an increased burden on medical services. When President Bill Clinton claimed that the number of Americans using drugs fell by 50 percent between 1979 and 1998, Republican Congressman Newt Gingrich retorted that narcotics use among teens rose by 70 percent between 1993 and 1998. The United States is at war with drugs, but does this fight entitle the country to intervene in the affairs of others in order to tackle the problem at source?

President George W. Bush's administration highlighted the increased tie-in between the drugs trade and terrorism when it claimed that one-third of the organizations on its register of terror groups are also active in the drug business. The DEA describes this combination as "narco-terrorism" and has vowed to stop it, maintaining that such action is all the more necessary after the September 11, 2001, attacks on the World Trade Center and the Pentagon.

> *"Evidence has emerged that Colombian army personnel trained by U.S. Special Forces have been implicated by action or omission in serious human rights violations...."*
> —AMNESTY INTERNATIONAL USA, CONGRESSIONAL TESTIMONY ON PLAN COLOMBIA, OCTOBER 12, 2000

Among the countries in which the United States is involved are several in Latin America. According to the State Department, "the Andes continues to produce virtually all of the world's cocaine and an increasing amount of heroin." Under the Andean Regional Initiative (the successor to the more narrowly targeted Plan Colombia) the United States provides money to several Latin American countries for antidrug

work and security and for economic and social development. In Colombia, for example, this money helps finance the Colombian government's war on insurgents of the Revolutionary Armed Forces of Colombia (FARC), which stands accused of financing its guerrilla campaign with cocaine profits.

Critics of U.S involvement in Latin America maintain that by working with local armed forces, the United States is militarizing what is essentially a civilian problem. At the same time, by training and arming the militaries, it is making it harder for the civilian governments concerned to control them. Further, some forces with which the United States is working have alleged links with the drug trade or with human rights abuses.

Concentrating on other ways of combating the drug menace would be preferable, according to critics. Some believe that since drug production is driven by fluctuations in the global economy, a campaign against narcotics will not succeed unless wider issues are also addressed. For example, when the price of coffee plummeted on the world market in 2001–2002, many farmers in Bolivia, Colombia, and Peru turned to growing coca and opium poppies. Other observers maintain that the priority should be to reduce the demand for narcotics in the United States and Europe.

In the articles that follow, Asa Hutchinson, director of the DEA, outlines the links between drugs and terror, and argues that the United States must intervene internationally to crush both. Peter Zirnite, on the other hand, in an extract from "Militarization of the U.S. Drug Control Program," argues that lack of foresight has led to the failure of current policies.

NARCO-TERROR: THE INTERNATIONAL CONNECTION BETWEEN DRUGS AND TERROR
Asa Hutchinson

YES

What kind of sacrifice do you think Hutchinson is referring to with regard to democracy?

We understand from our study of history that the maintenance of democracy requires in essence two things: sacrifice and participation. We also know from our study of current culture that sacrifice and participation are contrary to the concept of drug use.

Drug abusers become slaves to their habits. They are no longer able to contribute to the community. They do not have healthy relationships with their families. They are no longer able to use their full potential to create ideas or to energetically contribute to society, which is the genius of democracy. They are weakened by the mind-numbing effects of drugs. The entire soul of our society is weakened and our democracy is diminished by drug use.

Many, in the name of freedom, say drug use should be permissible. The argument is that the government should have a hands-off attitude toward drug use and that if individuals exercise their freedom, they should be able to exercise it toward drug use or drug abuse. But that very freedom is jeopardized by drug addiction. When an addict takes … drugs, he is not only changing the chemistry of the body, but little by little diminishing the character of a nation.

But there's another dimension to the abuse of drugs. Not only does it weaken the United States, but it also supports attacks against the judicial system in Mexico. It funds terrorism in Colombia and generally destabilizes governments from Afghanistan to Thailand.…

An extremist Muslim faction, the Taliban ("students"), took over the Afghan capital, Kabul, in 1996 and went on to control some 90 percent of the country before being ousted by U.S.-led military action at the end of 2001. For more information see http://abcnews.go.com/sections/world/DailyNews/taliban_intro.html.

The case of Afghanistan
Let's briefly look at the facts of the connection between drugs and terrorism, starting with Afghanistan. Afghanistan … [is estimated to have] produc[ed] in the year 2000 some 70 percent of the world's supply of opium.…

The Taliban, the ruling authority at the time, benefited from that drug trade by taxing and, in some instances, being involved in the drug trafficking.…

So it's clear that the Taliban benefited from the institutionalized taxation of heroin trafficking. Clearly, at the same time, the Al Qaeda network flourished from the safe haven provided by the Taliban.

Taken a step further, the DEA [Drug Enforcement Administration] has also received multi-source information that Osama Bin Laden himself has been involved in the financing and facilitation of heroin-trafficking activities. That is history now with the operation that has been taking place by our military in Afghanistan.

Now we can look to the future in Afghanistan. We're pleased that the interim president, Chairman Karzai, has banned poppy cultivation and drug production; but the United Nations, despite this ban that is currently in place, estimates that the area that is currently under cultivation could potentially produce up to 2,700 metric tons of opium in Afghanistan this coming year. This is an extraordinary concern to the DEA and the international community....

The situation in Colombia

In Colombia, we deal with three groups designated as terrorist organizations by the State Department: the revolutionary group called the FARC (Revolutionary Armed Forces of Colombia); the ELN (National Liberation Army); and a paramilitary group, the AUC (United Self-Defenses of Colombia). At least two of those, without any doubt, are heavily engaged in drug trafficking, receiving enormous funds from drug trafficking: the AUC and the FARC.

In the case of the FARC, the State Department has called them the most dangerous international terrorist group based in the Western Hemisphere. Two weeks ago [September 1998], the Department of Justice indicted three members of the 16th Front of the FARC, including their commander, Tomas Molina, on charges of conspiracy to transport cocaine and distribute it in the United States. It was the first time that members of a known terrorist organization have been indicted on drug trafficking charges.... The State Department estimates that the FARC receives $300 million a year from drug sales to finance its terrorist activities.

In March of this year, under the direction of President Pastrana, the Colombian Army and the Colombian National Police reclaimed the demilitarized zone from the FARC, based upon intelligence the DEA was able to provide. The police went in, and in the demilitarized zone that was supposed to be a peaceful haven, they found two major cocaine laboratories....

Osama Bin Laden (1957–) set up the Al Qaeda terrorist group in 1988. For more on Al Qaeda go to http://library.nps.navy.mil/home/tgp/qaida.htm. For a study of Bin Laden and his activities go to www.pbs.org/wgbh/pages/frontline/shows/binladen.

Both FARC (formed 1964) and ELN (formed 1965) are Marxist insurgent groups; AUC (formed 1997) is an umbrella organization for paramilitary groups opposed to the insurgents.

Andrés Pastrana Arango (1954–) was elected president of Colombia in 1998.

Prior to the seizure [of five tons of processed cocaine from the site], we knew the FARC was engaged in trafficking activities, but this is the first time we have had solid evidence that the FARC is involved in the cocaine trade from start to finish, from cultivation to processing and distribution.

According to the Amnesty International Report 2002 on Colombia, around 3,000 kidnappings occurred in the country during 2001, of which about 60 percent were carried out by guerrilla forces.

We should understand that's it's not just Colombian citizens that are impacted by the terrorist activities. Since 1990, 73 American citizens have been taken hostage in Colombia, more than 50 by narco-terrorists; and since 1995, 12 American citizens have been murdered.

So we see a clear connection by Al Qaeda and the FARC using drug proceeds to finance their terrorist activities. They are not by any means the only two groups.…

The toll on law enforcement. In the first few months of 2002, 13 law enforcement officers have been murdered in Mexico. You say, "this may not be terrorism." When you're going after government officials, judicial officials, to impact the stability of a government, in my judgment, it is terrorism.…

Is this a good definition of terrorism?

America's national interest. What is the national interest when it happens in faraway countries? It should be elementary: Drug production in Mexico, in Colombia, in Thailand, and in Afghanistan produces the supply of drugs that devastates our families and our communities.

If young Americans want to use narcotics, is it fair to blame the drug producers? Are the users the guilty parties?

The same illegal drug production funds that attack civilized society also destabilize democracies across the globe. Illegal drug production undermines America's culture; it funds terror; and it erodes democracy. And they all represent a clear and present danger to our national security.

A comprehensive strategy

What is our strategy to address this international difficulty?

• **Keeping our focus.** First of all, from the DEA's perspective, we intend to keep our focus. Since September 11, DEA's mission has not changed. Our focus is still the enforcement of our anti-narcotics laws domestically, but also to support the enforcement of the international laws against international drug trafficking.

So we intend to keep our focus; to engage in this effort; to be focused on our counter-narcotics mission knowing the contribution that that, in and of itself, makes to our effort against terrorism.

• **Adding value to intelligence collection.** The second thing that the DEA intends to do is to add value to our intelligence collection. Since September 11, our sources have been worked not just to identify narcotics trafficking, but also to learn information on terrorist activity.…

- **Accepting international responsibility.** The third part of our strategy is to accept our increased responsibilities internationally. The DEA has offices in 56 countries. We develop intelligence. We train and we build effective law enforcement in other countries, and this has given us successes in recent weeks....

Keys to future success

... We have to capitalize on this unique opportunity in history in which the international community is looking to the United States for consistent, dynamic, and timely leadership in going after the international criminal organizations that traffic in drugs and support terrorism.

- **Enhancing DEA's international presence.** To carry out that strategy, we have sent to the Hill, and OMB has approved, an Afghan initiative that includes enhancing our DEA presence in Afghanistan, opening an office there in Pakistan and Uzbekistan, in that region of the world, but developing that with a world-wide heroin strategy, looking at Southeast Asia and Mexico and Colombia, the four regions of the world that produce heroin.

It's like a commodity such as corn: If we reduce the supply in Afghanistan, that helps us on the streets of the United States....

- **Enhancing intelligence sharing.** Second, it is important that we continue to enhance our intelligence sharing....
- **Focusing American support.** Third, to have success in the future in Colombia, we must recognize that there is no distinction between the terrorists who kidnap presidential candidates and the traffickers who operate the cocaine labs and protect the coca fields. U.S. support should be limited in scope and restricted to avoid support for units that violate human rights.

But our logistical support for the Colombian government should not be restricted to the extent that we become ineffective in our primary mission of reducing illegal drug production and our secondary goal of strengthening the institutions of democracy in Colombia.

Under the current law, as you know, we have restrictions on our support in the counter-narcotics arena, but what if intelligence indicates that the FARC is going to set up a roadblock? Can we provide that intelligence to our counterparts in Colombia? Is it a counter-narcotics mission? Is it a counter-kidnapping mission? Is it a counter-terrorism mission? When they have a multifaceted problem facing them, then certainly our support should be in a broader context....

The Office of Management and Budget (OMB) comes under the Executive Office of the president. OMB's main mission is to assist the president in overseeing the preparation of the federal budget and to supervise its administration in the executive branch agencies.

Ingrid Betancourt, a candidate for the 2002 Colombian presidential elections who had accused the guerrillas of involvement in the drugs trade, was kidnapped by FARC in February 2002. At the time of writing, Betancourt had yet to be released.

MILITARIZATION OF THE U.S. DRUG CONTROL PROGRAM
Peter Zirnite (edited by Tom Barry and Martha Honey)

NO

At a time when fledgling civilian governments in Latin America are struggling to keep security forces in check, the U.S. has enlisted the region's militaries as its pivotal partners in international drug control. This militarization, which begins at the U.S.-Mexico border, is undermining recent trends toward greater democratization and respect for human rights, while doing little to stanch the flow of drugs into the United States.

Do you think that Americans would accept a more "militarized" police force if it would help win the war on drugs?

Washington's militarization of its anti-drug efforts is the product of a U.S. drug-control strategy that historically has emphasized reducing the supply of illegal narcotics rather than addressing the demand for drugs. In 1971, three years after the first declared "war on drugs," President Richard Nixon took a crucial step toward militarization by proclaiming drug trafficking a national security threat.

A national security issue

"Protecting the national security" has remained the rallying cry for providing more money and firepower to wage the war on drugs. Since the 1970s, U.S. spending on the drug war has risen from less than $1 billion to more than $16 billion annually. In the early 1980s, President Ronald Reagan raised the curtain on a rapid expansion of U.S. anti-drug efforts that continues unabated today. Reagan justified the expansion, in part, by developing the narco-guerrilla theory, which bolstered the national security rationale by positing ties between the Colombian cartels and Cuba, leftist guerrillas in Colombia, and the Sandinistas in Nicaragua.

The Sandinistas are members of the left-wing Sandinista Liberation Front (FSLN), formed in 1962. For a brief history go to www.infoplease. com/ce6/history/ A0843413.html.

The purported guerrilla-drug link has also been used to legitimize the approach the Pentagon has taken in carrying out its anti-drug mission in Latin America.... Shifting the Pentagon's posture in the region from the cold war to the drug war was easy because the new enemy included many old foes, allowing U.S. military personnel to employ the same tactics that they had used in fighting communism.

The National Defense Authorization Act of 1989 designated the Pentagon as the "single lead agency" for the detection and monitoring of illicit drug shipments into the United States. Soon after, President George Bush announced his Andean Initiative, a $2.2 billion, five-year plan to stop the cocaine trade at its source. Although U.S. military personnel had been involved in training, equipping, and transporting foreign anti-narcotics personnel since the early 1980s, the Andean strategy opened the door to a dramatic expansion of this role and to a significant infusion of U.S. assistance to police and military forces in the region.

In 2002 the administration of President George W. Bush launched its own Andean Regional Initiative as a follow-on to Plan Colombia and also embracing aid to Colombia's neighbors. For a fact sheet go to http://usinfo. state.gov/topical/ global/drugs/ 02032502.htm.

The Andean Initiative placed the spotlight on Colombia, Peru, and Bolivia. Yet the vast majority of the Pentagon's international drug spending still went to detection and monitoring operations in the Caribbean and Gulf of Mexico transit zones....

In late 1993, President Clinton shifted the emphasis of military operations ... from interdicting cocaine as it moved through the transit zones into the U.S to dismantling the so-called "air bridge" that connects coca growers and coca paste manufacturers in Peru and Bolivia with Colombian refiners and distributors. As a result, drug traffickers quickly abandoned air routes in favor of the region's labyrinth of waterways. The Pentagon responded by supporting interdiction operations that target the waterways in both source countries and neighboring nations.

Coca needs to be processed to produce the drug cocaine. To read a paper on coca and cocaine, including a diagram on how the drug is processed, go to www.cia.gov/ saynotodrugs/ cocaine.html.

Today, the vast majority of Washington's international anti-narcotics spending goes to Latin America and the Caribbean, where thousands of U.S. troops are annually deployed in support of the drug war, operating ground-based radar, flying monitoring aircraft, providing operation and intelligence support, and training host-nation security forces. Despite this militarization and the massive funding for Washington's drug war, illegal drugs still flood the United States. In fact, illegal drugs are more readily available now, at a higher purity and lower cost, than they were when the drug war was launched.

Do you agree that the drug war seems to be failing? If so, what alternatives are there?

Problems with current U.S. policy

... Washington's ambitious new strategy to "attack narcotics trafficking in Colombia on all fronts" underscores the fundamental problem with the U.S. approach to international drug control. The plan is premised on the Pentagon forging closer ties to Colombia's military with the aim of building what Gen. Charles E. Wilhelm, commander of U.S. military forces in Latin America and the Caribbean, describes as "marriage for life."

U.S. policymakers apparently believe that local militaries are their most capable and reliable allies in the war on drugs. Throughout Latin America, the resources and training that Washington provides to local armed forces in order to support their new role in domestic drug control operations—often in circumvention of congressional restrictions and oversight—are eroding the efforts of civilian-elected governments to consolidate their power.

Although counternarcotics operations are a law enforcement function reserved in most democracies for civilian police, the U.S. prefers to use military forces. When Washington does recruit police, it provides them with heavy arms and with training in combat tactics that are inappropriate for the role that police should play in a civilian society, thereby continuing to fuel human rights abuses. During the 1970s, Congress halted police aid programs because of widespread human rights abuses by U.S.-trained police in Latin America, but in the 1980s these programs resumed in Central America and have since spread to many other countries.

Do you think that human rights abuses in other countries are a price worth paying to defeat drug use in the United States?

A threat to regional security

The militarization of counternarcotics efforts in Latin America … also threatens regional security. In Colombia, where the line between fighting drug trafficking and combating insurgents is blurred, Washington risks becoming mired in the hemisphere's longest-running guerrilla war, possibly widening that conflict into neighboring countries. Citing the threat posed by Colombia's guerrillas, who earn much of their income by protecting coca and poppy fields and clandestine drug laboratories, the Pentagon has already expanded its operations in Ecuador and Venezuela.

By providing advanced military training and equipment to both Ecuador and Peru, the U.S. may also hamper efforts to resolve a longstanding border dispute between the two countries. In July 1998, the *Washington Post* reported that at the closing ceremony of a joint anti-drug operation conducted by U.S. special forces, Ecuador's military vowed to "never cede one millimeter of territory to the Peruvians."

The Latin America Working Group (www.lawg.org) strives "for U.S. policies that promote peace, justice, and sustainable development in the region."

In 1997, about 56,000 U.S. troops were deployed in Latin America, according to a July 1998 report by the Latin American Working Group (LAWG). Although many of these troops were involved in humanitarian projects, counternarcotics is the rationale for most U.S. troop deployments and for grant assistance to the region's militaries and police, which this year is expected to total more than $250 million.

Assistance to Latin American security forces stems from a tangled web of training and aid programs administered by a variety of government agencies, making it difficult to ascertain the exact extent and nature of U.S. anti-drug assistance and stymieing efforts to determine whether Washington is complying with congressional oversight and human rights requirements.

The perils posed by the lack of adequate controls can be seen in Mexico.... Despite restrictions limiting their use to anti-drug work, U.S.-supplied helicopters were used to ferry troops to quell the rebellion in Chiapas. Such dangers are likely to be heightened regionwide by a disturbing trend— an increasing amount of U.S. aid is being provided under Pentagon programs that are exempt from civilian oversight and human rights legislation.

If the United States supplies equipment to other governments, is it possible to limit its use to certain purposes?

Exempted training programs

Among the overseas training programs not subject to the restrictions and oversight that apply to other U.S. military operations are special operations forces Joint Combined Exchange Training (JCET) exercises, which involve Army Green Berets, Navy SEALS, and other special operations forces. The U.S. Southern Command plans to conduct nearly 200 of these specialized training exercises this year, with troops being deployed to all 19 Latin American countries and nine in the Caribbean, according to the *Washington Post*. More than 60% of these deployments will have a counternarcotics component.

Green Berets is an alternative name for U.S. Army Special Forces, further information on which can be found at www.specialforces.net/army/sf. SEAL (Sea, Air, Land) teams are part of the U.S. Navy; a fact sheet is available at www.chinfo.navy.mil/navpalib/factfile/personnel/seals/seals.html.

Even when programs are covered by restrictions, U.S. military personnel are loath to enforce them. In 1997, the White House responded to congressional pressure by limiting assistance to Colombia's armed forces, which have the most egregious human rights record in the hemisphere. Units receiving U.S. training are supposed to be vetted to ensure that they include no one accused of human rights violations, but screening, when it occurs, is cursory.

"Egregious" means "conspicuously bad."

As a result of both the lack of oversight and restrictions on some aid programs and of ineffective implementation of regulations when they do exist, U.S. troops work side by side with accused human rights violators throughout the region, not just in Colombia....

Ironically, the U.S. decision to engage armed forces as its principal allies in the drug war [also] has meant that the Pentagon is now providing counternarcotics assistance to militaries implicated in drug-related corruption, including those in Colombia, Peru, Guatemala, and Mexico....

159

Summary

Asa Hutchinson justifies the United States' overseas counternarcotics program by declaring that it is in America's national interest. According to Hutchinson, "illegal drug production undermines America's culture; it funds terror; and it erodes democracy. And they all represent a clear and present danger to our national security." The author emphasizes the links between the drug trade and terrorism. He singles out the protection enjoyed by Al Qaeda under the wing of the Taliban regime in Afghanistan, a regime that "benefited from the institutionalized taxation of heroin trafficking." Meanwhile, in Colombia, a major source of cocaine, the terror group FARC "receives $300 million a year from drug sales." Hutchinson argues that the international community is looking to the United States for leadership in the war on drugs and explains that reducing the supply at source will reduce the supply on the street.

Peter Zirnite counters that the U.S. strategy of reducing the supply of drugs at source in Latin America has not been successful and observes that "illegal drugs are more readily available now, at a higher purity and lower cost, than they were when the drug war was launched." He also casts doubt on the "purported guerrilla-drug link," which, he suggests, was a theory developed to strengthen "the national security rationale." More than this, Zirnite asserts, the U.S. policy of training and equipping Latin American armed forces to carry the war to the drug producers has resulted in the militarization of the program and a threat to democracy in countries whose civilian governments are still struggling to bring their armed forces into line. The author also argues that there is a "lack of adequate controls" on the assistance handed out to Latin American security forces, which can result in inappropriate use of aid or even in U.S. troops working "side by side with accused human rights violators."

FURTHER INFORMATION:

Books:

Dowd, Robert H., *The Enemy Is Us: How to Defeat Drug Abuse and End the "War on Drugs."* Miami, FL: Hefty Pr, 1997.

Gray, Mike (ed.), *Busted: Stoned Cowboys, Narco-Lords, and the Failure of Washington's War on Drugs.* New York: Thunder's Mouth Press/Nation Books, 2002.

Useful websites:

www.cia.gov/saynotodrugs/warondrugs.html
Central Intelligence Agency's war on drugs site.
www.csdp.org
Common Sense for Drug Policy site.
www.usdoj.gov/dea
Drug Enforcement Adminstration homepage.

The following debates in the Pro/Con series may also be of interest:

In this volume:

Topic 1 Does the United States have a duty to protect democracy and freedom overseas?

Topic 2 Is U.S. foreign policy too interventionist?

Topic 10 Has the United States exploited Latin America?

DOES THE WAR ON DRUGS GIVE THE UNITED STATES THE RIGHT TO INTERVENE IN OTHER COUNTRIES' AFFAIRS?

YES: Many organizations involved in drug production and trafficking are also terrorists

YES: Logic dictates that reducing the supply at source will reduce the supply on the street

TERRORISM
Is a foreign "war on drugs" justified because it is also a war on terror?

RESULTS
Is the policy of reducing the drug supply at source sound?

NO: Some of the purported links between the narcotics trade and terrorism are tenuous

NO: Illegal drugs are more readily available now than they were when the drug war was launched

DOES THE WAR ON DRUGS GIVE THE UNITED STATES THE RIGHT TO INTERVENE IN OTHER COUNTRIES' AFFAIRS?

KEY POINTS

YES: The trafficking and use of illegal drugs undermine democracy everywhere

YES: Besides providing foreign aid to combat the drug trade, the United States is committed to strengthening democracy

HUMAN RIGHTS
Can U.S. international action against drugs help protect democracy?

NO: The militarization of the antidrug program in Latin America threatens democracy

NO: The shortage of controls on aid means it can reach human rights violators

PART 4
FOREIGN POLICY AND TERRORISM

INTRODUCTION

On September 11, 2001, the world watched as New York and Washington, D.C., suffered the worst terrorist action that the United States has ever experienced. In the address to the nation following that catastrophic event George W. Bush stated, "Terrorist attacks can shake the foundations of our biggest buildings, but they cannot touch the foundation of America. These acts shatter steel, but they cannot dent the steel of American resolve."

The outcry against September 11 was heard not only in the United States but elsewhere in the world. Although terrorism on such a scale was unprecedented, people in many nations were already familiar with the effects of terrorist outrages. The British have suffered a bombing campaign at the hands of the Irish Republican Army (IRA), the Spanish of Basque separatists, the Russians of Chechens. Major terror campaigns have also struck as far apart as Sri Lanka, Indonesia, South Africa, and Peru.

As suspicion for the September 11 attacks fell on the fundamentalist Islamic group Al Qaeda, many Americans began to ask what their country had done to provoke such action and what it could do to prevent it from happening again. Many observers commented that U.S. interventionist foreign policy could

have angered terrorist groups around the world; in particular, U.S. moral and economic support of Israel is known to anger Arabs and other Muslims, who believe that Israel occupies land that belongs to the Palestinians. U.S. commercialism and exploitation of other countries is another possible cause of resentment. Even while discussing such possibilities, however, most people agreed that nothing America had done could possibly justify the September 11 attacks.

The Bush administration subsequently announced that it would engage in a global war against terrorism in order to shut down training camps and bring terrorists to justice, but also to prevent future threats from countries that are stockpiling chemical, biological, or nuclear weapons.

Foreign terrorist organizations

In October 2001 the Office of the Coordinator of Counterterrorism issued a report on foreign terrorist organizations listing 28 groups thought to be of extreme danger to U.S. citizens. They included Al Qaeda and the Revolutionary Armed Forces of Colombia (FARC). As a reminder that terrorism remains a living, changing threat, the list included two new groups—the Real IRA and the United Self-Defense Forces of Colombia

(AUC)—that were only added by Secretary of State Colin Powell in 2001.

While most people agree that terrorism is wrong, there is a central problem in defining what constitutes a terrorist act. It is summed up in an old saying that one man's terrorist is another man's freedom fighter. One group's violent struggle against a despotic regime, for example, could be perceived as terrorism by another country depending on its politics or particular viewpoint. Another problem is that, while terrorism appears easy to condemn, it is difficult to identify a no terrorist campaign has ever been defeated by military action alone: It is necessary to negotiate with the terrorists and listen to their demands, even if it means former terrorists achieving respectability, as was the case with Gerry Adams in Northern Ireland. Such people argue not only that economic sanctions and military intervention cannot defeat terrorism, but that such action in fact makes the situation worse by encouraging new recruits to join the terrorists.

The topics in this last section of the book look at crucial issues in foreign

---

"The terrible thing about terrorism is that ultimately it destroys those who practice it. Slowly but surely, as they try to extinguish life in others, the light within them dies."
—TERRY WAITE (1939–), BRITISH RELIGIOUS ADVISER
AND FORMER HOSTAGE IN LEBANON

---

single country that, according to some definitions has not engaged in some form of terrorist action at some time or another. This might be through directly funding groups but also through trading with despotic governments, imposing colonial rule on an unwilling people, or using armed police or military to control its own population.

Critics argue that despite problems of definition, terrorists cannot go unpunished for their crimes. Neither, they argue, should violent protest be seen to succeed. Terror must be defeated by military intervention and its proponents brought to justice. Opponents of such a course argue that policy and terrorism. Topic 13 begins by examining the historical development of terrorism, asking whether modern terrorism is different from terrorism of the past. Topic 14 addresses the relationship between terrorism and the states where it often begins, such as Afghanistan, Sudan, and Somalia. Do these so-called failed states breed terrorism? Whatever the causes of terrorism, what is the best way to tackle it? Topic 15 debates whether military force offers an effective solution. In the final topic Philip H. Gordon and President George W. Bush specifically consider U.S. responsibility for promoting peace in the Middle East.

Topic 13

IS MODERN TERRORISM DIFFERENT FROM TERRORISM IN PREVIOUS CENTURIES?

YES

FROM "OVERVIEW: THE ISSUE AT A GLANCE"
HTTP://WWW.PUBLICAGENDA.ORG/SPECIALS/TERRORISM/TERROR_OVERVIEW.HTM
PUBLIC AGENDA ONLINE

NO

INTRODUCTION, "TERROR IN HISTORY TO 1939"
THE INTERNATIONAL ENCYCLOPEDIA OF TERRORISM

INTRODUCTION

The *Random House Dictionary* defines terrorism as "the use of violence and threats to intimidate or coerce, especially for political purposes."
The practice of using terror to achieve power dates back to ancient times. However, the word "terrorism" emerged from the French Revolution's "Reign of Terror" (1793–1794), when revolutionaries used the guillotine to execute around 12,000 people deemed to be enemies of their regime.

Prior to the 1950s terrorism usually meant acts of terror carried out by governments as a means of repression. The tactics of the French revolutionaries were echoed by Lenin's secret police, the Cheka, founded to maintain the Bolsheviks in power after the 1917 Russian Revolution, and those of Hitler's Gestapo in Nazi Germany during the 1930s and 1940s.

During World War II (1939–1945) the tactics of state, or government-sponsored, terror were rivaled by those of antistate movements resisting Nazi occupation. They assassinated German officials and local collaborators, and destroyed railroads and bridges. To the Nazis this was the work of terrorists; to the resistance such tactics were a necessary part of the struggle to achieve liberation.

The postwar period saw people from Egypt, Algeria, and Rhodesia (now Zimbabwe) east to India and Vietnam rising up in revolt against colonial regimes. Although much of this protest was peaceful, some employed terrorist tactics—deliberately targeting civilians of the ruling country with random shootings and bombs in crowded cafes. Israeli terrorists employed similar tactics against the British in Palestine. During the Israeli struggle to create a homeland in the region, they assassinated British troops and blew up civilians in hotels.

After France executed two rebels in its colony of Algeria in 1956, the National Liberation Front of Algeria (FLN) killed 49 French citizens in just three days. Although French paratroopers eventually quashed the FLN terrorist network, the terror campaign ultimately led to Algeria's independence from France in 1962.

> *"Terrorism has become the systematic weapon of a war that knows no borders or seldom has a face."*
> —JACQUES CHIRAC, FRENCH PRIME MINISTER, 1986

The success of the FLN inspired others. Following the Israeli occupation of the West Bank and Gaza Strip in 1967, the Palestine Liberation Organization (PLO) adopted terrorist tactics. Other pro-Palestine groups followed suit, hijacking airplanes and murdering Israeli athletes at the 1972 Munich Olympics. Around the same time in Northern Ireland, the arrival of British troops on the streets led to the revival of terrorist campaigns by Catholic nationalists, which in turn provoked violence from Protestants who wanted the province to remain part of the United Kingdom.

The late 1960s and early 1970s saw militants in Europe and Japan also turning to terror. Marxist and extreme left-wing groups emerged—West Germany's Baader-Meinhoff Gang, Japan's Red Army, and Italy's Red Brigades—which carried out kidnappings and killings to protest the "fascist capitalism" of their home countries.

Historically the United States has suffered less from terrorist attacks than elsewhere in the world. However, the Weathermen, part of the 1960s antiwar movement, planted bombs in the Pentagon. U.S. embassies and army personnel overseas have also been targets—most often of Middle Eastern-based terrorists. In 1988 Pan Am flight 103 was brought down by a bomb planted by Libyan intelligence agents, killing 270 people. Since then America has come under attack at home, not only from Islamic extremists but also—as with Timothy McVeigh, who killed 168 people in Oklahoma City in 1995—from domestic terrorism.

The best-known terrorists at the start of the 21st century were Islamic fundamentalists: Al Qaeda, infamous for its attacks on the World Trade Center and the Pentagon on September 11, 2001; Hamas, Hezbollah, and others who orchestrate the campaign of suicide bombings in Israel. How do these groups compare in terms of their structure, funding, aims, and tactics with terrorists of the past? Are we facing similar patterns of disenfranchised and disaffected groups and individuals turning to violence as a last resort to highlight their grievances and bring about change? Or is there something different about the modern-day threat? Some people argue that suicide bombing on the scale witnessed on September 11, 2001, represents the new face of terrorism. Others point out that as far back as the 13th century the group known as the Assassins committed acts of suicidal violence. The following articles examine the debate.

OVERVIEW: THE ISSUE AT A GLANCE
Public Agenda Online

YES

✓ It was not the first time America was hit by domestic terrorism, but the September 11 attack—aimed at symbols of U.S. military and financial might—struck at the soul of the American people. It was the worst act of terrorism in modern history, and it left Americans feeling stunned and vulnerable. The damage still seems unimaginable: three of four hijacked airliners smashed into the World Trade Center and the Pentagon, and a fourth crashed in Pennsylvania, leaving about 3,000 people dead or missing by the latest count. The outpouring of grief has eclipsed even the deeply felt response to the Oklahoma City bombing in 1995—itself an unimaginable act, until it happened.

War unlike any other

Almost overnight, the "war on terrorism" became the nation's No. 1 priority. President Bush, targeting terrorist organizations with a "global reach," launched a military assault on Afghanistan, whose ruling Taliban party has harbored Osama Bin Laden, the suspected mastermind of the September 11 attacks. Among other actions, airports have tightened security and law enforcement has been given more leeway to wiretap and detain suspects....

But many challenges remain: Americans, still reeling from the shock of September 11, now find themselves facing the frightening prospect of bioterrorism, with numerous reports of exposure to the potentially lethal disease anthrax. America's postal system—apparently used to unleash the germ warfare—is under siege in an assault initially aimed at government offices, including Congress, and major news organizations. Only a handful have actually developed anthrax and only four have died, but thousands more have been forced to take antibiotics as a precaution. It's still not clear what connection—if any—there is between the September 11 attack and the outbreak of anthrax, but one thing is clear: In the fight against terrorism, America is engaged in a war unlike any other—one where the enemy is not so easily defined.

In launching military action against Afghanistan, President Bush warned that there could be significant U.S. casualties, and that retaliation against America was likely as a result of

Several weeks after the September 11 attacks America experienced a new panic as an individual or group began mailing anthrax—a deadly bacterial disease that can be produced as a biological weapon—to politicians and people who worked in the media. While many people believed that Al Qaeda—the chief suspects in the September 11 attacks—were behind the mailings, the FBI became increasingly convinced that the letters were the work of a U.S. citizen or citizens. By the end of 2001 there had been 18 confirmed cases of anthrax infection and five anthrax-related deaths.

In what way is "the enemy ... not so easily defined"? Is it not simply Osama Bin Laden and his Al Qaeda group?

military action. But there's also the risk that military action will increase instability in the Arab region. Even though President Bush has said the campaign is not aimed at Islam but at terrorist organizations and any governments that provide safe haven, many in the Arab world view the anti-terrorism campaign as anti-Islamic. ...

Some of the governments in predominantly Muslim countries that have supported the United States—most notably Pakistan, Saudi Arabia and Egypt—face considerable opposition from domestic groups that believe the West has exploited the region and supported oppressive regimes. Indeed, bin Laden is hoping the current conflict will foment uprisings within these countries. There also are concerns that, in the wake of military action against Afghanistan, bin Laden is trying to solidify his role as an anti-United States folk hero to some in the Arab world, particularly with the release of a videotape in which he taunted America and voiced support for the September 11 attack.

Why might groups in Pakistan, Saudi Arabia, and Egypt believe that their countries have been exploited by the West in the past? For one point of view—and links to others—go to www.csmonitor. com/2001/0927/ p1s1-wogi.html.

A recent report by the ... Congressional Research Service said the focus on Muslim terrorist groups raises the question of "how to condemn and combat such terrorist activity, and the extreme and violent ideology of specific radical groups, without appearing to be anti-Islamic in general."

A defining moment

The United States has struggled with [different forms of] terrorism for years. This was not the first attack on the nation's capital. In 1954 ... pro-independence Puerto Rican terrorists opened fire from the House of Representatives visitors' gallery, wounding five members of Congress.

Even Wall Street was a terrorist target as far back as 1920, when a massive bombing killed 30 people.... While the investigation centered on known Sicilian, Romanian and Russian terrorist groups, the case was never solved.

America also experienced a spate of plane hijackings in the late 1960s and 1970s that led to the placement of armed undercover guards ... on the nation's airliners, an idea that's been revived in the nation's current war on terrorism.

The deadly bombing of the American embassy in Beirut in 1983 marked the beginning of ... violence against U.S. targets by ... terrorist organizations ... in the Mideast. And the 1995 bombing of the federal building in Oklahoma City, in which 168 people died, raised the ... specter of homespun terrorism.

Some commentators suggest that it was U.S. involvement in Israel's 1982 invasion of Lebanon that prompted terrorist organizations in the Middle East to take action against the United States.

The world has seen terrorism become a weapon of war in domestic, regional and international disputes, sometimes linked to a specific conflict, as in Northern Ireland ... or

The "end of the Cold War" began in 1989 with the collapse of communist regimes in Eastern Europe; the Soviet Union finally broke up toward the end of 1991.

In the 1980s tensions between the Tamil and Sinhalese populations in Sri Lanka led to civil war. Tamil rebels, calling themselves the Liberation Tigers of Tamil Eelam (LTTE), carried out acts of terrorism with the goal of forcing the creation of a separate Tamil state in northern Sri Lanka. After a major LTTE suicide attack in 2001 the government signed a cease-fire with the rebels in 2002.

"Realpolitik" is practical politics, rather than politics based on ideological factors.

sometimes aimed at a broader target, as in Bin Laden's campaign against the United States and western influence in the Middle East. For Americans, though, the September 11 terrorist attack was a defining moment.

Politics of terror

The end of the Cold War, and the breakup of the Soviet Union, changed the very nature of many terrorist organizations. The Soviet bloc was believed to have provided considerable aid to terrorist organizations and nations that supported them.

Terrorists were forced to find other sources of funding, which reportedly have included such activities as drug trafficking, underground banking systems and money laundering. It's estimated that Bin Laden has at his disposal $300 million in personal wealth.

The problem of concerted terrorist activity is not limited to the Mideast, as seen in the rise of violent attacks in South Asia and the Pacific Rim, particularly in Sri Lanka.... [M]any of the rogue organizations that commit violence against the United States operate without respect to international boundaries. [However], for the United States, the current threat is distinctly rooted in the Mideast among Islamic extremists, and the stakes have been raised by the proliferation of chemical and biological weapons and fears that terrorists might get their hands on nuclear devices.

Shifting sands

For the United States, the issue of terrorism has been something of a foreign-policy netherworld often ruled by realpolitik. Alliances shift—yesterday's foe becomes today's friend—and infiltrating the world of terrorism sometimes requires dealing with people who have blood on their hands.

Five of the seven nations on the U.S. State Department's list of countries that sponsor terrorism are in or near the Middle East: Iran, Iraq, Libya, Syria and Sudan (Cuba and North Korea round out the list). Afghanistan, Pakistan, Lebanon and Yemen also have been cited as centers of major terrorist activity.

Now, however, Pakistan is playing a critical role in the anti-terrorism coalition; Washington also has consulted with Iran and Syria in an effort to bring them into the coalition.

The United States also finds itself in conflict with former allies. For example, the Islamic radicals who now rule Afghanistan [received U.S. assistance] when they were fighting the Soviet occupation. Saddam Hussein [also] received American support when Iraq was engaged in its decade-long war with Iran.

Officially, Washington says it will not negotiate with terrorists. As a practical matter, though, that policy has been waived with regard to the Palestinian Liberation Organization and the Irish Republican Army as an inducement to peace talks.

Does it matter if governments break their own rules?

In addition to the military campaign, the federal government has taken several steps to combat terrorism in the wake of September 11. President Bush has created a cabinet-level Homeland Security office to coordinate the nation's anti-terrorism efforts. Airports have put new security measures in place and law enforcement has been given broader authority to wiretap and detain terrorism suspects. The administration [is] also [tightening up] immigration provisions in an effort to keep terrorists out of the country.

Questions still remain

Other policy questions remain, though:

- Congress is considering having the federal government take over the job of airport security.
- There have been calls for a more aggressive counter-terrorism program with more covert activity, including assassinations of terrorist leaders.
- Tougher economic sanctions have been urged for nations that harbor or aid terrorists, along with a worldwide campaign to crack down on banks that launder money for terror groups.
- The establishment of an international court to try terrorism cases also has been suggested.
- And, in many regards, the issue of bioterrorism is uncharted territory. Several reports have warned that the federal government is ill-prepared to handle a major domestic incident of bioterrorism. Among the key questions: How would our public health systems … deal with a deluge of bioterrorism victims? It's not even clear if our health systems can detect a bioterrorism attack at its initial stage….

Is it important to uphold civil liberties at all costs? For a debate concerning the detention of suspected Al Qaeda and Taliban fighters at Camp X-Ray, Guantanamo Bay, Cuba, read Volume 9 Criminal Law and the Penal System, *Topic 14* Do prisoners have rights? *on pages 178–189.*

Finding a balance

As the federal government has moved to deal with the threat of terrorism, there have been concerns that civil liberties could be eroded. The Justice Department, for example, has detained more than 1,000 people since September 11, and critics say the government's refusal to identify many of them or specify charges amounts to secret detention.

"U.S. leaders must find the appropriate balance by adopting counterterrorism policies which are effective but also respect the democratic traditions which are the bedrock of America's strength," the National Commission on Terrorism wrote in a report to Congress last year.

TERROR IN HISTORY TO 1939
THE INTERNATIONAL ENCYCLOPEDIA OF TERRORISM

NO

X The word terrorism was coined in the guillotine days of the French Revolution, but the practice is much older. Terrorism stretches back in time to the bloody assassinations of the ancient Greeks and Romans and to barbaric customs such as suspending people over fires for not paying their taxes. Few parts of the world have escaped the brutalities and the climate of fear that terrorism creates. Among many examples, there were religious murder cults in the Middle East, massacres during the American Indian resistance, and Stalin's purges in Russia, when some 20 million people died at his hands to make sure that those still alive were cowed into submission.

It is a well-known saying that one person's terrorist is another's freedom fighter. Are some forms of terrorism more acceptable than others?

It is easy, in our concern about terrorism today, to lose sight of the historical perspectives on the subject that enable us to piece together a proper analysis of terror, and, therefore, to work out strategies for coping with it…. Terror can come from the state, from those resisting the state, from the excesses of warfare, from small dedicated ideological groups, and from clashes between different societies or views of society.

State terror

Set up in April 1793, the Committee of Public Safety was the first effective governing body in revolutionary France. The committee was largely responsible for the "Reign of Terror" in which thousands of citizens were put to death.

Examples of terror used by the state range from Imperial Rome to Stalin's purges in the Soviet Union. Both these examples demonstrate how a ruling class can be cowed by terrorist methods and forced to acquiesce in a dictatorship. The most famous introduction of terror by a state was that of the Committee of Public Safety in 1794. Under pressure from a European-wide coalition and having to deal with a series of revolts within France, the revolutionaries decided that they would terrorize their own population into obedience. The results were undeniably successful: the French armies defeated their enemies both on the frontiers and also within France.

This state terror has in turn produced theories that justify use of any means—including terror—to resist tyrants. Such ideas ("tyrannicide") were put forward in Ancient Greece and in the later Roman republic, the most famous example being the assassination of Julius Caesar. Some 1,800 years

This painting shows Gavrilo Princip, a member of the Serbian terrorist group The Black Hand, shooting Archduke Ferdinand of Austria as he drove through Sarajevo with his wife Sophie on June 28, 1914. The archduke's assassination was the immediate cause of World War I (1914–1918).

later the Russian anarchist terrorists cited ideas of tyrannicide in their attempts to murder the Czar.

Fear and terror are a necessary part of warfare. The knowledge that you are likely to die if you undertake a particular course of action—whether it be advancing across a fire-swept plain or climbing a scaling ladder to a fortress— is at the very heart of military science. However, to this can

171

COMMENTARY: The Assassins

The connection between terrorism and religion dates back more than 2,000 years. Extremist groups of the past have included the Zealots, a Jewish sect that between 66 and 73 A.D. carried out attacks and public acts of violence against the Roman Empire's occupation of the region that is now Israel, and the Thugs, a seventh-century religious cult in India that murdered travelers as sacrificial offerings to Kali, the Hindu goddess of terror and destruction.

Suicidal martyrdom

Among the most renowned of all early terrorists was a group known as the Assassins that, between 1090 and 1272 A.D., fought against the Christian crusaders then attempting to conquer the Holy Land, or present-day Israel and Syria. A highly secretive offshoot of the Ismaili branch of Islam, the Assassins considered acts of violence to be their divine duty. Their motivation was not only to vanquish their Christian enemies: In common with certain Islamic fundamentalists today, each Assassin believed that should he die in the course of carrying out an attack, he would immediately ascend to heaven. In carrying out an attack, the assassin made no plan of escape—consequently, suicide was the most common outcome.

Feared and hated by all

The Assassins were one of the first groups in history to make the planned, systematic, and long-term use of murder a political weapon. A product of centuries of divisions and splits in the Islamic faith, the group believed that anyone who did not follow their particular doctrine did not deserve to live. As such, they not only targeted Christians, but also prominent individuals in other branches of Islam, particularly the Sunnis. As a result, they were feared and hated by the majority of Muslims in the region.

"Hashish eaters"

The word "Assassin" is believed to be a mispronunciation of the Arab word "Hashishyum," which literally translated means "hashish eater." Hashish is another word for cannabis, which is prepared from the resin of the hemp plant and taken for its intoxicating qualities. Historians believe that the Assassins took hashish in ritual ceremonies before embarking on their murder missions. Members of the group were trained to use swords, daggers, and other weapons in order to carry out their work, and were able to also recognize and use various poisons.

The end of the Assassins came in the 13th century, when the Mongols reached the Middle East. With their arrival Assassin fortresses were burned to the ground, destroying many records of the group's existence. However, their legacy lives on with the word "assassin," used today to mean someone who commits murder either in return for money or for fanatical motives.

be added the aspect of deliberately threatening civilians. An obvious example of terror against civilians was in medieval siege warfare. Here, there were commonly understood rules about how long fortified places could resist before the inhabitants risked massacre. Similarly, the Mongols made it clear to their enemies that they would exact a savage vengeance if there was any resistance at all. During World War I [1914–1918], however, German threats against civilians in the territories they had occupied were more covert, an approach perhaps influenced by German policies toward subject populations in their colonies.

During the 13th century Genghis Khan, leader of the Mongols, founded an empire that would eventually stretch from China to the Middle East.

Modern terrorism

Much modern terrorism is carried out by small groups with a particular ideology or aim that they wish to force upon others. Again, there are examples of this throughout history. During the Middle Ages, the sect known as the Assassins in the Middle East, representing a particular schism within Islam, used selective assassination of enemy leaders as a weapon. The anarchists of the late nineteenth century also used terror for their ends. Such methods were again adopted by various nationalist groups in the early twentieth century, such as the Serbs who assassinated the Archduke Ferdinand in Sarajevo in 1914.

Think of some examples of "small groups with a particular ideology" that carry out terrorist attacks in the world today.

The use of terror policies may have taken most lives, however, in conflicts between different societies, or different views of society. Where two societies clashed, especially where they were at different levels of technological development, then terror was common. A typical example was in North America, where terror was used by both sides in the wars between the European settlers and the Indian tribes. The tide of European colonization across the world during the eighteenth and nineteenth centuries also saw the use of widespread terror. Massacre was used to terrify and subdue whole populations, and in retaliation by those being conquered.

Do you agree that the U.S. treatment of Native Americans in the 18th and 19th centuries was a form of terrorism? Research your answer by going to www.gliah.uh.edu/native_voices/native_voices.cfm.

But if different societies used terror against one another, so too did members of the same society who professed different views. These differences could be ideological, as in the Paris Commune, or in the civil war that broke out in the aftermath of the Russian revolution. In both cases, left-wing radicals fought reactionary conservative forces. Perhaps the most awful examples of this kind of terror took place where religious or racial differences were latched onto by the state. The brutal state-inspired Turkish treatment of Christian Armenians during World War I was an episode that prefigured the Nazi Holocaust.

Summary

The first article argues that the attacks of September 11, 2001, are evidence that the modern-day threat of terrorism is different from that of previous centuries. Terrorists are no longer the small, single-issue groups that have attacked America in the past. Rather, the aims and inspiration of Islamic extremists such as Al Qaeda are broadly anti-American and anti-Western. In addition, the end of the Cold War has meant the end of Soviet funding for some groups; instead, terrorists are increasingly turning to drug trafficking, underground banking, and money laundering. Finally, there is the question of tactics—modern terrorism has not only seen the advent of suicide bombings, but has also brought with it a new fear that groups might resort to chemical, biological, or nuclear weapons in pursuit of their cause.

By contrast, the *International Encyclopedia of Terrorism* implies that terrorism is much the same today as in the past. Terrorist tactics might come from the state, from those resisting the state, from the excesses of war, from small ideological groups, or from clashes between different societies or views of society. The essay contends that terrorists have used similar tactics throughout history. It cites examples of an Islamic sect known as the Assassins during the Middle Ages, late 19th-century anarchists, and early 20th-century nationalist groups, all of whom used terror in pursuit of their goals.

FURTHER INFORMATION:

Books:

Carr, Caleb, *The Lessons of Terror: A History of Warfare against Civilians*. New York: Random House, 2002.

Combs, Cynthia, *Terrorism in the Twenty-First Century*. Upper Saddle River, NJ: Prentice Hall, 1999.

Hoffman, Bruce, *Inside Terrorism*. New York: Columbia University Press, 1999.

Rubin, Barry, and Judith Colp Rubin (eds.), *Anti-American Terrorism and the Middle East: A Documentary Reader*. Oxford, UK: Oxford University Press, 2002.

Useful websites:

www.fas.org/irp/threat/terror.htm

Federation of American Scientists' resource page with links to articles and information on terrorism.

www.terrorismanswers.com

Council on Foreign Relations site. Provides information on terrorism and terrorist groups.

www.terrorism.com

Terrorist Research Center site. Provides profiles of terrorist organizations and counterterrorism groups.

The following debates in the Pro/Con series may also be of interest:

In this volume:

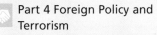 Part 4 Foreign Policy and Terrorism

Topic 14 Does terrorism arise from the problem of "failed states"?

Topic 15 Should the United States use military force against nations that harbor terrorists?

In *Criminal Law and the Penal System*:

Topic 14 Do prisoners have rights?

IS MODERN TERRORISM DIFFERENT FROM TERRORISM IN PREVIOUS CENTURIES?

YES: By contrast to nationalist groups such as the IRA, it is impossible to negotiate with fundamentalists like Al Qaeda whose ideology is broadly anti-American and anti-Western

YES: In the 1970s terrorism directed against the United States was supported by states such as Libya, Syria, and Iran, as well as the Soviet Union

AIMS
Are the aims of modern terrorism significantly different from those of previous centuries?

FUNDING
Does the manner in which terrorism is funded differ today from funding in the past?

NO: The extreme Marxist organizations of the late 1960s and early 1970s were bent on the overthrow of their "fascist" home governments; this aim is not so different from those of extreme Muslim groups—the overthrow of American influence and of "Western" ideology

IS MODERN TERRORISM DIFFERENT FROM TERRORISM IN PREVIOUS CENTURIES?
KEY POINTS

NO: Even following the end of the Cold War, there are still regimes prepared to covertly fund certain terrorist groups; drugs and money laundering have always been a source of funds for criminals

YES: The scale of suicide bombings—such as those of September 11, 2001—has taken the threat posed by terrorism to new levels

YES: Modern terrorism inevitably has the tools of modern technology at its disposal. For example, terrorists have used chemical agents such as the nerve gas sarin in recent years.

TACTICS
Are the tactics that the modern terrorist employs different from those of previous centuries?

NO: Extreme ideology, lack of hope, or desperation has always provoked extreme methods and the likelihood that a terrorist will make the ultimate sacrifice for his or her cause

NO: The tactics of terror—assassination, bombings, ambush, and sabotage—remain the same regardless of the modern means that are now available to pursue those tactics

SEPTEMBER 11, 2001

On September 11, 2001, four airplanes carrying a total of 266 people were hijacked by terrorists. Two of the planes crashed into the World Trade Center in New York; both towers, world-famous emblems of wealth and influence, later collapsed. The third plane smashed into the Pentagon, and the fourth crashed in Pennsylvania. The timeline below (according to Eastern Daylight Time) details the day's events as they unfolded.

08:40 The Federal Aviation Administration (FAA) alerts the North American Aerospace Defense Command (NORAD) that American Airlines Flight 11 has been hijacked. It had left Boston en route to Los Angeles carrying 81 passengers and 11 crew.

08:43 The FAA informs NORAD that United Airlines Flight 175 has also been hijacked. Two F-15 jet fighters take off from Otis Air National Guard Base in Falmouth, Massachusetts.

08:45 American Airlines Flight 11, a Boeing 767, crashes into the North Tower of the World Trade Center. It tears a gaping hole in the building, and fire breaks out.

09:03 United Airlines Flight 175 crashes into the South Tower of the World Trade Center and explodes. It originated in Boston and was bound for Los Angeles with 56 passengers and 9 crew on board.

09:10 In Sarasota, Florida, President George W. Bush is reading to children in a classroom when his chief of staff Andrew Card passes on news of the attacks.

09:21 The Port Authority of New York and New Jersey orders all bridges and tunnels in the New York area closed. The Stock Exchange, the Mercantile Exchange, and the financial district are evacuated.

09:29 Reports of casualties begin to pour in. On an average day up to 50,000 workers are based at the World Trade Center.

09:30 President Bush announces: "We have had a national tragedy. Two airplanes have crashed into the World Trade Center in an apparent terrorist attack on our country."

09:40 American Airlines Flight 77, carrying 58 passengers, 4 flight attendants, and 2 pilots from Washington, D.C., to Los Angeles, crashes into the west side of the Pentagon, the center of the United States' military, which houses about 20,000 people. Part of the building bursts into flames, and one side of its five-sided structure collapses. President Bush authorizes fighters to shoot down any other aircraft that threatens targets in Washington, D.C.

09:45 The White House and the Capitol are evacuated amid further threats of attack.

09:50 All U.S. airports are shut down, and commercial flights are grounded—the first time in U.S. history that air traffic nationwide has been halted.

09:58 An emergency despatcher in Pennsylvania receives a call from a passenger on United Airlines Flight 93 reporting a hijacking. Several passengers call relatives; they intend to tackle the hijackers.

10:05 The South Tower of the World Trade Center collapses, sending a massive pall of smoke and dust across Manhattan. Many emergency workers, firefighters, and people stuck in the building are crushed.

10:08 Secret Service agents armed with automatic rifles are sent into Lafayette Park across from the White House.

10:10 United Airlines Flight 93 crashes in Somerset County, 80 miles southeast of Pittsburgh. It was bound for San Francisco from Newark, New Jersey.

10:25 A car bomb is reported to have exploded outside the State Department in Washington, D.C.

10:29 The North Tower of the World Trade Center collapses. The southern part of Manhattan is covered with a thick layer of dust and debris from the building.

10:30 Governor George Palaki declares a state of emergency in the state of New York. He asks the president to declare New York City a federal disaster area.

12:39 President Bush makes a second statement in which he says: "Make no mistake: The United States will hunt down and punish those responsible for these cowardly acts."

13:20 President Bush leaves Barksdale Air Force Base in Louisiana. He is flown to Offutt Air Force Base in Nebraska.

13:44 The Pentagon says five battleships and two aircraft carriers will be deployed along the East Coast to provide air defense for the New York and Washington areas.

13:50 A state of emergency is declared by the city of Washington, D.C.

14:00 The United States Securities and Exchange Commission announces that all stock markets are closed for the afternoon.

14:48 Rudolph Giuliani, the mayor of New York, refuses to speculate on the number of fatalities, but he says that the eventual death toll will be "more than any of us can bear."

16:00 Officials state that Osama Bin Laden, head of the terrorist organization Al Qaeda, already suspected of coordinating bombings of the U.S. embassies in Kenya and Tanzania in 1998, may be involved in the attacks, based on "new and specific" information.

16:25 The American Stock Exchange, Nasdaq, and the New York Stock Exchange say they will remain closed on Wednesday.

16:30 President Bush leaves Offutt Air Force Base aboard Air Force One to return to the White House. He intends to make a televised address to the nation.

17:20 Building Number 7, a 47-story building adjacent to the ruins of the World Trade Center, collapses.

17:30 Officials say the plane that crashed in Pennsylvania could have been headed for one of three possible targets: Camp David, the White House, or the Capitol.

18:40 Defense Secretary Donald Rumsfeld holds a press conference in the Pentagon. He states that the building is still operational and says: "It will be in business tomorrow."

20:30 President Bush addresses the nation on television saying: "Thousands of lives were suddenly ended by evil." He hints at a strong U.S. response to the "terrorists who committed these acts and those who harbor them."

Topic 14

DOES TERRORISM ARISE FROM THE PROBLEM OF "FAILED STATES"?

YES

"RELIEF BODIES AS FRONTS FOR TERROR"
THE NATION (NAIROBI), DECEMBER 16, 2001
OPINION

NO

FROM "TERRORISM WORKS"
AL-AHRAM WEEKLY ONLINE, NOVEMBER 1–7, 2001
NOAM CHOMSKY

INTRODUCTION

A "failed state" is usually defined as one where—often as a result of war—the situation is so chaotic that its government can no longer function efficiently and cannot fulfill its obligations to its own citizens. It cannot, for example, provide security, basic education and health care, or freedom from want.

The War Against Terrorism, which was announced by President George W. Bush following the terrorist attacks of September 11, 2001, on the United States, provoked a crucial question: Are terrorist groups especially likely to arise from or to feed off of failed states? In other words, do chaotic and corrupt governments give such terrorist organizations as Osama Bin Laden's Al Qaeda opportunities to gain vital resources and recruits? Do disorderly states allow international criminals, including terrorists, freedom to maneuver and raise money that they would not have in a functioning state?

In the summer 2002 issue of the *Washington Quarterly*, political science author and president of the World Peace Foundation Robert I. Rotberg defined eight of the world's 191 nations as failed states: Afghanistan, Angola, Burundi, the Democratic Republic of Congo, Liberia, Sierra Leone, Somalia, and Sudan. Such areas of lawlessness and desperation, many people argue, are a breeding ground for terrorism. Extremist groups may be welcomed in such places if they can offer some of the basic securities that the state has failed to provide.

Somalia, where civil war has raged since 1991, is an example of a failed state under scrutiny for its terrorist associations. In a report of February 2002 the U.S. assistant secretary for African affairs noted how Al-Ittihad al-Islami, a radical Islamist organization responsible for terrorist operations in neighboring Ethiopia, had opened its own schools in some parts of Somalia and provided other services normally associated with government. The Somalis—otherwise living in a state of near-anarchy—may support the organization out of sheer desperation.

> *"Poverty does not cause terrorism…. Yet persistent poverty and oppression can lead to hopelessness and despair. And when governments fail to meet the most basic needs of their people, these failed states can become havens for terror."*
>
> —GEORGE W. BUSH,
> 43RD PRESIDENT, 2001

Despite such cases, the link between terrorism and failed states is not always clear. Some of the most poverty-stricken and ill-governed states in Africa—Niger and Chad, for example—do not seem to have had a significant role in the development of terrorist networks. Equally, wealthier Middle East countries—such as Egypt, the United Arab Emirates, and Saudi Arabia—have acted as crucial recruiting grounds.

There are opportunities for corruption in a failed state. In Sierra Leone, the Congo, and Angola in the 1990s terrorist groups profited from illegal diamond mining. But terrorists can play the system in strong states too. Al Qaeda, for example, used U.S. pilot schools to train the men who flew the planes in the September 11 attacks.

In the wake of those attacks President George W. Bush declared that states harboring terrorists would become targets for military action. The first such target was Afghanistan, a failed state used as a base by Al Qaeda, and a country where millions were at risk of starvation. Many people fear that the assumption that state failure automatically constitutes a threat to the security of the rest of the world may inevitably result in preemptive strikes against more of the world's poorest nations.

One powerful argument against the failed-states theory is that it distracts attention from other possible political injustices—such as those resulting from Israel's occupation of Palestine—that may be the root causes of terrorism. A further argument against it is that it may lead Western governments to reenact old imperial mistakes by intervening in the affairs of other nations, thereby fueling grievances and exacerbating the problem of terrorism.

Exploring the links between failed states, poverty, and terrorism, the following article from the Kenyan publication *The Nation* examines claims that non-Western aid agencies act as fronts for terrorist groups. While rejecting the idea that poverty is simply "fodder for terrorism," the piece highlights the need for Western aid and support for struggling states as a barrier against exploitation by terrorists.

In the second article the American radical activist and thinker Noam Chomsky questions the narrow definition of terrorism implicit in the failed-states argument. Pleading for a broader view of the issues, he argues that the United States has itself committed many acts that ought to be described as terrorism.

RELIEF BODIES AS FRONTS FOR TERROR
The Nation, Opinion

YES

☑ Until recently, almost all charity organisations in Kenya were from the West. But now, some relief organisations from the Gulf and Middle East countries have started to emerge on the scene, and some stand accused of being a front for terrorists.

Why does the West put conditions on the aid it gives to poor countries? Should it give aid unconditionally? See Topic 9 Should the United States give aid to developing countries irrespective of their politics? on pages 112–123.

Failed states a breeding ground for terrorism
Some Kenyans see the emergence of humanitarian agencies from non-Western states as the result of rising poverty and the stringent conditions the West have put on their aid. Questionable charities could be stepping in to fill the gap created by retreating Western agencies.

Dr Moustafa Hassouna, a senior lecturer at the Institute of Diplomacy and International Studies at the University of Nairobi, says:

The writer implies that the West has been largely responsible for the creation of failed states as a result of ignoring them. Do countries have the right to interfere in the affairs of other nation states? See Topic 2 Is U.S. foreign policy too interventionist?

> *There is definitely a search for alternatives. Countries that had been ignored by the West had to look for alternatives.*

Dr Hassouna says the lesson that must be learnt is that marginalisation of certain states "is not an option any more." He argues that failed states have created a vacuum being exploited by non-state actors like Al Qaeda to spread terror.

> *Somalia is thought to be harbouring terrorists because it has no government. It is a failed state. So was Afghanistan. I think we must all learn that failed states pose great danger. We must build bridges because if we don't, we promote a dangerous option for ignored states.*

Using quotations from other sources, particularly if they are experts, can help your argument. However, do you think the author's extensive use of them detracts from or enhances his case?

The lecturer says poverty is fodder for terrorism and it is possible that people join terrorist organisations in a desperate struggle for survival.

> *We can no longer have islands of prosperity in the middle of poverty. The real concern here is that the gap between the rich and the poor states has widened and we must close it, otherwise no one is safe.*

Osama Bin Laden took advantage of Afghanistan's marginalization by the West to organize camps there in which to train hundreds of volunteers for his Al Qaeda terrorist network.

Terrorism exploits rich and poor alike

Mr Mohammed Nyaoga, a Nairobi lawyer, does not entirely agree that there is a void the terrorist organisations are trying to fill. But he concedes that ignoring failed states is a dangerous undertaking.

> *"Bin Laden acted as a donor to Afghanistan. If a failed state is ignored, there is a chance for a terrorist 'donor' to come in with a lot of money and say 'I will bail you out, then I [will] operate from here,'" the lawyer said.*

But he says the agencies that serve as fronts for terrorists are not filling any gap.

> *Nobody has a monopoly over charity. The presence of Western donors never kept out those [terrorist groups] from the Islamic world.*

He sees as a contradiction the fact that some agencies can claim to be working in humanitarian activities and yet still spread mayhem.

The writer finds it unlikely that the same group of people could conduct charitable and terrorist activities simultaneously. Do you agree?

> *You cannot run a charitable organisation then at the same time front for terrorists. What is the point in giving help to somebody only to kill him.*

The financiers of terrorist acts are not poor, the lawyer says, ruling out the suggestion that people are driven to terrorism by poverty.

Are suicide attacks a modern phenomenon in terrorist activity? To find the answer, go to http://www.lib.umich.edu/govdocs/usterror.html #terrorism.

> *It is possible that the rich with grudges can take advantage of the poor by asking them to undertake acts of terrorism. But even that is hard to accept because most terrorists are keen on suicide attacks. How does it benefit you to take 10 million shillings because you are poor when you know you are going to commit suicide in the next minute? It is twisted logic.*

The lawyer argues that what the world has witnessed are the fruits of extremism—equally dangerous, he thinks, whether religious or political.

A complex problem

A U.S. embassy official close to the investigations agreed that there is a link between failed states and terrorism, but rejected the idea that the terrorist agencies are filling a gap.

Our analysis has shown that in Afghanistan, there is a strong sense of communal identity and solidarity. The same is the case with Somalia. In both countries, loyalty is expressed towards the family, then to the community, including religious orientation, then to the city or province and only to the country much later. That makes it hard to deal with them as states in the modern sense.

How should the United States try to "deal with" countries that do not act like "states in the modern sense"?

The embassy official said terrorist groups are not necessarily filling a void. Most may just be taking advantage of Kenya's good communication network, coupled with its weak policing.

We must also understand Kenya's location against that of states associated with terrorism. There is evidence that throughout the 1990s there were plans for expansion by terror groups in Egypt, Sudan and Somalia. And Kenya is a good ground for any group that wants rapid but secretive communications in the region.

The United States, the official said, thinks the states of Eastern Africa have managed to contain fundamentalists fairly well.

The Islamic fundamentalists in Sudan, Egypt and Somalia would have dominated here if Kenya, Tanzania and Ethiopia had not kept them at bay. I believe the states will succeed.

TERRORISM WORKS
Noam Chomsky

NO

Starting with the common assumption that what happened on 11 September is a historic event—one which will change history—the question we should be asking is exactly why is this so? Another question has to do with the "War Against Terrorism". Exactly what is it? And there is a related question, namely, what is terrorism?

This article appeared in the first week of November 2001. American-led bombing of Afghanistan—in response to the terrorist attacks of September 11—had begun on October 7.

The situation in Afghanistan

By far the most important question that we must ask ourselves after 11 September is what is happening right now? … According to *The New York Times* there are seven to eight million people in Afghanistan on the verge of starvation. That was true actually before 11 September. They were surviving on international aid. On 16 September, the *Times* reported that "the U.S. demanded from Pakistan the elimination of truck convoys that provide much of the food and other supplies to Afghanistan's civilian population." As far as I could determine, there was no reaction in the U.S. to the demand to impose massive starvation on millions of people. The threat of military strikes right after 11 September forced the removal of international aid workers that crippled the assistance programmes. …

The WFP website at www.wfp.org has a section on Afghanistan, with the latest information about the humanitarian crisis there.

The UN World Food Programme (WFP), which is the main aid programme by far, was able to resume food shipments in early October—at a much lower level. They do not have international aid workers inside Afghanistan, so the distribution system is hampered. Even this, however, was suspended as soon as the bombing began. The WFP then resumed, but at a slower pace, while aid agencies levelled scathing condemnations of U.S. airdrops of food packets as "propaganda tools which are probably doing more harm than good," the London *Financial Times* reported.

Do you agree that U.S. food drops were "propaganda tools"? Why might they have done "more harm than good"?

After the first week of bombing, *The New York Times* reported on a back page, inside a column on something else, that by the arithmetic of the United Nations, there will soon be 7.5 million Afghans in acute need of even a loaf of bread and there are only a few weeks left before the harsh winter will make deliveries to many areas totally impossible. But with bombs falling, the article said, the current delivery rate is down to half of what is needed. A casual comment, which tells us that Western civilisation is anticipating the slaughter of—well, do the arithmetic—between three or four million people.

Meanwhile, the leader of Western civilisation dismissed with contempt, once again, offers of negotiation for delivery of the alleged target, prime suspect Osama Bin Laden, and a request for some evidence to substantiate the U.S.'s demand for total capitulation. On the same day as this offer was categorically rejected, the special rapporteur of the UN in charge of food distribution pleaded with the U.S. to stop the bombing to try to save millions of victims. As far as I am aware, that plea went unreported by the media. A few days later the major aid agencies like OXFAM and Christian Aid joined in the plea. This too went unreported.

It looks like what is happening is some sort of silent genocide. It also gives a good deal of insight into the elite culture, the culture that we are part of. It indicates that whatever will happen, we do not know, but plans are being made and programmes implemented on the assumption that they may lead to the death of several million people in the next couple of weeks. Very casually, with no comment, no particular thought about it. That is just kind of normal, here...

Is Chomsky implying that the public perceived the death of several million people in a foreign country to be of lesser importance than the several thousand people who died on September 11, 2001? Do you think this would be a fair assessment of media and public opinion?

Terrorism in context

...Let us turn to the question of the historic event that took place on 11 September.... Unfortunately, there are terrorist crimes with effects a bit more drawn out that are more extreme. Nevertheless, 11 September was a historic event because there was a change. The change was the direction in which the guns were pointed. That is new. Radically new.

The last time the national territory of the U.S. was under attack, or for that matter, even threatened was when the British burned down Washington in 1814. In press reports following the attacks, it was common to bring up Pearl Harbour, but that is not a good analogy. Whatever you think about it, the Japanese bombed military bases in two U.S. colonies—not the national territory....

This time it is the national territory that's been attacked on a large scale, so ... this is unique.

During these close to 200 years, we, the United States, have expelled or mostly exterminated the country's indigenous population—that's many millions of people. We have conquered half of Mexico, carried out depredations all over the region, Caribbean and Central America, and sometimes beyond. We conquered Hawaii and the Philippines, killing

On August 24, 1814, during the War of 1812, the British seized Washington and burned down the Capitol and the White House. On December 7, 1941, Japanese planes attacked the U.S. naval base at Pearl Harbor, Hawaii, bringing the United States into World War II.

hundreds of thousands of Filipinos in the process. Since the Second World War, the U.S. has extended its reach around the world in ways I don't have to describe. But it was always killing someone else, the fighting was somewhere else—it was others who were getting slaughtered.

In the case of Europe, the change is even more dramatic because its history is even more horrendous than that of the U.S. The U.S. is an offshoot of Europe, basically. For hundreds of years, Europe has been casually slaughtering people all over the world. That's how they conquered the world—not by handing out candy to babies....

But during this whole bloody, murderous period, it was Europeans slaughtering each other, and Europeans slaughtering people elsewhere. There are again small exceptions, but pretty small in scale.... This is the first change. The first time that the guns have been pointed the other way.

> In what way might the rest of the world perceive events in the United States differently from Americans?

The world looks very different depending on whether you are holding the lash, or whether you are being whipped by it for hundreds of years—very different. So I think the shock and surprise is very understandable. That is the reason why most of the rest of the world looks at it quite differently. Not lacking sympathy for the victims of the atrocity or being horrified by them, that is almost uniform—but viewing it from a different perspective. It is something we might want to understand.

Is the United States a terrorist state?

Well, let us go to the question of terrorism. What is the "war against terrorism"? The war against terrorism has been described in high places as a struggle against a plague, a cancer which is spread by barbarians, by "depraved opponents of civilisation itself".... I am quoting President Reagan and his secretary of state. The Reagan administration came into office 20 years ago declaring that the war against international terrorism would be the core of U.S. foreign policy....

> In 1981 the U.S. government began backing Contra rebels in Nicaragua who were attempting to overthrow the Marxist government, which the Reagan administration believed a threat to U.S. interests. Although Congress outlawed such activity, it continued—secretly and illegally—for several years.

The Reagan administration responded to this "plague spread by depraved opponents of civilisation itself" by creating an extraordinary international terrorist network, totally unprecedented in scale, which carried out massive atrocities all over the world. I will not run through the whole gamut of it, but just mention one case which is totally uncontroversial: the Reagan-U.S. War Against Nicaragua. It is uncontroversial because of the judgments of the highest international authorities: the International Court of Justice, the World Court and the UN Security Council. So this one is uncontroversial, at least among people who have some minimal concern for international law, human rights, justice and other things like that.

The case of Nicaragua is a particularly relevant one, not only because it is uncontroversial, but because it does offer a precedent as to how a law-abiding state would respond—did in fact respond—to a case of international terrorism, which is uncontroversial. A case of terrorism that was even more extreme than the events of 11 September. The Reagan–U.S. war against Nicaragua left tens of thousands of people dead, the country ruined, perhaps beyond recovery.

Nicaragua did respond. They did not respond by setting off bombs in Washington. They responded by taking the U.S. to the World Court, presenting a case for which they had no problem putting together evidence. The World Court ruled in Nicaragua's favour, and condemned what they called the "unlawful use of force," which is another term for international terrorism. They ordered the U.S. to terminate the crime and to pay massive reparations. The U.S., of course, dismissed the court judgment with total contempt and announced that it would not accept the jurisdiction of the court henceforth. Nicaragua then went to the UN Security Council, which considered a resolution calling on all states to observe international law. No one was mentioned but everyone understood. The U.S. vetoed the resolution. It now stands as the only state on record which has been condemned both by the World Court for international terrorism and has vetoed a Security Council resolution calling on states to observe international law.

Nicaragua then went to the UN General Assembly, where there is technically no veto, but a negative U.S. vote amounts to a veto. The General Assembly passed a similar resolution— with only the U.S., Israel, and El Salvador opposed. The following year Nicaragua took its case again to the General Assembly. This time the U.S. could only rally Israel to the cause, so two votes opposed observing international law. At that point, Nicaragua had exhausted all available legal measures, concluding that they do not work in a world that is ruled by force.

Terrorism, on the other hand does work, and is the weapon of the strong. It is a very serious analytic error to say, as is commonly done, that terrorism is the weapon of the weak. Like other means of violence, it is primarily a weapon of the strong—overwhelmingly, in fact. It is held to be a weapon of the weak because the strong also control the doctrinal systems and their terror does not count as terror.

If the United States' use of force in Nicaragua was unlawful, does it follow that the United States was guilty of terrorism?

See www.icj-cij.org for more about the World Court—or International Court of Justice (ICJ). Do you think the United States was right to disregard its findings?

Why might Israel support the United States when every other country chose not to? Go to http://www.lib. umich.edu/govdocs /usterror.html#arabis, and see if you can find out.

Summary

The author of the first article, from *The Nation,* asks three citizens of the
Kenyan capital Nairobi about claims that non-Western relief organizations
in the country are a front for terrorists. One argues that if poor countries
are ignored by the West, they may look for help from terrorist groups instead.
A lawyer argues that even if the West helps poor countries, it may not keep
terrorists out. He claims that political and religious extremism, not poverty,
causes terrorism. The third, a U.S. embassy official, says not all countries work
as "states" in the modern sense, which can make them a prey to terrorists.

Noam Chomsky counters that it is the strongest states that usually carry
out the worst acts of unlawful violence, which is how he defines terrorism.
He describes the withdrawal of aid from Afghanistan after September 11
as "genocide" and claims that President Reagan's administration committed
many acts that should be described as terrorism, including in Nicaragua.
He argues that terrorism is a weapon of the strong, not of the weak, and
that the strong are better able to disguise it as legitimate violence.

FURTHER INFORMATION:

Books:

Bergen, Peter L., *Holy War, Inc.: Inside the
Secret World of Osama Bin Laden*. New York:
Touchstone Books, 2002.
Chomsky, Noam, *9-11*, New York: Seven Stories, 2002.
Goodson, Larry P., *Afghanistan's Endless War: State
Failure, Regional Policy, and the Rise of the Taliban*.
Seattle, WA: University of Washington Press, 2001.

Useful websites:

www.cato.org/pubs/pas/pa429.pdf
"Old Folly in a New Disguise: Nation-building to Combat
Terrorism" by Gary T. Dempsey.
www.twq.com/02summer/rotberg.pdf
"The New Nature of Nation-State Failure" by
Robert L. Rotberg.
www.state.gov/p/af/rls/rm/7872.htm
"Weak States and Terrorism in Africa: U.S. Policy Options
in Somalia" by Walter Kansteiner.
www.twq.com/winter00/231Byman.pdf
"Afghanistan: The Consolidation of a Rogue State" by
Zalmay Khalilzad and Daniel Byman.
http://academicinfo.net/afghan.html
Good links to up-to-date articles on political events
in Afghanistan.

www.reliefweb.int
The United Nations' site provides information about
humanitarian operations, including on Afghanistan.
www.state.gov/s/ct/rls/pgtrpt/2001
State Department site with Counterterrorism Office's 2001
"Patterns of Global Terrorism" report.

The following debates in the Pro/Con series may also be of interest:

In this volume:

Topic 9 Should the United
States give aid to developing
countries irrespective of their
politics?

Topic 15 Should the United
States use military force
against nations that harbor
terrorists?

Part 4: Foreign Policy and
Terrorism

DOES TERRORISM ARISE FROM THE PROBLEM OF "FAILED STATES"?

YES: Poverty exacerbates anger and feelings of injustice. It can lead people to take desperate measures to change their circumstances.

YES: It is difficult to obtain arms and recruit people in states with strong and efficient law-enforcement agencies

POVERTY
Does poverty drive people to join terrorist organizations?

LAWLESSNESS
Do terrorist groups exploit the weak policing of failed states?

NO: Few suicide bombers are motivated by financial considerations. Terrorist leaders, including Osama Bin Laden, often come from wealthy backgrounds.

NO: Recruits for terrorist organizations are as likely to come from functioning states as from failed states

DOES TERRORISM ARISE FROM THE PROBLEM OF "FAILED STATES"?
KEY POINTS

YES: Acts of violence committed by democratic countries in order to preserve and strengthen democracy in the world are not acts of terrorism

YES: An act of terrorism is by definition something carried out by nonstate actors. It is not the same thing as "war," which is conducted by states.

DEFINING TERRORISM
Does the West define terrorism fairly?

NO: The United States and its allies have committed many unlawful acts of violence that they ought to acknowledge as terrorism

NO: If people who are desperate have no state to act for them, they have a legitimate right to improve their situation, even through violence

Topic 15

SHOULD THE UNITED STATES USE MILITARY FORCE AGAINST NATIONS THAT HARBOR TERRORISTS?

YES

"STATE SPONSORS OF TERRORISM SHOULD BE WIPED OUT, TOO"
AMERICAN ENTERPRISE INSTITUTE, SEPTEMBER 18, 2001
RICHARD N. PERLE

NO

"MAKING THE WORLD MORE DANGEROUS"
THE GUARDIAN, JULY 28, 2002
MARRACK GOULDING

INTRODUCTION

Soon after the terrorist attacks on New York and Washington, D.C., on September, 11, 2001, President George W. Bush pledged to "rid the world of evildoers" and declared that the United States was at war with terrorists. His words were directed not only against the world's terrorist networks, such as Osama Bin Laden's Al Qaeda organization, but also against any governments that sheltered terrorists and sponsored their activities.

The term "terrorist" is an emotional one that has always been open to wide interpretation. To some people a suicide bomber is a criminal mass-murderer, while to others he or she is a brave martyr, killing for a righteous cause. As the old saying goes: One person's terrorist is another person's freedom fighter. There is no better example of this contradiction than

Nelson Mandela (1918–), who in 1964 was sentenced to life imprisonment for acts of sabotage, treason, and violent conspiracy against the South African government. To black South Africans, however, Mandela was a hero who led resistance to the country's system of apartheid (ethnic segregation and discrimination). In 1990, with a change in South Africa's government and public opinion, Mandela was released from prison. The following year he was elected president of South Africa.

Until 2001 most terrorism targeted at the United States took place beyond its borders. U.S. Army personnel stationed in Lebanon, Saudi Arabia, and Yemen were all victims of terrorist attacks, and in 1998 American embassies were blown up in Kenya and Tanzania. After several of these attacks the United States responded with military force. Osama Bin Laden and

Al Qaeda were blamed for the African embassy bombings, and air strikes were launched against suspected bases in Afghanistan and Sudan. Over a decade earlier President Ronald Reagan had created the precedent for such action when he ordered the bombing of military and government targets in Libya. Reagan's orders were a response to the killing of American soldiers in a German discotheque in 1986, an attack linked to the Libyan regime run by Muammar Gaddafi.

> *"If we propose some principle that is applied to antagonists, then we must agree that the principle apply to us as well."*
>
> —NOAM CHOMSKY (1928–),
> POLITICAL COMMENTATOR

However, does this sort of unilateral military retaliation work in practice? In 1987 the United Nations (UN) drafted a resolution condemning terrorism in an attempt to reach international agreement on how to deal with the problem. The United States and Israel were the only member states to oppose the resolution, disagreeing with its wording that "Nothing in the present resolution could in any way prejudice the right to self-determination, freedom, and independence … particularly peoples under colonial and racist regimes and … foreign occupation."

Israel was concerned that the resolution would legitimize Palestinian action to end Israeli occupation of its territory. The United States withdrew its backing because the resolution made it harder to support South Africa—an important anticommunist ally at the time—and also because it would have prevented the U.S. government from dealing with terrorists as it saw fit.

During the early days of the War Against Terrorism Afghanistan was at the top of the list of terrorist states. The Taliban—the then ultraorthodox Islamic rulers of Afghanistan—provided a safe haven for Osama Bin Laden and Al Qaeda, and refused to give them up for investigation into their suspected terrorist activities. Following a UN mandate, a U.S.-dominated force allied with rebel Afghan factions attacked the Taliban in October 2001.

Within a matter of weeks the government in Afghanistan had been replaced. Nobody knows if Bin Laden survived, but thousands of his followers escaped. The United States retains the right to use force in self-defense against other states, such as Iraq, Iran, and Syria, which have links to anti-American terrorist activity.

In the first of the two articles that follow, former defense adviser Richard N. Perle argues that military action against terrorists can only reduce their operations. He believes that attacking the states that sponsor them would also put an end to their activities for good.

In contrast, the second article contends that military action does not solve the problems that drive terrorists to act in the first place. The author, former UN Under Secretary-General for Peacekeeping Marrack Goulding, argues that such action will simply make existing conflicts worse.

STATE SPONSORS OF TERRORISM SHOULD BE WIPED OUT, TOO
Richard N. Perle

"Vichyite" describes someone who collaborates with the enemy. The word originates from the town of Vichy in southern France, where some French leaders formed a new government in collaboration with the Nazis after the country surrendered to Germany in 1940.

Are sanctuary, intelligence, and so on really things that "only states can provide"?

YES

There is an air of Vichyite defeatism about some of the commentary in Britain on the current war on terrorism. We constantly hear the reiteration of such themes as "We don't know who the enemy is," "We don't know where to strike them," "Even if we could find them, it would simply create more martyrs" and that "The Wretched of the Earth" (to use the title of Franz Fanon's famous anti-colonial tract) are so desperate that they would not fear honourable death at the hands of what they see as the "Great Satan [United States]."

Need for decisive action
The U.S. Defence Secretary, Donald Rumsfeld, and other senior Administration officials are quite right to say that it is a totally new kind of war which the Free World now faces. But even though it is new, the Vichyite contingent would be quite wrong to extrapolate from that that the U.S. and its allies are impotent. Even if we don't yet know the whole story about last week's atrocities, we know enough to act, and to act decisively.

The truth is that the international community has not created a new world order in which sponsorship of terrorism by states is beyond the pale. Without the things that only states can provide—sanctuary, intelligence, logistics, training, communications, money—even the bin Laden network and others like it could manage only the occasional car bomb. Deprive the terrorists of the offices from which they now work, remove the vast infrastructure now supporting them and force them to sleep in a different place every night because they are hunted—and the scope of their activity will be sharply reduced.

Regimes supporting terrorism have many different motives. Some, such as Afghanistan, Iraq, Iran and Syria, do so because they agree with the fanatical outlook of their proteges. Saddam Hussein, crazed by a desire for vengeance, pays the families of suicide bombers. The Saudis tolerate terrorism out of fear and weakness, hoping thereby to deflect them on to other potential victims.

Precedent for applying pressure

We can, we must get governments out of the terrorism business. We do enjoy economic, political and military leverage over sovereign states, whose leaders do not crave martyrdom. There are, of course, precedents for such action. The Syrians permitted Armenian terrorists to operate freely from territory they control—until intolerable pressure from the Turkish government forced the Ba'athist regime to expel their "guests." This resulted in a precipitate drop in terrorist attacks.

In recent years, there has been no penalty for tolerating or even abetting terrorism. After the bombing of the United States al-Khobar barracks in Saudi Arabia in 1996, the local authorities feared the consequences of further aggravating the perpetrators more than they feared American displeasure, and the investigation went nowhere.

Lessons from the past

As the United States builds a coalition to combat terrorism, it must remember that including states that are themselves sponsors of terrorism, or ready to tolerate it, carries a heavy price. The last time around, in building the coalition to liberate Kuwait in 1990–1991, we paid a cost which we should never again bear.

For example, Syria was invited to join the Gulf war coalition. Its military contribution to the campaign was minimal, yet in exchange for getting inside the western tent it obtained the latitude to continue the use of and the sponsorship of terrorism—especially in Lebanon. It has continued to destabilise the region. There are those who argue that even Yasser Arafat, a terrorist himself, who has recruited suicide bombers, commemorated their murderous acts, and ordered the assassination of American diplomats, should join the campaign to combat terrorism.

Today, there is even talk about bringing Syria, Iran and Libya into a new anti-terrorism front. But if these regimes want to get into the creditors' club, as it were, then they must cease to be debtors. That means renouncing terrorism in word and apprehending terrorists in deed, now.

Repressive regimes must be excluded

Depth of genuine commitment to the anti-terrorist cause must not be sacrificed for the sake of breadth. In other words, breadth and "inclusivity" must not become ends in themselves, especially if they compromise the moral basis of avenging the slaughter of innocents.

The Ba'ath Party is the name of an Arab political party found in Iraq as well as in Syria. Its ideology is based on secularism, socialism, and union among all Arab states.

Since the terrorist attacks of September 11, 2001, the Bush administration has worked to build an international coalition against terrorism. The United Nations passed resolutions in 2001 and 2002 requiring states to take measures to combat terrorism.

Do you believe that former terrorists can successfully join the peace process? Doesn't that just reward the use of violence with political power?

Although he has been part of the political process since entering into peace talks with Israel in 1993, many people still see Palestinian leader Yasser Arafat as a terrorist.

For example, Iran has its own reasons for supporting military action against the Taliban regime in Afghanistan. But no one should confuse Iranian support for such action with an Iranian commitment to oppose terrorism. It is unthinkable that we could admit them into the coalition. An anti-terrorist coalition that has any reasonable prospect of success will be made up of countries that value democratic institutions, individual liberty and the sanctity of life.

It cannot include countries who repress their own people, violate fundamental human rights and scorn the fundamental values of western civilisation. Momentary, fleeting collaboration for immediate tactical advantage may make sense, as Churchill understood in joining with the Soviet Union to defeat Nazism. No coalition to defeat terrorism can include countries that countenance campaigns of hate and vilification. Countries that tolerate the incitement to kill civilians—Americans, Britons, Israelis and others—have no legitimate role in the war against terrorism.

Some countries may be unwilling or unable to participate in a coalition that demands a respect for the values and norms of western civilisation. The nature of their hold on power may be inconsistent with genuine opposition to terrorism. Such countries are part of the problem, not the solution, and we neither need their help nor would benefit from their professions of support.

War against regimes, not individuals

Those countries that harbour terrorists—that provide the means with which they would destroy innocent civilians— must themselves be destroyed. The war against terrorism is about the war against those regimes. We will not win the war against terror by chasing individual terrorists, any more than we will win the war against drugs by arresting the "mules" who pass through Heathrow. It is the networks that send young men on suicide missions and their sponsors that must be destroyed.

Should the United States only form partnerships or coalitions with other democracies? How successful would the Gulf War have been without the support of Saudi Arabia? Is the author being realistic here, do you think?

Does the United States, as the world's only superpower, actually ever need help from other nations?

Do you agree with Perle that the only way to combat terrorism is to go after the countries that harbor terrorists rather than individuals?

MAKING THE WORLD MORE DANGEROUS
Marrack Goulding

Sir Marrack Goulding is the former under secretary for political affairs at the United Nations 1993–1997. He was chief peacekeeper at the UN for seven years.

President George Bush called for a "war" against terror after September 11. But is war the right way to deal with the likes of Osama Bin Laden and Al-Qaeda? Here a self-confessed "bleeding heart" answers no to that. It's an assessment based on years in charge of the UN's [United Nations] peacekeeping operations.

The attacks on September 11 were unparalleled in their ingenuity, in their planning and in the political, material and psychological impact they had on the terrorist's enemy. They revealed that a clandestine group could set up a worldwide network and that that network, using modern communications and other technology, could, out of the blue, launch simultaneous and devastating attacks on two cities in the most powerful country in the world. The resources used by the terrorist network—estimated at less than $100,000— amounted to only a tiny proportion of the costs of more than $400 billion faced by the victim....

This contradicts what the author of the previous article said. He argued that with limited funds, terrorists would "manage only the occasional car bomb."

First moves

In the aftermath of September 11, the Bush administration launched a huge effort to discover how this disaster had come about and take action to ensure that those responsible for it were punished and that it would not be repeated.

Initially there seemed to be grounds for hoping that Washington would draw on lessons about how to deal with conflict which the international community had learnt since the end of the Cold War. Much, for instance, was said about the need to clarify what had motivated nineteen educated young men to sacrifice their lives in this way. This implied recognition that conflicts cannot be resolved unless their root causes are addressed. Washington already knew that there was great resentment at American policy in the Arab and Muslim worlds. After September 11, there were signs that the U.S. and its allies recognised that, if future attacks were to be prevented, a more serious effort was needed to resolve existing conflicts such as those between Israel and the Arabs, between the United States and Iraq and— though this was not much mentioned at the time—the very dangerous conflict in Kashmir.

The Cold War started to end in 1989 with the fall of communist governments in Eastern Europe. Finally, on December 25, 1991, the Soviet Union ceased to exist.

What aspects of foreign policy have led to resentment in the Arab and Muslim worlds, do you think?

It was also said that an international coalition should be created to try to ensure that such attacks were never repeated. This seemed to indicate recognition … that a campaign against an aggressor gains legitimacy and effectiveness if it is carried out by a large and representative group of countries, as was demonstrated by the coalition so successfully assembled by Washington to liberate Kuwait in 1991.

The hope that a similar coalition would be formed this time was strengthened by the UN Security Council's adoption, on September 28, of a U.S.-sponsored resolution requiring all member states to report in detail on the measures they had taken to block the formation of terrorist networks on their territories and the further measures they had in mind.

Military action was, of course, being prepared to punish those responsible for September 11 and to destroy their capacity to launch further attacks, but there was in those early days as much talk of political as of military action.

How would foreigners have seen the United States if it had not used military force against Al Qaeda? How would Americans have seen themselves?

The wrong road

If these priorities had prevailed, it would have been possible to say that September 11 had to some extent helped international peacemaking by enhancing the legitimacy and effectiveness of the techniques developed since the end of the Cold War to deal with regional conflicts in Africa, Central America and Southeast Asia.

But that, alas, did not happen. The wisdom of the initial reaction to the New York and Washington attacks was overtaken by President George Bush's declaration of a "war" on terror. This borrowing from the political vocabulary of Israel had a number of unfortunate consequences. It implied that military action was to be the primary response to the terrorist attacks, and that little interest remained in finding political ways of removing factors that had made the terrorist attacks possible. It also implied that, as often happens in war, civil liberties might be curtailed … if this was deemed necessary in order to win the war. That has happened in the United States and other countries. In addition, Bush invited states to declare that they were with the United States in its assault on terror. To fail to do so or to question its wisdom or legitimacy was tantamount to supporting terrorism.

What "factors … made the terrorist attacks possible"? How could such factors be removed using political, rather than military, means?

This declaration rolled out a bandwagon on to which a number of other leaders jumped. Those who were facing insurrections in their own countries or in territories occupied by them were delighted to be able to say that forceful military action against their opponents was all part of the war on terror.

Israeli Prime Minister Ariel Sharon is the obvious example here. Can you think of any others?

Is it possible to see Palestinian suicide bombers as anything but terrorists?

Finally, Bush seemed to sympathise with Israeli Prime Minister Ariel Sharon's position that Palestinian opposition to Israel's occupation of the West Bank and the Gaza Strip is to be characterised as terror. This led him to espouse the view that there can be no negotiation until all violence has ceased. This was, and is, a mistake. It is not the norm to delay peace negotiations until violence has ended. The norm in conflicts which the U.N. helped to resolve after the end of the Cold War was that talks began while the fighting continued. Fighting often reached its most intense level on the eve of the final agreement. If we had insisted that there could be no negotiation before fighting stopped, there would have been no peace settlement in Namibia, Cambodia, Mozambique, El Salvador, Guatemala or Bosnia. Moreover, if you say that there can be no talks unless violence ends, you are putting the peace process into the hands of the extremists on both sides. It takes only one terrorist to bring it to a halt….

The new context

It can however be argued that the September attacks were unprecedented and quite different in kind from the interstate and civil wars in which the international community developed its current techniques for peacemaking, peacekeeping and peacebuilding and that those techniques would not therefore have worked successfully.

Why would it be difficult to negotiate with Osama Bin Laden and Al Qaeda using traditional methods? Is there any point in negotiating at all?

There is some force in that argument. September 11 did introduce us to a new and frightening threat and new techniques must be developed to deal with it. But those techniques should not be exclusively military nor should they be applied in a way that strengthens the grievances which facilitated the organisation and execution of the terrorist attacks. It is far from evident that military action is an effective way of destroying terrorist networks. The first defence of democratic countries against such networks should be their domestic and external intelligence services and their systems of criminal justice….

If proven terrorists cannot be brought to justice because they are not within our jurisdiction, there may be a case for using force of arms to eliminate them. But such actions can easily backfire, as Britain found when its forces killed IRA [Irish Republican Army] terrorists in Gibraltar.

In 1988 members of the Special Air Service (SAS) Regiment shot dead three IRA terrorists who were planning to plant a bomb in Gibraltar, a British colony. However, the terrorists were unarmed, and the operation turned into a propaganda disaster for the British government.

It doesn't work

Major punitive operations of the kind which the United States and some of its allies have been engaged in in Afghanistan and which Israel is currently undertaking in the occupied Palestinian territories seem even more likely to be counterproductive. First, as U.S. Defense Secretary Donald Rumsfeld shows us daily, it is difficult to avoid giving the impression that revenge is the primary purpose of the operations.

Secondly, they inevitably cause unintended collateral damage. The technology may be brilliant but it cannot ensure that only proven terrorists are eliminated. The blowing away of a wedding party because someone is foolish enough to fire a rifle in the air just fuels the hatred that led to the earlier terrorism. The arrogance of invading forces and their sometimes brutal treatment of civilians has the same effect.

Thirdly, there is the question of what happens next, after the invading forces have destroyed the institutions of the country or territory that has been harbouring terrorists. If there are no longer any functioning political and administrative institutions, how will it be possible to negotiate agreements to prevent the re-establishment of terrorist facilities? And who will have the authority to implement agreements if these can be negotiated?... What the international community, led by the West, needs to do is what it has done in Bosnia and Kosovo: blanket the country with a substantial political and military presence for at least five years—preferably more—until an effective government is in place to provide security and justice for its citizens.

Setbacks to conflict resolution

The horrible events of September 11 and the reaction to them of the United States and some of its allies, especially Britain, have disrupted the laborious progress towards developing peaceful means of preventing and resolving conflict between states, or between states and non-state actors, of whom Osama Bin Laden is one. The horrors were different, at least in size and impact, from what happened in earlier conflicts, and if international peacemaking has been hindered by them, the responsibility and the blame clearly lie with the originators of the attacks on New York and Washington.

Nevertheless, the reliance on military action in the aftermath of September 11 has been a major setback for two reasons. It will not stop future terrorist attacks. On the contrary, it is likely to stimulate them by fuelling hatred and the desire for revenge. It has also returned us to the age of Ronald Reagan, when military action was the favoured response to trouble in the third world and political action, if considered at all, was a secondary option.

> *Why is it counter-productive to give the impression that the United States is taking revenge for the attacks of September 11?*

> *Do you think the author is correct in his assessment that the action taken by the United States in Afghanistan or in the future will likely provoke further terrorist attacks?*

Summary

Richard Perle begins his argument by rebutting another made by people opposed to plans to use military force against terrorists. He says that contrary to the belief of these opponents, military action could be targeted at the perpetrators of an atrocity and would not kill more innocents than guilty. He says that military action will keep targeted terrorists on the run so they cannot regroup and plan more attacks. Turning his attention to states that shelter terrorists, Perle gives examples of how terrorists have been allowed to operate with impunity in certain nations. He explains that some of these nations were included in the UN coalition during the Gulf War, even though they were sponsoring terrorism at the time. Perle says that such compromises should never be made in the War on Terror since the only way to defeat terrorism is to destroy the states and networks that sponsor it.

Marrack Goulding outlines his disappointment that the United States chose to take military action after the September 11 attacks. He also argues that President Bush's use of the word "war" to describe the response has been copied by leaders around the world, allowing them to escalate their own conflicts and gain support from the United States. Although the size of the attacks on America was unprecedented, Marrack says that this is no reason not to explore political solutions. He argues that military force should only be used if terrorists lie outside of the jurisdiction of a democratic state. Marrack predicts that a military campaign to remove a terrorist state will fail in the long run. It would look like revenge, it would kill innocent people, and peacekeeping forces would have to fill the resulting power vacuum for years.

FURTHER INFORMATION:

Books:

Carr, Caleb, *The Lessons of Terror: A History of Warfare against Civilians*. New York: Random House, 2002.
Corbin, Jane, *Al Qaeda: In Search of the Terror Network That Threatens the World*. New York: Thunder's Mouth Press/Nation Books, 2002.
Hamilton, John, *Behind the Terror (War on Terrorism)*. Minneapolis, MN: Abdo & Daughters, 2002.

Articles:

The Friends Committee on National Legislation (FCNL), "If Not War, Then What? Alternatives to the 'War Against Terror.'" *FCNL*, January 2002.

 Useful websites:

www.lib.umich.edu/govdocs/usterror.html
The University of Michigan Documents Center. A comprehensive source on the attacks of September 11, previous terrorist attacks, background information on the terrorists, states that harbor terrorists, and so on.

The following debates in the Pro/Con series may also be of interest:

In this volume:
Topic 1 Does the United States have a duty to protect democracy and freedom overseas?

Topic 13 Is modern terrorism different from terrorism in previous centuries?

SHOULD THE UNITED STATES USE MILITARY FORCE AGAINST NATIONS THAT HARBOR TERRORISTS?

YES: Any decision to use military force to find terrorists must have the backing of the United Nations

YES: The United States intelligence services are the best experts in identifying anti-American terrorists

UNITED NATIONS
Should any military action have the support of the United Nations?

TERRORIST OR FREEDOM FIGHTER?
Is it up to the United States to decide which terrorists to attack?

NO: The UN is a peacekeeping organization; it is not in its interests to resolve conflicts by military force

NO: It should be left to the international community to decide if military action against a rebel group is acceptable

SHOULD THE UNITED STATES USE MILITARY FORCE AGAINST NATIONS THAT HARBOR TERRORISTS?

KEY POINTS

YES: Attacks on states harboring terrorists will remove terrorists' access to finance and other forms of support; terrorist networks will be undermined for good

YES: Terrorists cannot plan new attacks if they are always on the run from the military

FORCE
Will military force prevent future terrorist attacks?

NO: There is no precedent of a terrorist campaign being ended by violence, only by dialogue

NO: Resentment against U.S. military action will only serve to encourage more people to become terrorists

Topic 16
SHOULD THE UNITED STATES TAKE MORE RESPONSIBILITY FOR PROMOTING PEACE IN THE MIDDLE EAST?

YES
"U.S. MUST TAKE A RISK ON MID-EAST"
THE AUSTRALIAN FINANCIAL REVIEW, APRIL 8, 2002
PHILIP H. GORDON

NO
"PRESIDENT TO SEND SECRETARY POWELL TO MIDDLE EAST"
SPEECH IN THE ROSE GARDEN, APRIL 4, 2002
GEORGE W. BUSH

INTRODUCTION

For centuries there has been unrest in the Middle East, much of it centering on the land at the Eastern end of the Mediterranean Sea that has variously been called Palestine and Israel. Jewish settlement of Palestine began in the 18th century, when it was ruled by the Turkish Ottoman Empire. When the Turks left in 1916, Palestine came under a British mandate, and in 1917 the Balfour Declaration established support for the creation of a Jewish national home in Palestine that respected the rights of the majority Arab population.

When the British mandate ended in 1947, the United Nations (UN) recommended that Palestine be divided between the Arabs and Jews. Fighting broke out between Arab and Jewish armies that resulted in the creation of the state of Israel in 1948. A series of wars followed, most significantly in 1967, when territories exceeding the

UN boundaries, including the Golan Heights and the West Bank, were ceded to Israel.

Israel continued its expansionist policy of creating settlements close to Arab communities. In 1987 a Palestinian revolt, the intifada, began in the Gaza Strip and West Bank. Israel and Jordan signed a peace treaty in 1994 that led to Israel's withdrawal from the Gaza Strip and most of the West Bank by 1996, when the Palestinians took control of those areas. But negotiations for a final settlement broke down, and violence erupted again in 2000.

By late 2002 the Israeli–Palestinian conflict was spiraling out of control. A wave of attacks by young Palestinian suicide bombers followed on civilian targets in both Israeli and Jewish settlements in the Occupied Territories, land claimed by Palestinians, but under Israeli military occupation. In response

Israeli forces targeted suspected terrorist enclaves in Palestinian towns and refugee camps. The violence escalated by the day.

This was the situation facing President George W. Bush's government. How should it use its influence to promote a lasting settlement to this bitter quarrel? Should it get more closely involved? Those who agree with the last question point to many reasons why the United States should play a stronger role in solving the Israeli–Palestinian problem. First, there is the moral issue. As the world's superpower, the United States has a duty to end further violence in the area.

"Only a negotiated settlement can resolve the conflict between Israelis and Palestinians."

—COLIN POWELL,

SECRETARY OF STATE,

APRIL 17, 2002

Second is the question of U.S. interests. U.S. support for Israel already puts pressure on U.S.-Arab relations. Failure to step in could be seen as an abandonment of the Palestinians, which would further discredit the United States in Arab eyes. At risk would be U.S. commercial interests, the use of military bases in the region, and even the free flow of Middle Eastern oil.

In the wake of George W. Bush's declaration of a war on terrorism following the events of September 11, 2001, America's allies in the Arab world

stressed that achieving a just settlement to the Israeli–Palestinian conflict was an essential prerequisite to defeating terrorism. As long as the Arabs resented the Israelis, they said, terrorists would find no shortage of recruits fueled by a hatred of Israel and also of its supporter, the United States.

Those people who would prefer the United States to limit its role in the Israeli–Palestinian conflict counter that some 30 years of U.S. diplomatic intervention in the region have had little success in bringing about peace. They point to the failure of President Bill Clinton's administration in brokering a deal between Israel and the Palestinian Authority.

Some people also argue that since the collapse of the Soviet Union in 1991 the United States' attention in the Middle East has shifted to Saddam Hussein's Iraq. On the subject of terrorism, meanwhile, many people take issue with those who see a just settlement as the way to end the terror. They argue that Palestinian suicide bombers are terrorists and are therefore enemies in the war on terrorism.

The following two pieces present differing views on how the United States should handle this issue. The author of the "yes" argument, Philip H. Gordon, believes that the United States must be more proactive in trying to resolve the Middle East crisis. He says it should move heaven and earth to bring the parties together since failure to do so will have dire consequences. The "no" argument is the transcript of a 2002 speech by Bush on the Middle East. It outlines his administration's policy for the region that in essence calls for an end to Palestinian violence and a withdrawal of Israeli forces as a condition of renewed talks.

U.S. MUST TAKE A RISK ON MID-EAST
Philip H. Gordon

YES

☑️ As world leaders and experts … debate the reasons for and ways to stop the violence that is spinning out of control in the Middle East, they seem to agree on only one thing: the United States needs to do something, and fast.

All these observers, of course, have different views as to what that "something" should be, and the United States itself, reluctant to take the political risk of failing, seems unable to decide among the options.

President Bush's decision last week to send Secretary of State Colin Powell to the region for consultations, and his phone call to Israeli Prime Minister Ariel Sharon, were positive steps toward greater engagement, but with the situation rapidly spinning out of control the most striking thing about the US initiative was its modesty.

Failed summit and fighting on the ground

The impression of an America reluctant to get bogged down in the Arab-Israeli dispute results in part from the Bush administration's initial philosophy about the conflict. Bush saw how much his predecessor, Bill Clinton, invested in seeking a resolution to the conflict, and he also saw the result: a failed Camp David summit and fighting on the ground.

With other foreign policy priorities—building a national missile defense, changing the regime in Iraq, and after September 11 of course the war on terrorism—Bush had little desire to tackle the situation between Israelis and Palestinians. The administration put the conflict in the "too hard" box, significantly downgraded the level of engagement, and hoped that things would work themselves out, or at least that the violence would not get out of hand.

That approach is now unsustainable. With the death toll on both sides continuing to rise, order in the Palestinian territories rapidly disintegrating, and the entire Arab world erupting with anger at Israel and the United States, the costs of American inaction are rapidly becoming greater than the costs of action, whatever the risks.

It is, of course, unfair to blame Bush or any Americans for what is going on. The responsibility for the current conflict lies primarily with the parties on the ground, their

What is the "risk" for the United States of being seen to "fail" in the Middle East?

Ariel Sharon, a former senior army officer, became prime minister of Israel in February 2001. For more biographical detail go to www. us-israel.org/ jsource/biography/ sharon.html.

The Palestinian territories comprise parts of the West Bank and the Gaza Strip. These areas, within what is called the Occupied Territories, have been under limited Palestinian rule since 1994. For a map go to www. pbs.org/newshour/ bb/middle_east/ conflict/map.html.

Should the United States take more responsibility for promoting peace in the Middle East?

Israel's Prime Minister Ariel Sharon (left) with Secretary of State Colin Powell in Jerusalem, April 12, 2002. Powell's visit to Israel was part of an attempt by President George W. Bush to achieve a cease-fire between Palestinians and Israelis. It failed, however, to halt the violence.

predecessors over the past years and decades, and the basic structural factor of different peoples wanting to live on the same land.

Still, while there is no guarantee that greater US engagement from the start would have avoided or limited the current violence, it should have always been clear to the administration that leaving the parties to themselves was not going to work—and it is certainly not going to work now.

Even more clear is that by appearing to stand aside, Bush gave the impression to the world—and especially to the Arab world—that the United States, obsessed with Iraq and beholden to Israel, did not really care about Palestinian casualties or the Palestinian state of affairs. The result is that Bush is being blamed for the tragedy unfolding during his watch, whether he could in fact have done anything about it or not.

Cease-fire first demand will not work

So what to do now? The current approach, of insisting on a cease-fire before any serious political process begins—or before senior administration leaders get directly involved—will not work. Bush and other administration officials can keep repeating the need to stop the violence and to implement the Tenet and Mitchell plans until they are blue in the face, but doing so will have no effect, however right they might be on the level of principle.

Another option the administration is considering—to unambiguously support Sharon's efforts to use force to crush the Palestinian terrorist infrastructure—would also fail. This approach, reportedly backed by a range of administration hard-liners, would have the merits of showing the Palestinians that terror does not pay, would be consistent with the principles of Bush's war on terrorism, and would presumably be popular with pro-Israel voters at home.

The problem, however, is that, like the current approach, it would also have little prospect of bringing about long-term success. Palestinian violence and terrorism would continue, Israelis would get stuck trying to manage several million unwilling Palestinians on the West Bank and in Gaza, and U.S. cooperation with the Arab world—not least for a potential military operation in Iraq—would become vastly more difficult.

Thus the only real option for the administration is a risky one: to try to start a political process at the same time that it seeks a cease-fire, seeking to offer both sides a way to save face, claim victory, and go home.

The Tenet and Mitchell plans are formulas for peace between Israel and the Palestinians. Former Senator George Mitchell led an international fact-finding committee, which produced its report and recommendations at the end of April 2001. CIA Director George Tenet proposed his cease-fire plan in June of the same year. For details of the plans go to www.cbsnews. com/stories/ 2002/04/03/world/ main505244.shtml.

Does America's failure to support military action against the Palestinians contradict the aims of the War Against Terrorism? Do you think that all terrorists are as bad as each other?

To do this, Bush would probably have to take the political risk of calling for an international conference—perhaps together with Arab and European leaders—that would seek to offer Israelis and Palestinians a track toward a political outcome that they will now never agree upon by themselves.

Bush and the other leaders would have to put themselves on record as supporting a peace plan not too different from the one Clinton offered in his final weeks in office, and which almost everyone agrees must be the basis for a final settlement. With broad international backing—perhaps including a UN seal of approval, American peacekeeping forces, European and Arab money for reconstruction, and an end to conflict based on a two-state solution—the parties might, just might, end their logic of war.

There would be no guarantees, and of course Bush could end up with a failed summit on his hands just like the predecessor whose efforts he once scorned. But with the situation on the ground rapidly deteriorating, risking potential failure seems wiser than accepting the certain failure unfolding before our eyes.

Having failed to broker a peace between Israel and the Palestinians at Camp David in the summer of 2000, then President Bill Clinton made another attempt to reach a settlement that winter. To read excerpts from the Clinton peace plan, visit www. us-israel.org/ jsource/Peace/ clintplan.html.

PRESIDENT TO SEND SECRETARY POWELL TO MIDDLE EAST
George W. Bush

NO

The President: Good morning. During the course of one week, the situation in the Middle East has deteriorated dramatically. Last Wednesday, my Special Envoy, Anthony Zinni, reported to me that we were on the verge of a cease-fire agreement that would have spared Palestinian and Israeli lives.

That hope fell away when a terrorist attacked a group of innocent people in a Netanya hotel, killing many men and women in what is a mounting toll of terror.

In the days since, the world has watched with growing concern the horror of bombings and burials and the stark picture of tanks in the street. Across the world, people are grieving for Israelis and Palestinians who have lost their lives.

When an 18-year-old Palestinian girl is induced to blow herself up, and in the process kills a 17-year-old Israeli girl, the future, itself, is dying—the future of the Palestinian people and the future of the Israeli people. We mourn the dead, and we mourn the damage done to the hope of peace, the hope of Israel's and the Israelis' desire for a Jewish state at peace with its neighbors; the hope of the Palestinian people to build their own independent state.

No negotiations with terrorists
Terror must be stopped. No nation can negotiate with terrorists. For there is no way to make peace with those whose only goal is death.

This could be a hopeful moment in the Middle East. The proposal of Crown Prince Abdullah of Saudi Arabia, supported by the Arab League, has put a number of countries in the Arab world closer than ever to recognizing Israel's right to exist. The United States is on record supporting the legitimate aspirations of the Palestinian people for a Palestinian state.

Israel has recognized the goal of a Palestinian state. The outlines of a just settlement are clear: two states, Israel and Palestine, living side by side, in peace and security.

This can be a time for hope. But it calls for leadership, not for terror. Since September the 11th, I've delivered this message: everyone must choose; you're either with the

Can you think of any reasons why so many Palestinian bombers are young people? Do you think it is because young people are more idealistic? Or perhaps because they are put under pressure to act by their elders?

The Arab League, or League of Arab Nations, was formed in Cairo in March 1945 to aid coordination and cooperation among members. To learn more, visit www.infoplease. com/ce6/history/ A0804481.html. To place Crown Prince Abdullah's peace plan in context, go to www.cbsnews. com/stories/2002/ 04/03/world/ main505244.shtml.

civilized world, or you're with the terrorists. All in the Middle East also must choose and must move decisively in word and deed against terrorist acts....

At Oslo and elsewhere, Chairman Arafat renounced terror as an instrument of his cause, and he agreed to control it. He's not done so.

The situation in which he finds himself today is largely of his own making. He's missed his opportunities, and thereby betrayed the hopes of the people he's supposed to lead. Given his failure, the Israeli government feels it must strike at terrorist networks that are killing its citizens.

Yet, Israel must understand that its response to these recent attacks is only a temporary measure. All parties have their own responsibilities. And all parties owe it to their own people to act.

We all know today's situation runs the risk of aggravating long-term bitterness and undermining relationships that are critical to any hope of peace. I call on the Palestinian people, the Palestinian Authority and our friends in the Arab world to join us in delivering a clear message to terrorists: blowing yourself up does not help the Palestinian cause. To the contrary, suicide bombing missions could well blow up the best and only hope for a Palestinian state.

Not martyrs but murderers

All states must keep their promise, made in a vote in the United Nations to actively oppose terror in all its forms. No nation can pick and choose its terrorist friends. I call on the Palestinian Authority and all governments in the region to do everything in their power to stop terrorist activities, to disrupt terrorist financing, and to stop inciting violence by glorifying terror in state-owned media, or telling suicide bombers they are martyrs. They're not martyrs. They're murderers. And they undermine the cause of the Palestinian people.

Those governments, like Iraq, that reward parents for the sacrifice of their children are guilty of soliciting murder of the worst kind. All who care about the Palestinian people should join in condemning and acting against groups ... which opposed the peace process and seek the destruction of Israel.

The recent Arab League support of Crown Prince Abdullah's initiative for peace is promising, is hopeful, because it acknowledges Israel's right to exist. And it raises the hope of sustained, constructive Arab involvement in the search for peace. This builds on a tradition of visionary leadership, begun by President Sadat and King Hussein, and carried forward by President Mubarak and King Abdullah.

Yasser Arafat (1929–) is president of the Palestinian Authority and has been involved in the Arab-Israeli conflict since the 1940s. For a biography go to www.us-israel.org/jsource/biography/arafat.html. The 1993 Oslo Accord paved the way for limited Palestinian self-rule. For more on this visit www.cnn.com/interactive/specials/0007/mideast.documents/oslo.html.

Abdullah ibn Abdul Aziz (1924–) is crown prince of Saudi Arabia. Anwar al-Sadat (1918–1981) was president of Egypt from 1970 to 1981, when he was assassinated and succeeded by Hosni Mubarak (1928–). King Hussein of Jordan (1935–1999) was succeeded by his son, Abdullah II (1962–).

Now, other Arab states must rise to this occasion and accept Israel as a nation and as a neighbor. Peace with Israel is the only avenue to prosperity and success for a new Palestinian state. The Palestinian people deserve peace and an opportunity to better their lives. They need their closest neighbor, Israel, to be an economic partner, not a mortal enemy. They deserve a government that respects human rights and a government that focuses on their needs—education and health care—rather than feeding their resentments.

It is not enough for Arab nations to defend the Palestinian cause. They must truly help the Palestinian people by seeking peace and fighting terror and promoting development.

United Nations Security Council Resolution 242 was adopted after the Arab–Israeli War of 1967 and includes a call for Israel to withdraw from the territories it had occupied (among them the West Bank and Gaza Strip). Resolution 338 was adopted during the 1973 Arab–Israeli War. It reiterates 242 and calls for talks for "a just and durable peace." To read the resolutions, go to www.usembassy-israel.org.il/publish/peace/242.htm and www.usembassy-israel.org.il/publish/peace/338.htm.

Hard choices

Israel faces hard choices of its own. Its government has supported the creation of a Palestinian state that is not a haven for terrorism. Yet, Israel also must recognize that such a state needs to be politically and economically viable.

Consistent with the Mitchell plan, Israeli settlement activity in occupied territories must stop. And the occupation must end through withdrawal to secure and recognized boundaries consistent with United Nations Resolutions 242 and 338. Ultimately, this approach should be the basis of agreements between Israel and Syria and Israel and Lebanon.

Israel should also show a respect, a respect for and concern about the dignity of the Palestinian people who are and will be their neighbors. It is crucial to distinguish between the terrorists and ordinary Palestinians seeking to provide for their own families.

The Israeli government should be compassionate at checkpoints and border crossings, sparing innocent Palestinians daily humiliation. Israel should take immediate action to ease closures and allow peaceful people to go back to work.

Israel is facing a terrible and serious challenge. For seven days, it has acted to root out terrorist nests. America recognizes Israel's right to defend itself from terror. Yet, to lay the foundations of future peace, I ask Israel to halt incursions into Palestinian-controlled areas and begin the withdrawal from those cities it has recently occupied.

I speak as a committed friend of Israel. I speak out of a concern for its long-term security, a security that will come with a genuine peace. As Israel steps back, responsible Palestinian leaders and Israel's Arab neighbors must step forward and show the world that they are truly on the side of peace. The choice and the burden will be theirs.

The world expects an immediate cease-fire, immediate resumption of security cooperation with Israel against terrorism. An immediate order to crack down on terrorist networks. I expect better leadership, and I expect results.

These are the elements of peace in the Middle East. And now, we must build the road to those goals. Decades of bitter experience teach a clear lesson: progress is impossible when nations emphasize their grievances and ignore their opportunities. Storms of violence cannot go on. Enough is enough.

And to those who would try to use the current crisis as an opportunity to widen the conflict, stay out. Iran's arms shipments and support for terror fuel the fire of conflict in the Middle East. And it must stop. Syria has spoken out against Al Qaeda. We expect it to act against Hamas and Hezbollah, as well. It's time for Iran to focus on meeting its own people's aspirations for freedom and for Syria to decide which side of the war against terror it is on.

Al Qaeda, Hamas, and Hezbollah are terrorist groups. For profiles visit http://library.nps. navy.mil/home/tgp/ tgpndx.htm#2000.

Powell's quest for support

The world finds itself at a critical moment. This is a conflict that can widen or an opportunity we can seize. And so I've decided to send Secretary of State Powell to the region next week to seek broad international support for the vision I've outlined today. As a step in this process, he will work to implement United Nations Resolution 1402, an immediate and meaningful cease-fire, an end to terror and violence and incitement; withdrawal of Israeli troops from Palestinian cities, including Ramallah; implementation of the already agreed upon Tenet and Mitchell plans, which will lead to a political settlement....

UN Security Council Resolution 1402 was adopted on March 30, 2002, in view of the worsening Middle East situation. It included a call for a cease fire and the withdrawal of Israeli troops from Palestinian cities. To read the resolution, go to www.state. gov/p/io/rls/othr/ 2002/9105.htm.

We have no illusions about the difficulty of the issues that lie ahead. Yet, our nation's resolve is strong. America is committed to ending this conflict and beginning an era of peace.

We know this is possible, because in our lifetimes we have seen an end to conflicts that no one thought could end. We've seen fierce enemies let go of long histories of strife and anger. America itself counts former adversaries as trusted friends: Germany and Japan and now Russia.

Conflict is not inevitable. Distrust need not be permanent. Peace is possible when we break free of old patterns and habits of hatred. The violence and grief that troubled the Holy Land have been among the great tragedies of our time. The Middle East has often been left behind in the political and economic advancement of the world. That is the history of the region. But it need not and must not be its fate....

Summary

The difference in the views expressed by President George W. Bush and foreign policy expert Philip H. Gordon is one of emphasis. In his speech of April 4, 2002, and in subsequent pronouncements on the issue the president lays great stress on the need first and foremost to end the violence—"Enough is enough." But any cycle of violence and retaliation can be viewed from two sides. From Bush's speech it is clear that he sees Palestinian terrorism, in particular the suicide bombings, as the prime cause and the Israeli incursions into Palestinian-controlled areas as the response. So while he calls on the Israelis to stop their incursions and begin withdrawing, the burden of his speech is directed at Yasser Arafat, who, according to Bush, has not used his influence to stop the violence. The president repeats his familiar challenge, "You're either with the civilized world, or you're with the terrorists."

Philip H. Gordon believes the president needs to be more proactive, despite the specter of failure, because the United States is being blamed for the tragedy "whether he [Bush] could in fact have done anything about it or not." As Gordon points out, "leaving the parties to themselves was not going to work"; nor is the insistence on a cease-fire before serious negotiations can begin; nor would supporting the Israeli prime minister's efforts "to crush the Palestinian terrorist infrastructure." According to Gordon, the United States has no alternative but to take the plunge and set to work for a political settlement at the same time as demanding a cease-fire—even though there are no guarantees of success.

FURTHER INFORMATION:

Books:

Bard, Mitchell Geoffrey, *Myths and Facts: A Guide to the Arab–Israeli Conflict.* Chevy Chase, MD: American–Israeli Cooperative Enterprise, 2001.

Journalists of Reuters, *The Israeli–Palestinian Conflict: Crisis in the Middle East.* Upper Saddle River, NJ: Prentice Hall, 2002.

Mattar, Philip (ed.), *Encyclopedia of the Palestinians.* New York: Facts on File Inc., 2000.

Neff, Donald, *50 Years of Israel.* Washington, D.C.: American Educational Trust, 1998.

Useful websites:

http://fyi.cnn.com/fyi/interactive/0108/mideast
CNN Middle East backgrounder.

www.us-israel.org
Jewish Virtual Library—a division of the American–Israeli Cooperative Enterprise.

www.wrmea.com
The Washington Report on Middle East Affairs site.

The following debates in the Pro/Con series may also be of interest:

In this volume:

Topic 1 Does the United States have a duty to protect democracy and freedom overseas?

Topic 2 Is U.S. foreign policy too interventionist?

Topic 4 Should the United States show a greater commitment to the UN?

SHOULD THE UNITED STATES TAKE MORE RESPONSIBILITY FOR PROMOTING PEACE IN THE MIDDLE EAST?

YES: Negotiating with the Palestinians while suicide bombings continue is inconsistent with the war on terrorism

YES: Seeming to do nothing makes the administration look uncaring and has angered the Arab world

PRECONDITIONS
Is America right to insist on a cease-fire before negotiations can begin?

INFLUENCE
Should the United States do more to curtail Israeli military operations?

NO: Realistically there will be no end to terrorism unless the Palestinians feel that they are making some progress

NO: Only the Palestinian leadership can stamp out terrorism, and Israel's response is appropriate as a temporary measure

SHOULD THE UNITED STATES TAKE MORE RESPONSIBILITY FOR PROMOTING PEACE IN THE MIDDLE EAST?

KEY POINTS

YES: The United States must provide leadership. The parties cannot resolve the issue alone.

YES: The United States must intervene decisively and promote a cease-fire and a political process simultaneously

LEADERSHIP
Is U.S. leadership indispensable to an Israeli–Palestinian settlement?

NO: Arab governments must step forward and take a full part in the peace process

NO: It is not within U.S. power to broker a lasting peace, as years of trying have demonstrated

GLOSSARY

Al Qaeda an international terrorist group led by Osama Bin Laden, it is thought to be behind several acts of terrorism, including the events of September 11, 2001. It was initially formed to unite Arabs fighting in Afghanistan against the Soviet Union.

Arab League a popular name for the League of Arab States, formed in 1945 in an attempt to give political expression to the Arab nations. The constitution of the league provides for coordination among the signatory nations on education, finance, law, trade, and foreign policy, and it forbids the use of force to settle disputes among members.

AUC (United Self-Defenses of Colombia) an umbrella organization for paramilitary groups in Colombia formed in 1997.

Bay of Pigs a landing in Cuba on April 17, 1961, of about 1,300 members of a CIA-supported counterrevolutionary Cuban exile force. The military operation failed.

cartel a national or international organization of manufacturers or traders allied by an agreement to fix prices, limit supply, divide markets, or to fix quotas for sales, manufacture, or division of profits among the member firms.

Cold War the conflict between the United States and the Soviet Union over ideological differences, carried on by methods short of sustained overt military action. The Cold War lasted from the end of World War II until the breakup of the Soviet Union in 1991.

containment the policy of preventing the expansion of a hostile power.

coup d'état the sudden overthrow or alteration of an existing government, usually by a small armed group.

developing countries the nations of Africa, Asia, and Latin America that are still struggling to establish stable governments and economies. *See also* World Bank.

dictatorship a government ruled by a person or small group that exerts absolute power.

diplomacy the art and practice of conducting negotiations between nations.

FARC (Revolutionary Armed Forces of Colombia) a group of Marxist rebels established in 1964 as the military wing of the Colombian Communist Party.

Federal Republic of Yugoslavia (FRY) formerly a federation of six republics: Serbia, Croatia, Bosnia and Herzegovina, Macedonia, Slovenia, and Montenegro. In the early 1990s the federation split along ethnic lines. Slovenia, Croatia, Bosnia and Herzegovina, and Macedonia became independent states. In 1992 Serbia and Montenegro formed a new federation.

globalization the growth of ideas or organizations on a worldwide scale.

gross domestic product (GDP) the total value of the financial output within the borders of a particular country. It is used to measure a nation's economic performance.

Hamas a Palestinian Islamic fundamentalist organization established in 1987. An offshoot of the Muslim Brotherhood, it operates mosques, schools, and social programs. Its military wing has carried out numerous terrorist attacks on Israelis.

imperialism the policy or practice of extending the power or dominion of a nation, especially by territorial acquisition.

International Monetary Fund (IMF) an organization established to promote international monetary cooperation and orderly exchange arrangements, to foster economic growth and high levels of employment, and to provide temporary financial assistance to countries to help ease balance-of-payments adjustment.

isolationism a policy of abstaining from any alliances or other international and economic relations to concentrate on domestic affairs.

intifada a term used to describe the uprising of Palestinian Arabs in the Gaza Strip and West Bank, beginning in late 1987 and continuing sporadically into the early 1990s, in protest against Israeli occupation of these territories.

North American Free Trade Agreement (NAFTA) an accord signed in 1992 by Canada, Mexico, and the United States, which took effect on January 1, 1994, and established a free-trade zone in North America.

North Atlantic Treaty Organization (NATO) a treaty signed on April 4, 1949, creating an alliance of 12 independent nations. The role of NATO is to safeguard the freedom and security of its member countries. As of 2002 it had 19 members.

Palestinian Liberation Organization (PLO) the coordinating council for Palestinian organizations founded at the first Arab summit in 1964. Composed of various guerrilla groups and political factions, the PLO is dominated by Al Fatah, its largest group, whose leader, Yasser Arafat, has been chairman of the PLO since 1968.

quota a proportional share assigned to a group or each member of a group.

sanctions an economic embargo or boycott taken against a nation as a penalty for disapproved conduct, such as human rights violations or undue aggression against other nations, to enforce certain laws or standards. Although primarily economic, it can also involve military action.

Security Council an executive organ of the United Nations whose main responsibility is to preserve peace. *See also* United Nations.

Taliban an Islamic fundamentalist group composed of Afghans trained in religious schools in Pakistan as well as former Islamic fighters or mujahedin. *See also* Al Qaeda.

tariff a schedule of duties or charges that are imposed by a government on imported or exported goods.

terrorism the unlawful or threatened use of force or violence by a person or an organized group against people or property with the intention of intimidating or coercing societies or governments, often for ideological or political reasons.

United Nations (UN) an international organization founded after World War II to maintain world peace and security and to foster cooperation in solving economic, social, cultural, and humanitarian problems. *See also* Security Council.

USA PATRIOT Act (Uniting and Strengthening America through Providing Appropriate Tools Required to Intercept and Obstruct Terrorism) an act introduced after the terrorist action of September 11, 2001. It increased the powers of the Immigration and Naturalization Service, allowing it to arrest and detain immigrants. It also extended the powers of the Military Order, which allowed tribunals to try noncitizens who have been charged with terrorism.

World Bank (International Bank for Reconstruction and Development) a specialized United Nations agency set up in 1945, when 28 countries ratified the agreement; it now has 183 members. The bank makes loans to member nations and, under government guarantee, to private investors for the purpose of facilitating productive investment, encouraging foreign trade, and discharging the burdens of international debt. *See also* International Monetary Fund.

World Trade Organization (WTO) an international organization founded in 1995 as a result of the final round of the General Agreement on Tariffs and Trade (GATT) negotiations, called the Uruguay Round. It monitors national trading policies, handles trade disputes, and enforces the GATT agreements, which are designed to reduce tariffs or other barriers to international trade and to eliminate discriminatory treatment in international commerce.

Acknowledgments

Topic 1 Does the United States Have a Duty to Protect Democracy and Freedom Overseas?

Yes: "A Post-Wilsonian Foreign Policy" by Irving Kristol, American Enterprise Institute, August 1996 (www.aei.org/oti/oti6856.htm). Copyright © 1996 by Irving Kristol. Used by permission.

No: From "U.S. 'Global Leadership': A Euphemism for World Policeman" by Barbara Conry, Policy Analysis No. 267, February 5, 1997 (www.cato.org/pubs/pas/pa267.htm). Copyright © 1997 by the Cato Institute. Used by permission.

Topic 2 Is U.S. Foreign Policy Too Interventionist?

Yes: From "A Sad State of Affairs" by Rep. Ron Paul. Speech to the U.S. House of Representatives, October 25, 2001. Courtesy of the U.S. House of Representatives.

No: "Saving America from the Coming Civil Wars" by Steven R. David. Reprinted by permission of *Foreign Affairs*, January/February 1999. Copyright © 1999 by the Council on Foreign Relations, Inc.

Topic 3 Should the United States Have Relations with Fundamentalist Regimes?

Yes: "Iran: Time for Détente" by Stephen Zunes, *Foreign Policy in Focus* Policy Briefs, Vol. 4 No. 28, November 1999 (www.fpif.org/briefs/vol4/v4n28iran.html). Copyright © 1999 by *Foreign Policy in Focus*. Used by permission.

No: From "On to Iran!" by Reuel Marc Gerecht, American Enterprise Institute, February 18, 2002 (www.aei.org/ra/ragere020218.htm). Copyright © 2002 by Reuel Marc Gerecht. Used by permission.

Topic 4 Should the United States Show a Stronger Commitment to the United Nations?

Yes: From "Choosing Engagement: Uniting the UN with U.S. Interests" by William H. Luers. Reprinted by permission of *Foreign Affairs*, September/October 2000. Copyright © 2000 by the Council on Foreign Relations, Inc.

No: From "Paving the Road to Hell: The Failure of U.N. Peacekeeping" by Max Boot. Reprinted by permission of *Foreign Affairs*, March/April 2000. Copyright © 2000 by the Council on Foreign Relations, Inc.

Topic 5 Does Big Business Have Too Much Influence on Foreign Policy?

Yes: From "Get Tough" by Seth Gitell, *Boston Phoenix*, April 12, 2001. Copyright © 2001 by Boston Phoenix Inc. Used by permission.

No: "Many Constituencies Influence U.S. Foreign Policy-making" by I. M. Destler, *U.S. Foreign Policy Agenda*, May 1996.

(www.usinfo.state.gov/journals/itps/0596/ijpe/pj4destl.htm). Copyright © 1996 by I. M. Destler. Used by permission.

Topic 6 Does NAFTA Work?

Yes: "NAFTA's (Qualified) Success" by J. Bradford DeLong, July 2000 (http://econ161.berkeley.edu/totw/nafta.html). Copyright © 2000 by J. Bradford DeLong. Used by permission.

No: From "North American Free Trade Agreement" by Sarah Anderson, John Cavanagh, and Saul Landau, *Foreign Policy in Focus* Policy Briefs, Vol. 2 No. 1, January 1997 (www.fpif.org/briefs/vol2/v2n1naf_body.html). Copyright © 1997 by *Foreign Policy in Focus*. Used by permission.

Topic 7 Should Economic Sanctions Be Used to Promote Human Rights?

Yes: "The Role of Sanctions in Promoting Human Rights" by Kenneth Roth, Testimony before the Senate Task Force on Economic Sanctions, September 8, 1998. Copyright © 1998 by Human Rights Watch. Used by permission.

No: "Human Rights and International Trade: Right Cause with Wrong Intentions" by Pradeep S. Mehta, Consumer Unity and Trust Society's (CUTS) Centre for International Trade, Economics, and Environment (www.cuts.org/2001-3.htm). Copyright © 2001 CUTS. Used by permission.

Topic 8 Should the United States Be More Open to Exports from Other Nations?

Yes: From "The Wrong Enemy: Why We Shouldn't Fear Low-wage Imports" by Jay Mandle. Reprinted with permission from *The American Prospect*, Vol. 9, No. 37: March 1, 1998. *The American Prospect*, 5 Broad Street, Boston, MA 02019. All rights reserved.

No: "Address to the Chicago Council on Foreign Relations" by Patrick J. Buchanan, November 18, 1998 (www.chuckbaldwinlive.com/read.freetrade.html).

Topic 9 Should the United States Give Aid to Developing Countries Irrespective of Their Politics?

Yes: From "Redesigning Foreign Aid" by Carol Lancaster. Reprinted by permission of *Foreign Affairs*, September/October 2000. Copyright © 2000 by the Council on Foreign Relations, Inc.

No: From "Think Again: Debt Relief" by William Easterly, *Foreign Policy*, November/December 2001. Copyright © 2001 by William Easterly and *Foreign Policy*. Used by permission.

Topic 10 Has the United States Exploited Latin America?

Yes: From "A 'Killing Field' in the Americas: U.S. Policy in Guatemala" by Third World Traveler (www.thirdworldtraveler.com/US_ThirdWorld/US_Guat.html).

No: From "The Prospect for U.S.–Latin American Relations" by Mark Falcoff, American Enterprise Institute, December 2000 (www.aei.org/lao/lao12349.htm). Reprinted with the permission of the American Enterprise Institute for Public Policy Research, Washington, D.C.

Topic 11 Should the United States Normalize Relations with Cuba?

Yes: "No Sanctions, No Castro" by James K. Glassman, American Enterprise Institute, March 1998 (www.aei.org/oti/oti8885.htm). Copyright © 1996 by James K. Glassman.

No: "Should America Lift Sanctions on Cuba"? by Stephen Johnson, The Heritage Foundation, May 20, 2002 (www.heritage.org/Press/Commentary/ed052002a.cfm). Copyright © 2002 by Stephen Johnson and the Heritage Foundation. Used by permission.

Topic 12 Does the War on Drugs Give the United States the Right to Intervene in Other Countries' Affairs?

Yes: From "Narco-terror: The International Connection between Drugs and Terror" by Asa Hutchinson (Director, Drug Enforcement Administration), speech to the Institute for International Studies, April 2, 2002. Courtesy of the Drug Enforcement Administration.

No: From "Militarization of the U.S. Drug Control Program" by Peter Zirnite (edited by Tom Barry and Martha Honey), Foreign Policy in Focus Policy Briefs, Vol. 3 No. 27, September 1998 (www.fpif.org/briefs/vol3/v3n27drug_body.html). Copyright © 1998 by Foreign Policy in Focus. Used by permission.

Topic 13 Is Modern Terrorism Different from Terrorism in Previous Centuries?

Yes: From "Overview: The Issue at a Glance" (www.publicagenda.org/specials/terrorism/terror_overview.htm). © Public Agenda 2002. No reproduction/distribution without permission. www.publicagenda.org.

No: Introduction, "Terror in History to 1939," The International Encyclopedia of Terrorism. Chicago, IL: Fitzroy Dearborn, 1997.

Topic 14 Does Terrorism Arise from the Problem of "Failed States"?

Yes: "Relief Bodies as Fronts for Terror," Daily Nation, December 16, 2001. Reprinted with permission from Daily Nation, Kenya's largest independent newspaper.

No: From "Terrorism Works" by Noam Chomsky, speech to the Massachusetts Institute of Technology. Al-Ahram Weekly Online, November 1–7, 2001, Issue No. 558. Copyright © 2001 by Noam Chomsky. Used by permission.

Topic 15 Should the United States Use Military Force against Nations That Harbor Terrorists?

Yes: "State Sponsors of Terrorism Should Be Wiped Out, Too" by Richard N. Perle, American Enterprise Institute, September 18, 2001 (www.aei.org/ra/raperl010918.htm). Copyright © 2001 by Richard N. Perle.

No: "Making the World More Dangerous" by Marrack Goulding, The Guardian, July 28, 2002. This article first appeared as "No Military Solution," The World Today, August/September 2002. Copyright © 2002 by The World Today. Used by permission.

Topic 16 Should the United States Take More Responsibility for Promoting Peace in the Middle East?

Yes: "U.S. Must Take a Risk on Mid-East" by Philip H. Gordon, The Australian Financial Review., April 8, 2002. Copyright © 2002 by The Australian Financial Review. Used by permission.

No: "President to Send Secretary Powell to Middle East" by President George W. Bush. Speech in the White House Rose Garden, April 4, 2002 (www.whitehouse.gov/news/releases/2002/04/20020404-1.html).

The Brown Reference Group plc has made every effort to contact and acknowledge the creators and copyright holders of all extracts reproduced in this volume. We apologize for any omissions. Any person who wishes to be credited in further volumes should contact The Brown Reference Group in writing: The Brown Reference Group plc, 8 Chapel Place, Rivington Street, London EC2A 3DQ, UK.

Picture credits

Cover: The Brown Reference Group; Hulton/Archive: 171; **PA Photos:** EPA 105; **Rex Features Ltd:** Sipa Press 181, 194, 205; Richard Jenkins, 34/35; **Robert Hunt Library:** 143, 148/149; **U.S. Customs Service:** James R. Tourtellotti 176/177

SET INDEX

Page numbers in bold refer to volume numbers; those in *italics* refer to picture captions.

A

abortion 1:188–201; 7:148; 11:144
  legalizing the abortion pill RU-486 10:9, 48–59
  violent protest by antiabortionists 7:141, 142–50
  see also Roe v. Wade
accountability 3:68–69
acid rain 4:86–87, 110, 138–39
ACT-UP (AIDS Coalition to Unleash Power) 10:41
acupuncture 5:66; 10:88, 92, 97
Adams, John 2:103; 7:20
address, terms of 12:78, 82
Adolescent Family Life Act (AFLA; 1981) 11:127
adoptions
  gay couples as parents 11:16–17, 40–43, 44, 48–49, 62–73
  single-parent 11:48, 56–59, 60
  transcultural 11:82, 84, 85
  transracial 11:49, 74–85
  in the United States 11:57
advertising 3:203, 205; 6:88–99
  body image and 6:74–77, 82
  and business ethics 3:171, 198–209
  negative 3:199
  and objective journalism 6:87, 126–37
  political 6:87, 138–49
  tobacco 3:171; 6:87, 104, 112–23, 125
  to children 6:86–87, 100–111
affirmative action 1:9, 72–85
Afghanistan
  drugs and terrorism 8:152–53
  Internet usage 6:171
  prisoners of war in 9:179, 180–87
  U.S. foreign policy and 8:25, 43
  War on Terrorism 8:166–67, 184–85, 190–91
AFL-CIO 8:67
  and equal pay for women 11:189, 190–93, 198
Africa
  foreign aid for 8:115–16
  privatization in 3:44
  reparations to 1:179–81
  Third World debt 3:158, 161
African Americans
  the Constitution and 7:64–65
  and corporal punishment 11:120–21
  and crime 9:8
  and illegal drugs 7:69; 9:129–30
  prejudice against 11:23
  in prisons 7:67–69
  racial profiling of 9:126
  single mothers 11:53–54
  and transracial adoption 11:74–75, 80–82

Tulia trial 11:23
  see also civil rights; segregation; slaves/slavery
Agnew, Spiro 2:206, 208
agriculture *see* farming
aid, foreign 4:38, 39; 8:112–23
  see also relief bodies
AIDS *see* HIV/AIDS
AIDS Prevention for Adolescents in School 11:132
Aid to Dependent Children (ADC) 7:83
air pollution 4:139
  "pay to pollute" systems 4:86–97
  see also acid rain; global warming
alcohol, advertising 6:104–5
Algeria, terrorism 8:165
Allende, Salvador 8:125
Allport, Gordon 11:28
Al Qaeda 8:23, 25, 111, 153, 179, 190–91; 9:214
  prisoners of war 9:179, 180–88
Alzheimer's disease 10:80
Amazon.com 3:48, 49, 54–55, 57, 58
Amazon rain forest, and capitalism 3:23, 24–25, 32
American Arts Alliance 12:35, 36–39
American Association of Retired People (AARP) 1:18
American Civil Liberties Union (ACLU) 1:100–101
  and abortion 1:190–93, 198; 7:147–48
  and antiabortion violence 7:145, 146–49, 150
  and artistic freedom 12:47, 48–51, 56
  and the death penalty 9:120
  and disability rights 7:89, 94–97, 98
  and English language 1:87, 92–95, 96
  and gay adoption 11:63, 64–67, 72
  and gay marriage 1:61, 62–65
  and gays in the military 7:104–5, 113
  and hate speech 1:139, 140–43, 148; 7:129, 131
  and Internet censorship 6:155, 158, 160–63, 164
  and medical marijuana 5:113, 118–20, 122
  and pornography 7:156–57
  and racial profiling 9:131
  and sex education 11:127
  and warning labels on music 12:203, 208–11, 212
American Dream 1:8; 6:90
American Family Association 6:162–63
American History X (film) 12:149, 163, 164–72
American Liberty League 2:143
American Management Association (AMA) 7:194, 195
American Medical Association (AMA) 5:127–29; 10:62
American Revolutionary War 7:10, 12

Americans with Disabilities Act (ADA; 1990) 7:89, 95–97; 12:158
Amin, Idi 8:88
Amish, and education 1:51, 115, 117–23, 124
Amnesty International 9:115, 166, 168, 179
Andean Regional Initiative 8:151, 157
Angkor Wat 12:87, 88
animals
  cloning 4:174–85; 5:22–23, 26, 34–35, 165, 174
  ethical dilemmas and 4:123
  medical research on 5:63, 150–61
  sacrificed in the Santeria religion 7:115, 116–19, 124
  in zoos 4:123, 162–73
  see also wildlife
Annan, Kofi 8:51, 55–56
anthrax, in the mail 8:166
antibiotics, in farming 4:48; 10:151, 152–53, 160
antidepressants, overprescribed? 10:162, 164–75
anti-Semitism 7:135; 11:23; 12:214
antitrust laws 3:172
apartheid 1:126, 131
Aquinas, Thomas 5:61
Arafat, Yasser 8:193, 194, 209
Arbenz Guzmán, Jacobo 8:126, 127
architecture, and Nazi politics 12:177, 178–81, 186
Argentina, privatization in 3:43
argumentation skills 3:60–61
aristocracy 2:16
Aristotle 3:60; 6:37, 43
arms industry, U.S. 8:63, 73
arthritis 10:120
artificial insemination 4:182, 183
artists
  installation artists 12:12–15, 20
  politics of 12:174–87
  responsibility 12:190–201
arts 12:8–9, 110–11, 148–49
  benefit the rest of the school curriculum? 12:149, 150–61
  can pornography be art? 12:111, 136–47
  censorship 6:17–19, 20; 12:48–51, 58–59
  corporate sponsorship 12:9, 96–107
  and creativity 12:8–9, 22–33
  does art matter? 12:10–21
  First Amendment protects artistic freedom? 12:9, 46–59
  is rap an art form? 12:111, 124–35
  modern art 12:11, 21
  political correctness and 12:80
  and politics 12:174–87
  and racism 12:149, 162–73
  response to September 11 attacks 12:9, 10–20
  should artifacts be returned to their original countries? 12:84–95

SET INDEX